Educating the Postmodern Child

Also available from Bloomsbury

Education and Technology, Neil Selwyn

Education in a Post-Metaphysical World, Christopher Martin

Pedagogy, Oppression and Transformation in a 'Post-Critical' Climate,
Andrew O'Shea and Maeve O'Brien

Educating the Postmodern Child

The Struggle for Learning in a World of Virtual Realities

Fiachra Long

Bloomsbury Philosophical Studies in Education

B L O O M S B U R Y
LONDON · NEW DELHI · NEW YORK · SYDNEY

Bloomsbury Academic
An imprint of Bloomsbury Publishing Plc

50 Bedford Square
London
WC1B 3DP
UK

175 Fifth Avenue
New York
NY 10010
USA

www.bloomsbury.com

First published 2013

British Library Cataloguing-in-Publication Data
A catalogue record for this book is available from the British Library.

ISBN: HB: 978-1-4411-0387-1
ePDF: 978-1-4411-2542-2

Library of Congress Cataloging-in-Publication Data
Long, Fiachra.
Educating the postmodern child : the struggle for learning in a
world of virtual realities / Fiachra Long.
p. cm. – (Continuum philosophical studies in education)Includes
bibliographical references and index.ISBN 978-1-4411-0387-1 (hardcover) –
ISBN 978-1-4411-3266-6 (ebook) – ISBN 978-1-4411-2542-2 (pdf) 1. Problem
children–Education. 2. Children–Social conditions. 3. Postmodernism. I. Title.
LC4801.L66
2013371.93–dc23
2012036133

Typeset by Newgen Imaging Systems Pvt Ltd, Chennai, India
Printed and bound in Great Britain

Contents

Foreword

Although children could be said to be the raw materials of schooling, the family and community, serious philosophical work on this subject has, until relatively recently, been noticeable by it absence. The omission might be traced to the schools of thought that have informed and shaped the evolving philosophy of education over the years. Political and social theories took a surprising amount of time to recognize children as active and important agents within society; until they came to this realization, children were seen as either passive or invisible.

Matters have changed considerably since then. Led by revolutions in psychology that have shown traditional presumptions to have dramatically underestimated children's capacities to think and act, and by an increasingly nuanced sociological understanding of the social contexts of school and the family, scholarly study of children's lives is now a serious area of research.

Part of the great appeal of Fiachra Long's timely and valuable book is that he brings the mind and approach of a philosopher to a subject that has always tended to be owned by the social sciences. In doing so, he brings fresh insights, challenges cosy assumptions and inspires the reader to look again at concepts and experiences that one might previously have taken for granted. Long's monograph explores a host of issues and challenges that confront children in a postmodern world.

This book offers a lens through which the reader is able to look at the context of childhood in new ways. More generally, Long also offers a conceptual bridge between philosophy and the social sciences. For both of these, he deserves to be applauded and thanked.

Richard Bailey
Writer and researcher

Acknowledgements

I want to thank Professor Kathy Hall for allowing me to free myself from Teaching Practice for a period in order to complete this book. I also appreciate her counsel and intellectual engagement on many topics, including the topic of childhood. I would like also to thank colleagues who have read chapters of this work in an early stage and some in latter stages. Professor Denis O'Sullivan perused the first half of the manuscript in early draft form. His words of assurance helped me advance to other levels and I thank him for this support. Thanks also to Dr Steven O'Brien and Dr Karl Kitching for carefully reading two chapters and follow-up conversations. I could always rely on other colleagues past and present for words of encouragement. I am indebted to my class of Masters' students from 2011 for discussions on elements in my chapter on talent and colleagues from other institutions who also helped by conversations and inquiry, in particular, Dr Kevin Williams and Professor Joseph Dunne.

I owe a lot to other colleagues in the frontline office who could be relied upon to ease my administrative burden through some heavily congested periods, Hannah Joyce, Angela Desmond, Claire Dooley, Anita Cronin, Carol Kennedy, Stephanie Larkin and Lorraine Crossan. I would like to thank Dr Finbarr O Leary for his insights into the psychiatry of children, and my good friend Dr Tom Mullins who regularly invited me away from the desk, often without success, eventually waving off my version of childhood with an encouraging hand.

I owe much to the support of family and friends and especially my children, Cillian and Bláthnaid, who appeared in cameo and unknowingly in some of my chapters, and through whom I had a sense of children growing up and teenage experience. And to my wife Siobhán, a constant support and companion to me over the years nothing but a poem would suffice.

On the publishing side, Professor Richard Bailey's early encouragement tipped the balance in favour of writing or not writing this book. His considered arrangement with Continuum publishers led me into contact with Rosie Pattinson who nudged me forward to see this project through, while Alison Baker has kept a much appreciated watchful eye. I thank all the team at Continuum for their careful support.

Part I

Context

1

Childhood and the Child

Then, my good friend, I said, do not use compulsion, but let early education be a sort of amusement; you will then be better able to find the natural bent.

Plato, *Republic*, vii 537a, translated by B. Jowett

Introduction

It is perhaps too commonplace to think of children as individuals with their own personalities and to presume therefore that this individuality stands apart from the context in which they operate. This book and indeed this chapter will in contrast argue that the individuality of children is derivative and a function of a set of relations impacting on the child. In many ways, this thesis would not be controversial were it not for the fact that children educated in a postmodern setting are already 'global' in an important and still undefined sense. They derive their individuality from a culturally novel set of global coordinates. What makes the education of a child unique at this time is the increased range of cultural influences that intervene directly to shape the individuality of the child, conferring upon it a texture of speed and density that both challenges the human reality and increases the vulnerability of the human species.

It is interesting that Jowett's 1888 translation of the passage from the *Republic* above manages to avoid the term 'children' altogether, even though some variation of the Greek word for child, *pais*, is at work through the passage. A more modern translation by Grube and Reeve is made to read: 'Then don't use force to train the children in these subjects; use play instead. That way you'll also see better what each of them is naturally fitted for' (Cooper, 1997). It might well be possible to bemoan the disappearance of 'children' from such a text or else congratulate us wise moderns for having made children reappear again but perhaps childhood in its modern appearances has its own problematic significance. Indeed this chapter looks at some of the historical elements that may have led to our contemporary understanding of children in terms of chronology or age. I need to spend some time reflecting on the historical elements which provide the context for this understanding, using the now famous study of Philippe Ariès and more contemporary authorities like Hugh Cunningham and Stephen Humphries. I argue here that the historical collective, meaning the family unit or the group unit, which posited identification with the group as the primary mark of one's identity has now been replaced by age-specific social cohorts, each positioned by legislative and cultural instruments. For adults, young mortgage holders, senior citizens, these separations are not controversial but for children, who do not yet have any experience of the world, the separation into an age cohort is at least dramatic and may indeed be damaging. Former understandings centering on the vulnerability of children or the competence of children seem to have been set aside in contemporary culture while advanced communications teachnologies now enable children of different ages to connect with one another, often with only the slightest awareness of parents.

For a time, two issues, age and competence, competed with each other to define the nature of childhood. Postman argued that the link between literacy and numeracy competence in schools eventually created 'childhood' as we know it, for it was the need for technical competence identified by parents, the need to prepare children to read and write that underscored the importance of schooling and hence created childhood (Postman, 1994/1982). He concluded that since reading and writing in this old sense is now no longer needed, 'childhood' will soon disappear. Postman's view echoes the fact that while age seemed to be important in the past, it was the competence or ability of children as judged by parents that set them apart. Some aspects of children's current grasp of technology, however, might reverse the issue of competence, establishing youth culture on an age basis primarily and not on a competence basis. So all in all, there are in the main four pressures that currently separate children from their parents or, in more generic terms, currently combine to break up the historical collective. They are the fact that (i) children control communications technologies at least as well and often better than adults; (ii) the traditional historical development of the child is no longer valued because of the rapidity of cultural change; (iii) children who have some control over the technology imagine that they have improved economic prospects and (iv) that the influence from the United States in the way childhood has developed is unavoidable. Nowadays a combination of forces, some stemming from children themselves and the industries that support children's tastes, some coming from the adult world have turned a drift into a rift. Where before World War I almost 500,000 juveniles worked part-time in Britain, this number for various reasons (to do with social policy, compulsory schooling at primary level, improved prospects for individual children, changing technologies, reduced stability factors binding communities together) had reduced to between 80,000 and 90,000 in 1931 (Cunningham, 1995, p. 174). Children had begun to see themselves as state assets or resources while parents began to see children as costs rather than resources, while a reduction in child mortality led to smaller families, not larger ones. With increased wealth, the trend worldwide has been towards smaller families (Schell, Reilly, Rosling, Peterson and Ekström, 2007) while a widening gap between childhood and adulthood is now a constant feature in sociological analysis (James, Jenks and Prout, 1998).

Events in the United States also had a marked influence. The trend to favour age rather than competence therefore had already been noticed in the United States where strong child-centred approaches to education had begun to take root. English visitors to the United States had been shocked by the precocious behaviours of American children. These youngsters had freedoms not yet heard about for children in Europe (Rapson, 1965). Yelvertos described American children in 1875 as 'diminutive men and women in the process of growing into big ones' (as cited in Rapson, 1965, p. 521). These were future-looking kids, their minds orientated away from the past and towards the ever-refreshing prospect of eternal youth. And the thought to identify children as an intergenerational resource and indeed a source of joy and enrichment for a family began to compete with the idea that children had their own existence within a micro-culture so that already quite soon the child had already ceased being a family member and had learned to think of itself as a economic citizen of the State.

Hence the breakup of the historical collective and the rediscovery of the importance of age were signalled by a few cultural features. They began to feel secure more quickly with the technology they would need and had learned to move more quickly than age suggested. They started feeling that they should look forward not backward and resonated with the American attitude to freedom and consumption, as mediated through American culture and products. As a result, children ceased to look backwards and started looking uniquely forward. It was their lives that mattered and parents told them so. Their lives existed in the future and they were happy to learn how to have mastery over them. This attitude contrasted with a generation before when children preferred to leave school to help out at home and sometimes even refused scholarship[s] if it meant being absent from the family home (Humphries, 1981, p. 60; Cunningham, 1995). Moreover children began to see themselves more as consumers and people of the future (Cunningham, 1995, p. 177). Or as Mark Poster rightly remarks, they had experienced the way 'consumer culture no longer trickles down from the leisure class but climbs up from society's lower reaches' (2004, p. 416).

Following the breakup of the historical collective into discrete age groups, children would have to be understood as belonging to the world of 'childhood' and subject for the first time to forms of visibility that would invade their territory more effectively than they had done in the past. New frames of visibility based on age came to the fore, shaped carefully by commercial markets. Broken up in this way, childhood had become the time without human speech (0–2 years), early childhood (2–6 years), middle childhood (7–10 years), late childhood (11–14 years), tweenagers (10–12) or the teenagers traditionally described using the term 'adolescence' (13–18 years). As these age visibilities have increased in focus, commercial interests specializing in precise sections of the market heightened awareness of teenage fashion and 'cool' dietary behaviour (Grimstad Klepp and Storm-Mathison, 2005; Schor and Ford, 2007). Hidden in all these precisions, however, is the assumption that children of any age should be expected to carry the weight of society on their shoulders. They should either be the lever that leads parents away from poor or *laissez-faire* practices of child-rearing, as judged by wider society, or they should be the targeted scapegoats (yobbos, scum bags, hooligans, riff-raff) in which uncivilized practices can be located and criminalized. In either case, society could hold its head high by staunchly thinking of all its children as 'subject' to its normative ideals.

Historical traces, defining the child

Age or Competence?

According to Joseph Kett, in the United States in the 1860s, one could commonly still find 25-year-olds in elementary school and 30-year-olds at College (Kett, 1971, p. 292). This state of affairs was also rather common in Europe in the twelfth century, according to Philippe Ariès. Even at the cathedral schools of the thirteenth century, adults mixed with children without distinction, indicating that the focus of attention lay critically on competence rather than development and on standards of attainment rather than processes of learning. This mix was also evidence of a belief among educators that stable knowledge served as the benchmark of progress. Levels were marked by sets of outcomes (we seem to be returning to this today) rather than by age, method, process of learning, maturity or development. Indeed the link between schools and children's ages, which is generally assumed today, following Ariès, did not begin to occur before the fourteenth century.

In the medieval curriculum, a line could be traced from the beginning of a basic literacy in Latin to the study of rhetoric and Aristotle's logic, the culmination of undergraduate study. Infancy could easily extend to the age of 10 while some pupils could emerge quite young from the study of Aristotle's logic, ready for university study, as the Tudor baron Francis Bacon did at the age of 14. This was a trend across Europe. Ariès details the development of the child prodigy, Crosley, born in Troyes in 1718, who began rhetoric at the age of 11, and finished logic at the age of 14 with a Baccalauréat (p. 208). Figures given for the school Sainte-Barbe in 1816–17 (p. 220) indicate that a norm for rhetoric at about 16 or 17 years of age had been established while it was usual to spend a further number of years to control the different modes of the syllogism, the square of opposition and the study of various fallacies detailed in Aristotle's *Organum*. Quite a few more years would be needed in the study of law, theology or medicine before a candidate could emerge as a master with the authority to take in students of his own. For a time at least this process replicated the long number of years given to mastery in the guilds, so much so that a constant rivalry existed between the guilds and the universities, to say nothing of the university schools.

Because of the general common belief that knowledge itself was stable and stood apart from knowers as a content that could be passed from person to person and from generation to generation, the child could be defined by reference to their competence to do certain things. The skill of reading could be seen in similar terms to the skill of working in the fields – a capacity of some sort. The stress on a universal standard of attainment and on a stable form of knowledge that could outlast centuries also meant that it would outlast learners so that even while changes were occurring in the institutions of learning such as the founding of schools and the opening of education to the poor, the same standards would apply in the same ways to everyone. There was no mystery about it. From a time when all age groups mixed indiscriminately (as they still do in families) alternatives to the University school, the Collèges in France, the *pensions* as boarding facilities, the little schools run mainly by clerics and scribes to which boarding houses could be attached, and cathedral schools, which grew up around music and liturgy, all tended to stratify the students into competence groups rather than age groups. Practices began to be established around these norms, which roughly replicated family life. Parents who could pay fees could be assured their children would be legitimately engaged in the work of scholarship and brought to a particular level by a good master. Ariès mentions the case of an impoverished Irishman, John Callaghan, who, being of good ability and having finished his schooling at the Port-Royal Collège of La Flèche, studied philosophy and then theology in 1630. As the master in charge of his class had been appointed to serve as Master of Novices at a nearby abbey in 1633, John Callaghan received these students as a parting gift, along with the school, and the main reason given was that it offered the Irishman a means of subsistence (p. 267). The assumption was that he would uphold proper standards and competence levels, not that he would offer a caring environment for the growth and development of young children, even though there was no reason to believe that this would not happen.

In the following centuries other factors seem to have played an equally important role in defining education, including the discovery that knowledge is not stable but rather very much empirically based and temporally located, while Marxist thought proposed that knowledge too is very much governed by the power claims that operate on social and political structures generally. The acceptance that knowledge now had feet of clay meant that in the long run it could no longer serve as a yardstick for competence and opened up issues that are still relevant in contemporary sociological analysis (Cunningham, 2009). One can see the challenge of this to the historical collective linking parents to children through this mind-set change. Where before children thought of themselves as net contributors to family income and culture, willing to work in the fields alongside their parents or to climb up chimneys in Victorian London, once they were strong enough and had the ability to do so, their age rather than their competence began to come to everyone's attention, while shifts in the nature of knowledge itself began to play a determining role in separating children's concerns from the adult world.

Discipline

For Ariès, the critical distinction in the old world between adults and children not only involved the child's ability to do adult things but it also centred on the way children, as distinct from adults, could be disciplined. Discipline could be thought of as a way of distinguishing 'childhood' from adulthood that either enhanced the historical collective or undermined it. The issue for parents and children alike was the matter of discipline – what discipline meant, why it was needed, how it came to be administered. This was always the key issue. Ariès suggests that after the sixteenth century, the birch had become commonplace in the disciplining of children of all ages outside the home, but that already by the eighteenth century this use had been abandoned for rhetoricians at 15–17 years of age (p. 250). It was as if reaching adulthood had conferred the right on children not to be beaten and that the subjection to certain kinds of punishment was a child's lot. Here small changes in the child's age could have big consequences in their treatment in school, perhaps holding the birch in place longer in public settings than in private ones. For whatever reason, Ariès notes that the birch was slower to leave the public setting. And it was the thought that lay behind the disciplining of children as much as the manner of its application that widened the rift between a child of one age and a child of another. After the banishment of the Jesuits from France in 1763 and the abandonment of their disciplinary methods, other models began to come into play. Jean Baptiste de la Salle promoted the abandonment of the birch in French schools. La Salle, on Ariès' account, also limited the monitor system, already prevalent in England since Tudor times, which had given proxy powers to unqualified senior pupils to manage large groups of pupils and which itself had led to some excesses (p. 252). Lasallian culture led to the promotion of proper teacher training for all teachers and lessened reliance on the birch, which became illegal in France after the reforms of 1763, but not in Great Britain and Ireland. In these latter countries, the stoic ideal still held sway, namely that boys had to take their punishment, even unwarranted punishment, and that they should face up to these trials like men, even if no men at the time had to suffer the types of humiliation and exposure to unlimited adult power sometimes evident in public floggings at school.

Domestic stability

The contexts for discipline also varied. Ariès details how childhood *en famille* was liable to end abruptly when employment became possible. Children could be exposed to sudden domestic changes by being sent in to service elsewhere or to boarding school and this kind of change probably became a childhood dread. Ariès says that children, as young as age 6, could be sent away to apprenticeship. They could find themselves pledged to guilds where guild masters would take on the child as an extra member of their family. This state of affairs, which may have opened the prospect of eventual well-paid employment for the child, also led to experiences of rupture in the child's life and may have precipitated Ariès' remarks about a lack of sentiment between parents and children. The family structure seemed 'unable to nourish a profound existential attitude between parents and children' (p. 356). It is always difficult to measure the true effects on parents of poverty, high child mortality rates, damp and unsanitary living conditions, cramped spaces, large families, the fear of plague, the need to supplement family income, limited access to paid work, obstacles put in their way by a 'grace and favour' employment system, the reality of illness and shorter life expectancy. Access to employment by means of school certificates or references from master teachers, proposed to open doors to employment and would offer great liberation from the old structures. It contributed widely to greater mobility but did parental moves to avail of these chances signal an unfriendly attitude?

The fact that school masters tended to be seen as guild masters simply meant that, for a time at least, going by what Ariès recounts, the relation between schoolboy and school master was similar to that between apprentice and master tradesman. In such circumstances parenting had come to an abrupt end. Some of the drawbacks of the old system continued as a result – access to reputable masters was uneven, as it has been for the trades and guilds, encouraging parents to send their children longer distances at younger and younger ages in order to secure places with the best masters. Ariès details the growth of boarding schools, *pensions* and the attractiveness of large towns as centres of learning for rural populations, factors that naturally took children out of the direct care of parents and left them exposed, on some occasions, to unscrupulous masters, devious perverts and even pedagogically incompetent tutors. These latter were sometimes paid to accompany boys to their destination schools and oversee their instruction. As surrogate parents, however, they could turn out to be hostile and unfriendly, increasing the likelihood that children far from home would feel particularly isolated and afraid. The pressures of attending these schools may have worsened the normal pressures of growing up.

While a separation of disciplinary modes accepted in French public schools contrasted with the discipline acceptable in homes and while the harshness of emotional separation due to attendance at boarding school might be considered as two pieces of evidence supporting the suggestion that children were being constructed in a separate cultural space, it may be an exaggeration to contend that schools had largely become instruments of oppression. Foucault alleges that 'in the course of the seventeenth and eighteenth centuries the disciplines became general formulas of domination' (Foucault, 1979, p. 137) and furthermore that they produced 'docile bodies' (p. 138). There is no account here of the way such discipline could be seen contra Foucault as a liberation from domination, which was closer to the original intention of some of these disciplinary practices. Jean Baptiste de la Salle irked many by opening his schools to the poor, even if paradoxically his schools drew the rich and well connected to its well-organized and potentially beneficial structures[1] (Ariès, 1962, p. 293). One example of the revolutionary character of these schools centred on a legal action undertaken in 1661 and which demanded a limit to what La Salle schools could teach since the guild of scribes had traditionally controlled the art of writing and claimed the ancient right to be teachers of this craft. This successful legal action by the guild excluded writing for a time from the curriculum of these schools but La Salle and others succeeded in having this law reversed and responded by being even more prescriptive about how writing should be done, detailing in exact ways how writers should sit at their desk, hold their pen etc. Without having to pay the guild master's fee, the poor child could perfect a skill traditionally closed off to it and would embrace the required precision of bodily practice, paying due attention to detail all the more assiduously in the hope of one day being employed as a clerk or a legal secretary. This, however, is not the impression given by Foucault's quotation from La Salle's *Conduite*:

> A distance of two fingers must be left between the body and the table . . . The right arm must be at a distance from the body of about three fingers and be about five fingers from the table, on which it must rest lightly. The teacher will place the pupils in the posture that they should maintain when writing, and will correct it either by sign or otherwise, when they change this position. (as quoted in Foucault, 1979, p. 152)

This perspective sets in context the disciplined body which Foucault complains about. While my remarks do not discredit Foucault's basic thesis about 'docile' bodies, it is clear that corporal discipline was not by definition oppressive. The pupils who were learning how to write may not have found these regimes oppressive, even though, by modern standards, without understanding the context in which they took place, they might seem so. The context was the political liberation of the poor and disenfranchised from the wealth tracks limited to a small group in society.

Moreover a negative view of bodily disciplinary devices tends to reflect current misgivings about the authority role of adults in the lives of children. People today accept more readily the account that discipline involves the oppressive 'subjectification' of children to powers of domination. A more historically resonant view would also have to point to the positive contribution of discipline, including bodily discipline, in servicing the historical collective and in promoting children's prospects of employment. It may well be that the supposed rift between child and family is a result of a number of interpretative options, including this one of choosing to view discipline in a Rousseauian spirit as an emblem of subjectification.

Moral discipline: Monsters or angels?

It is at this moment of our analysis that a distortion comes into play in the understanding of the historical collective which placed it in a position of extreme danger. The switch from a political concern for poverty experienced by the whole family, as they surveyed their own circumstances aided by the social innovators of the time, switched to a moral concern. Poverty had usually not been a moral concern, although Victorian England set about forging links between moral and political poverty. However in every age, vagabondage had been considered as mildly immoral. In the Middle Ages (it gave rise to the response of the mendicant orders criminalized in Paris from the fourteenth century on, so it was an old thought to link poverty to moral shortcomings, laziness or desultory living. This mind-set switch became the trap for the religiously minded just as it did for social reformers who now could criminalize beggars for being poor.

Religious groups arguably confused their work to counter the injustice of exclusion from the wealth of society by means of their schools with a campaign to map these political inequalities onto moral ills, attributing their causes too easily to moral problems in adults such as drunkenness, laziness etc., and finding themselves amenable to judgements about the wildness and wilfulness of untamed children. Indeed two moral views began to dominate, often divided on social class lines, but nonetheless valuable as categories in their own right. The Puritan view of the need to curb the wilfulness of children characterized children as chaotic pre-civilized animals while the Rousseauian view located the child in a prelapsarian space, identifying the child with innocence, freshness, newness, angelic behaviours (Demos, 1971; Cunningham, 1995). But this was the mistake that moralized adult relations with children and offered a higher moral ground by which to adjudicate on parental practices. Poverty and squalor could be presented in moral terms and justify withdrawal of children from parents as the moral innocence of childhood could be contrasted with the moral corruption of adult society generally. Alternatively, the corruption of an entire group of people could be contrasted with the progressive attitudes of church and state. At the turn of the twentieth century, the divisive norm situated children in a 'wild' space, encouraging teachers in particular to think of poor urchins as requiring strong control and rigorous moral training for the salvation of their souls. Education accordingly began to root itself in two alternative constructions of childhood – monsters or angels.

The monster model of childhood suggested the need for firm measures to curb the wilfulness of children (thus giving the disciplines a moral purpose) while the angelic model lauded the innocence of children, almost removed the need for discipline at all and thought of children as 'angels, messengers from God to a tired adult world' (Cunningham, 1995, p. 62). From the Puritan perspective, this romantic reading tended to encourage 'the egoism latent in all children' (Vachel as quoted in Rapson, 1965, p. 525) which, as a thought, could all too easily compromise child-centred approaches. Nietzsche, for example, saw this movement in the 1870s as a general pandering to youthful subjectivism (Nietzsche, 1973, par. 207). For others, child-centredness was the key to the future. What else could explain the wild enthusiasm of Sir Philip Gibbs who described American children as 'free from that juvenile snobbishness which is still cultivated in English society, where boys and girls of well-to-do parents are taught to look down with contempt upon children of the poorer classes' (as quoted in Rapson, 1965, p. 532). What else could explain Wordsworth's resounding words:

> The child is father of the man
>
> And I would wish my days to be
>
> Bound each to each by natural piety

When Europe met the United States in the space of the child, these two great moral 'models' of childhood began to battle with each other – the angelic and the demonic. In the US context, having removed the darker picture of the wilfulness of children, it became less and less clear why children should be disciplined at all. What had become defunct in the American system was not the need for discipline but the *moral grounds* upon which this need had been based in the old world. And this basically meant parental authority. The key difference between the new world child and the old world child lay in the absence of moral discipline which new world parents were not now prepared to exercise over their young. European visitors sometimes thought of American children as 'rude' (p. 528) while Walt Whitman and Matthew Arnold were loud in their praise of the freedom of the American child.

Breaking up the historical collective

Apart from the divisions between childhood and adulthood implied by a 'moral' discourse, a social engineering element began to play its part, especially since the middle of the nineteenth century. With discipline no longer a factor in defining childhood in the public arena of schools in Great Britain and Ireland, since the regimes were universally harsh, what some commentators called the 'social risk model' prevailed and resulted in the development of an industrial school system for waifs and strays (O'Sullivan, 1979, p. 211). This generated a logic that would still be in vogue in Ireland in the Cussen Report of 1936 (Cussen,

1936) and indeed, O' Sullivan argues, into the 1960s (p. 212). Moves to introduce compulsory schooling in the 1880s began to set up their own backlash among the working classes, resulting in what Humphries calls 'subsistence truancy', truancy precipitated by poverty that was usually aided and abetted by parents to create 'a fierce solidarity in opposition to the school authorities and a collective resistance to the inflexible imposition of attendance regulations' (1981, p. 66). The social stigma of children as economically non-viable and thus not 'producers' of family wealth, when viewed from society as a whole, stood in stark contrast to actual contributions made by children's part-time work to needy families. The social view prevailed among the middle classes, however, who were not gripped by need and saw the long-term benefits of a proper education. Predictably there had been resistance in France and England when primary schooling became compulsory in the 1880s, not because people objected to the discipline of schools or the knowledge available there, but because families objected to the loss of their children as economic resources available to work, if needed. Rather than alleviate poverty, compulsory schooling placed poor families in a worse position because poor families often relied on the small sums children could earn to keep them above the breadline (see Humphries, 1981).

In just a short space of time, children began to be constructed as beings belonging to the future, not the present. They began to be associated with their own children in the future rather than with the families of their birth. This development, however, took place more slowly among the working classes or at least basic poverty led to greater resistance to this trend. Cunningham notes the difference this made in England and Wales where the participation of children in school from ages 5 to 14 rose from 24% in 1870 to 48% in 1880 to over 70% in 1900 but while middle-class England could congratulate itself about this advance, it remained blind to the damage done to the family unity of poorer classes and the resulting fracture of the historical collective. Soon children of whatever class were not able to see themselves as complicit producers in a local breadline economy (p. 165).

Now that childhood had been separated from adulthood, the antagonistic perspectives (which to a large extent determine the modern space of childhood) provided the template for further fractures, setting up childhood as a cultural entity in its own right governed by its own set of rules and manifestations. Not only entire classes could be sacrificed for the sake of the better social good but family unity also could be sacrificed to save the child in some abstract sense. And in this manner poverty could be criminalized and the working classes turned into potential outlaws. And so '[t]he critical element in the entire process of classification and segregation was the removal of children from families considered to be morally and physically degenerate' (Humphries, 1981, p. 213).

Reform schools

Humphries identifies three aspects of reform schools that would be compatible with what I am calling here the breakup of the historical collective. First there is the invasion by the institution of every sphere of personal life: children were to have no rights, no privacy, no free time, lest a corrupted seed find root in idleness: the child needed to be set upon in order to survive. Second, there is the control of time, the sequencing of tasks, the monotonous daily grind of activities, meals, lessons, work, that would drum out all initiative and eliminate the potential perniciousness of independent thought. This thought is singularly well developed in passages from Foucault's *Discipline and Punish*, which has become a standard reference text to represent the oppression of children by institutions (James et al., 1998, p. 43). Third, there would be a regime of harsh physical punishment, an element downplayed in the French system, but one held to be central to the control of children throughout the British system and in the Stoical Far-East. The regime was to be supported by harsh impersonal and disproportionate discipline taking the form of liberal doses of the birch or the cane. In accordance with this view, the logic of reform schools was deliciously vague. They promised a better future but insisted on sound moral and physical discipline as a means to achieve this with transgressions being punished severely. Reform schools had made visible the banishment of the historical collective in its worst possible light. On the surface it promoted itself as a moral agency but mixed children of different psychological profiles together, failing to distinguish the genuine orphan from the delinquent and the school prankster and proclaiming 'the homogeneity of the school population' (O'Sullivan, 1979, p. 221). To place side by side the impoverished and bewildered child, the joker who was unlucky to be caught, and the more violent child who had learned the way of devious aggression, simply reinforced stereotypes about the monster child and brought all together under the same disciplinary regime. The merging of these three types of child, if one can call them types, increased the terror experienced by the destitute but innocent child. Such children were further terrorized by the link made between poverty and delinquency. Poverty itself could be considered as evidence for delinquency in institutions that blended together all in a common basket: 'Their enforced confinement in institutions that had little to offer apart from rote learning, rigid discipline and training in manners and morals that were often alien and meaningless led to a constantly antagonistic atmosphere' (Humphries, 1981, p. 70).

This dark atmosphere, in some cases amplified by episodes of particular physical and sexual abuse, simply fuelled the resentment former boarders expressed years later and directed backwards at all known authorities responsible for their personal histories (Touher, 2007). Such children, now grown up, resented the law and its visible presentations, the policemen on the beat, religious authorities who ran these institutions, teachers who never softened in applying strong disciplinary measures, masters who applied the strap mercilessly, disciplinarians who oversaw the malevolent withdrawal of privileges, together with occasional teacher practices that were cruel and sadistic. Many practices could be hidden behind the cry for discipline just as many ways could be found to impose middle-class values as the norm.

It is somewhat ironic that the adoption by society of a 'high moral' ground in opposition to the historical collective resulted in such a dark recent history of childhood for a number of children. My argument has been that the historical collective began to disintegrate under the strain of moralized social policy agendas and that the gap widened extensively when children became identified by the commercial forces that play on their insecurities. One hundred years ago it may have been an aspiration to begin again, as it were, and free society of its ills by measures of cleansing and general enlightenment that would rid society of its poverty and its benighted practices but today it is clear that other forces are at work to make sure other agendas are served now that children have, as it were, come into the marketplace.

Where is the postmodern child?

In the main, the Rousseau ideal of the natural goodness of the child has prevailed over the image of the 'wicked' child as is evident in legal instruments designed to protect children and a general emphasis on children's 'rights'. Due to the breakup of the historical collective, it is now becoming the norm for messages about healthy eating, exercise, lifestyle balance to be communicated directly to children bypassing parents. Indeed it is often parental education that is the focus of some of these programmes (Evans, Rich and Holroyd, 2004; Rich and Evans, 2005). The dominant romantic view considers childhood to be an important resource through which various social reforms can be achieved. On a world level, and dating from 2007, UNICEF published a report (Progress for Children:

A Report Card on Maternal Mortality No. 7)[2] which offered what it called the first comprehensive assessment of the well-being of children worldwide. Legal, medical and sociological factors combined with educational elements to suggest six dimensions of importance: material well-being, health and safety, education, peer and family relationships, behaviour and risks and young people's own subjective sense of well-being. This landmark report resulted from a survey of 21 OECD countries, which corresponded to one of the recommendations of the *Convention on the Rights of the Child* and concluded that it was continually seeking '[t]o identify areas where societies could do better in supporting every child to be and become all that s/he can be over and above generally universal access for every child to basic services in education, health, nutrition, shelter'.[3] It is hard then not to notice the hyperbole in these remarks and the Rousseau-like assumptions that lie behind them.

These views tie in with concerns expressed in several individual countries which have deliberately undertaken a whole child perspective. *The National Children's Strategy of Ireland* (2000) struck a clear educational note when it set out to highlight what it called '[t]he capacity of children to shape their own lives as they grow, while also being shaped by the world around them' (Government of Ireland 2001, p. 9).[4] The educational tone is set by the insistence on a 'dialectical' power exercised between self and world where the child is presumed to have achieved sufficient autonomy and indeed agency to shape the world around it and to accept in filtered form some of the world's influences in return. This mutually nurturing arrangement, which educators feel is central to a successful childhood and which is filtered through legal and administrative measures is only softly influenced by parents and carers, who themselves fall under scrutiny and could apparently be replaced should their standards not be high enough. On the one hand, there is suspicion; on the other hand, there is a global optimism. Matters are advancing because the legal instruments have been put in place. Or so it is thought.

But the fact that childhood has now become identified as an autonomous world constitutes a significant change in the life prospects of the postmodern child. It means that childhood has become a separate culture supported by its own forms of visibility while the commercial visibility of children can now be targeted by commercial interests only too happy to divide children into many competing peer consumer groups (Kenway and Bullen, 2001, p. 63).

As I end this chapter, I watch scores of youths on Sky News rampaging through London high streets, looting shops, burning cars and properties and terrorizing inhabitants. Although much could be said about the way these events have been inflated by the media, the key issue is not poverty, race or working-class versus middle-class values. Nor do I want to call them yobbos, hooligans, scum, thugs, even criminals. What is evident in the behaviour of these youths is membership of a different kind of 'collective'. At the turn of the twentieth century, bonds of affection reinforced the historical collective and justified petty larceny in the minds of children as an answer to the family's need for food and fuel (Humphries, 1981). One hundred years later, children from the same social class now see themselves as social looters who offer no comparable rationale. On television interviews, suitably muffled and disguised, they talk about their present lives and their prospects in the future. The talk is about the future rather than the past. Their awareness is guided by their desire for consumer goods, not food; they steal from sports shops, not food shops. They want sneakers of a particular brand or clothes that they respect and covet and that are 'cool' enough either to wear or to trade. They have become the emblems of a new age. They leave bookstores untouched, perhaps evidence that Postman was right – a new literacy is in place and books and institutions based on books are no longer relevant. Large numbers of youths obviously think of themselves as separate from the society they are happy to loot. Luckily there are other youths who are happy to help with the clean-up lest anyone think that 'all' youth are looters. But the manifestation of haphazard looting and an indifference concerning the destruction of local amenities has demonstrated the irrelevance of parental restraints. The widespread contagion raises the serious question about how children in an autonomous state of 'childhood' have come to understand themselves and how they are motivated to act in the 'world' they find already constructed around them.

Notes

1 Ariès cites H. Joly here, *Traité historique des écoles épiscopales et ecclésiastiques*.
2 www.unicef.org/publications/index_45454.html
3 Summary at www.unicef.org/media/media_38299.html as accessed 21 October 2010.
4 Government of Ireland, 2000, accessed at www.dcya.gov.ie as accessed 3 November 2011.

Child's Play

Introduction

The Ancient Greeks associated the word 'play' with children since they linked the very word *paidia* (play) to the word *paideia* (play, education or formation) and referred both back to the word for child, *pais*. There is no reason to retain this strict association with children, as tradition has shown since play has often been associated with adults also, even if it is true that play is normally associated with children. If play only described non-serious behaviour, then it would overlook the serious function of play in the child's development and dismiss the adult need for play. If we restricted its reference points, adults per se would set this behaviour aside and only resort to it for recreation purposes rather than as part of their activity processes (including work). Generations have followed Aristotle in seeing play as a kind of recreation (*Pol* viii, 3, 133b 39; *Nicomachean Ethics* x, 6 1176b 33)[1] but the result of this move has been to think of adult play as peripheral to ordinary behaviours, a kind of immature escape, a kind of rest from the strains of a hard day's work. It is perhaps better to think of play as enhancing the creativity of any activity and lessening its drudgery and for this reason 'child's play' is a feature of all human behaviour.

Frost has recently offered a comprehensive history of play (Frost, 2010), while some writers have focused on one important feature that they take to be central, such as the ambiguity of play (Sutton-Smith, 1997). Indeed the Norwegian researcher, Arne Trageton has assembled an impressive compendium of these central features, presenting them as a astonishing list: play is action, symbol making, the work of edifying (Comenius, 1632); children's art (Schiller, 1793); the highest point of development in childhood (Froebel, 1826); surplus energy (Spencer, 1855); practice training for adult life (Groos, 1899); an emotional outlet (Freud, 1920); the expression of self-mastery (Erikson, 1941); assimilation of the world (Piaget, 1962); development of abstract thinking (Vygotsky, 1933); process, creativity, flexibility (Sutton-Smith, 1971; Bruner, 1972); group adapting, reflection of reality (Leontiev, 1977); work itself (Goodman, 1974); fantastics, aesthetics (Rodari, 1991); communication (Bateson, 1955; Garvey, 1979; Olofsson, 1987); ecological cooperation, interaction (Bae, 1988); culture teaching (Opie and Opie, 1969); culture creation (Huizinga, 1938; Gadamer, 1965; Sutton-Smith, 1990); *Spiel* (Wittgenstein, 1932; Papert, 1983; Rasmussen, 1990; Bauer, 1996) (see Trageton in McMahon, Lytle and Sutton-Smith, 2005, p. 161). This list is quite astonishing and I do not claim to understand it all. Instead in this chapter and mindful of the possibility that postmodern culture is a culture in which play is significant – the play of signifiers, for example, the play of multiple selves, the play of multiple worlds, many of them virtual, I am going to narrow the discussion to what I take to be two conditions of play and three manifestations. These features will later enable a comparison to be made between traditional play and postmodern play.

Two conditions

First, the two conditions. The child is clear on the distinction between play and play-acting. If children play-act, they are quickly brought back into line by their peers, since the entire universe of the life of the child is built around play, not play-acting. Messing actually is an attack on play itself. In children it is the reassertion of the egotistic ends of play over any collective ends, ultimately destroying the world which play creates and the enjoyment and instant connectivity which play generates among children. The messer runs away with the ball or lets the dogs loose at the picnic or in some way makes the game impossible to play. This destroys the collective experience of fulfilment in play and children therefore are usually annoyed. Adults recognize messers at work too – egotistical sabotage designed to break up a collective action whether at work or in games. Blondel noted that the play-actor or dilettant is acting out a contradiction and effectively making action itself impossible, betraying in his attitude a deeper commitment to nothingness, nihilism, 'inaction'. To this extent, the adult dilettant, like a child messer, foregoes the more satisfying experience of the collective creation in order to undermine the structures provided. Paradoxically the last thing play-actors want is to be entirely successful because, if the game collapses, they are left without a world to undermine. The messer is the one who wants to enjoy the being that others present while remaining committed to the negation of that being (Blondel, 1984, p. 34), an attitude that might be formulated as a particular type of nihilism and anarchy. Play, on the other hand, is central to the positivity of participation and production and is not a withdrawal from life or a retirement from learning about it.

In a certain sense, therefore, play is serious, not frivolous and from this fact it is possible to see why play, as a behaviour, has been so valuable to humans and indeed to other animals, as a survival mechanism. When John Ssebunya disappeared into the Ugandan bush in the 1990s, he began to play with juvenile vervet (green) monkeys and this helped him to blend in with the group as a non-threatening juvenile. Other research has shown that monkeys use play to learn how to *assess* a social situation so as to determine their place in it. This knowledge allows them to operate with confidence from the bottom up as it were so that beginning from an inferior and unthreatening position they can eventually grow in status among the group. They do not become either overly timid or overly aggressive as adult troop monkeys, but manage to discern their appropriate place and develop the emotional ability to hold themselves in that place. On the other hand, monkeys kept in cages and deprived of play became socially inhibited and, despite physiological maturity they became 'incompetent in virtually every aspect of monkey social activity'. Indeed Harlow found that '[w]ire-cage reared adults will viciously attack a helpless neonate or they may suicidally attack a dominant male – an act few socially sophisticated animals are stupid enough to attempt '(Suomi and Harlow, 1975 in Bruner et al., 1976, p. 492).

If play expresses some key learning features of the child's world, this is because it offers not simply practice in agility, as it did for the green monkeys (practice play), but it also represents an imaginative association with the real world. This is the second condition I would like to mention. D. W. Winnicott noted that play enables a juvenile (or indeed adult) to stand apart from reality in a certain way. Winnicott felt that play is a 'basic experience of living' (Winnicott, 2005/1971, p. 69). There is an imagined equality in play that ultimately facilitates entry into the inequality of society. Play enables the child to step back from the world and think for a moment. One might have no difficulty in saying that play is the expression of a child's world but the key interest is the way play balances itself against reality in the child's mind. Children recognize immediately the difference between the context of a meal where everyone 'has to eat their dinner' (serious) and the context of a game with the dolls' house where the dolls are eating their dinner prepared by the child (play). Along these lines Vygotsky had tried to suggest that all games are rule bound and that games shroud actions with a kind of veil. The 'real' world is now governed by the rules that are given to it by the child and this is 'play'. The child's world has become knowingly limited, bordered, within the safe environment provided by carers who need to be somewhere near in case things get a little scary. Vygotsky gives the example of two sisters playing as 'sisters' in the game 'let us play sisters'. The key contrast for these girls in Vygotsky's view is the one between action and meaning-making, between the engagement in actions as real sisters and the engagement in a veiled form of action explicable in terms of meaning-making and the exploration of being 'sisters'. Play allows the child to step aside for a moment and to reflect and make meaning out of an experience, even the experience of being someone's 'sister'. In general this reflective bubble is very enjoyable, social and safe, a bubble from which the stresses of the real world have been removed. The contrast is therefore not between fantasy and reality but between a 'safe' presentation of reality, which is essentially fun and the real experience about which the child is still a little unsure:

> I do not think that play is the dominant type of child activity. In fundamental everyday 'situations' a child behaves in a manner diametrically opposed to his behaviour in play. In play, action is subordinated to meaning, but in real life, of course, action dominates over meaning. (Vygotsky, 1976/1933, p. 551)

Three features of play

Drawing on these conditions, I would like to highlight three important features of play I have witnessed and which are particularly pertinent to education in a broad sense. The first feature is the ability of children to lose themselves in play. This is not the full story in any game but it is an important feature and it applies also to teenage and adult day-dreaming. Anyone can observe this in children apparently 'lost' in their own world. I remember one incident vividly.

Most of the boys I saw playing football had lost the awareness of being in the schoolyard. Had they been taken up by a spaceship and transported a thousand miles away, barely any of these children would have noticed. To an onlooker like myself, they seemed lost in a shared inner world. But the strange thing was that rather than being cut off in their own inner world, they seemed to dip in and out of it as they pleased. They could imagine themselves at Old Trafford only to recognize a split second later that the ball needed to be retrieved from over the schoolyard wall. A brief dispute would establish whose responsibility it was to retrieve the ball: 'You kicked it out, you get it' or 'No, it hit Jamie last, Jamie, you get it'.

They were learning not only about football but about themselves. No one was duped by the claim of some players to be famous footballers and yet these identity claims were respected for the duration of the game. When one little chap claimed, after he had won the ball, that it was 'Man United on the ball', he was forced back to reality when he lost control after a mistimed lunge forward. Any claim to be Manchester United now had been momentarily silenced, and yet all this make-believe was part of the fun. An occasional event like scoring a goal or accidentally doing something interesting with the ball was quickly celebrated. Players could become the hero of a moment, and for a short time, they could indulge their fantasy. They could imitate with remarkable precision the antics of professional footballers when they scored a goal or narrowly missed a sitter. It is obvious that in a playful way, our footballers had transformed ideas about themselves into ideals to be tested out. Certain micro-practices, how to trap the ball, how to pass, how to head the ball, how to dive, how to celebrate on scoring a goal, how to shout instructions as a goalkeeper, how to walk, everything had been noted, scrutinized and playfully recreated.

Although these boys were momentarily lost in their own collective world, boredom was prevented because they seemed happy to experiment with several symbolic identities at once and easily shifted from the reality of their performance to the imaginary excesses and perfections of their performance in the dream world. These children fancifully constructed their surface identities by drawing together mental and physical, private and public aspects of their actions. Within this fanciful world, they played every character they imagined on the playing field, each identified by an action – defensive work like player A, blocking a goal attempt like player B, a slick pass like player C, stopping the ball going out, like player B again, going over to congratulate a goal-scorer like players remembered for doing so on the television, each action 'sponsored' perhaps by a different imaginary person. The variety here prevented boredom or the 'captivation' Heidegger noticed in all boring experiences (Heidegger, 1995) because these players constantly changed their perspective in the game, effectively playing several roles at once.

This leads to the second feature of play and suggests that play lies *between two 'worlds'* – the world of the self, which incorporates the phantasmagorical just mentioned (see Sutton-Smith, 1997, p. 151) and selected elements from the real world, which is always acknowledged as existing 'out there'. This feature may lack precision in very young children and in children raised away from nurturing human company. If we remember Lacan, we would have to expect the child to allow just enough reality into its subjective circle to deal with it as part of an imagined game so that the representation is neither entirely contrived nor entirely literal – Vygotsky's observed game of 'let us play sisters'. The objective, as Piaget has well described it, is to assimilate aspects of the world to already well-established subjective schemas, which have safe boundaries and definite rules assigned to them. Players do not accommodate themselves to the world in its totality, even though they 'lose' themselves in games, because being between two worlds is essential to the game while avoiding responsibility for the world is also a key feature. Had some advanced scout for Manchester United appeared in the schoolyard, the 'game' would have changed dramatically and much of the enjoyment would have disappeared.

This lack of responsibility points to a conscious feature in the child's play and suggests evidence that children are not entirely 'lost' in their games. The 4-year-old child knows that if you ask her to get the dinner, she will do so in her own playful way and the last thing she wants is for the other members of the family to sit around the table, fork in hand, waiting for her to supply their dinner. The child knows full well the difference between the real situation and her own more intimate constructions. She knows what is a game and what is reality. The child often needs reassurance that no real demand is being made on her as part of her play. Somewhat relieved and excited, she uses play to cast both a temporal and a spatial veil over reality, echoing Vygotsky's comments, in order to construct its outline in softer terms. In this context, events can be 'remembered', but there is no immediate urgency about adaptation to real-time demands and so the precise details can be left out. From Piaget we have learned that the ability to abstract from present time and to engage in 'play time' provides the condition for deferred imitation and concept making (however unstable) in young children. Even the magical interpretation of events, which children can make, would not be possible without this kind of playful disengagement, reflection and connection – call it a kind of paradoxical relation to the real world that Piaget noted:

> Generally speaking, we find in every ludic symbol this *sui generis* combination of distorting assimilation, which is the basis of play, and a kind of representational imitation, the first providing what is 'signified' and the second being the 'signifier' of the symbol. (Jean Piaget, 1951/1976, p. 564)

A third feature is the *spatio-temporal structure* of play, its bordering and possible displacement. In this context Heidemann distinguishes between temporal and spatial features in a child's play. The temporal quality, its repeatability – *Wiederholbarkeit* (Heidemann, 1968) – creates a security and helps the child to assimilate new experiences without having to make all the psychic adjustments of imagination and emotion real encounters entail. Piaget called this 'practice' play (Jean Piaget, 1951, p. 89). The child will identify particular sequences as safe and repeatable in isolation from what a fuller encounter beyond the field of recognition would entail and the feature of time is also significant as games wear thin after a while. Not only does the end of any game, its *Erreichbarkeit* (Heidemann, 1968, p. 35) structure the game around some purpose or outcome but its satisfaction rating as a game must also be maintained. The dinner is 'cooked' when all the plastic food has been identified, located and placed on the plate and offered to the recipient with a plastic knife and fork. Immediately the child goes off to cook the dinner again. A succession of events is then ordered as a unit and turned into a repeated game, a succession of temporally limited actions with a beginning point and an end point and an element of fatigue is also built into the picture. So when the 4-year-old child brings over the dinner made up of plastic food, it is immediately withdrawn once I have even made a move to eat it and the question is promptly asked to restart the game, 'What would you like for dinner?' In this case the end of game A marks the beginning of game B, the temporal limit of the game also having spatial consequences – the plate is withdrawn and brought into a make-shift kitchen. Once the novelty is lost, however, the game is abandoned and sometimes abandoned for good.

The spatial use of a shape to the game also invests places with meaning, as spatial features are intertwined with a temporal loop, and it is possible for children to reverse or abandon the game at any time if the spatial conditions alter (a missing Teddy or a different companion might be enough to end the game), just as children may at any moment redefine the meaning of the space around them in relation to the needs of the game. A rise of ground can be the 'safe-house' in a game of chasing on one day only the following day to transform magically into a den of aliens or vampires. Changes are not always safe and can cause interest to die away sooner than expected or a new game to form outside the old parameters altogether. Similar issues happen with adults also. You might like playing scrabble in this kind of circumstance but not in another while pub managers dread the kill-joy sitting at the bar when they see other drinkers finish up and head away early, tired of the same old stories (the pub game).

Play as learning and relating

These three features of play can be summarized by saying that play is *an emotionally safe way to open up* to the world, not simply learning in a general way about the world 'out there' but rather picking out elements of it that initially appear safe enough, structuring them in a certain way using rules and sequences of a certain duration and repeating them in a way that does not replicate the real world exactly. Once we switch our attention away from play to games with rules, then we are dealing with bounded events in more formal terms but the basic use of play as an experimental field is still intact. For this reason, Heidemann identifies rules with the autonomy of the game, the fact that this game exists in the abstract as separate from other games, whereas the style of play, the precision of movement, the excellence of visible skill can equally be attributed to the confluence of different play rhetorics (Heidemann, 1968, p. 61). Heidemann interprets this flexibility to be a strength not a weakness, leading to the thought that the definitiveness of a game in space-time is always relative, a way indeed of bringing together the two elements that are normally thought to be opposite, namely, freedom and determination (Heidemann, 1968, p. 65). This is related to the non-boring feature of play, the fact that multiple perspectives are 'inhabited' by the child at the same time.

It is well known that the link between play and learning has been used as a tool for recovery in trauma situations as patients are brought back to trauma and the potential for healing by means of situations that are conjured up and presented for the purpose of healing and analysis. Scenarios are already softened by the familiar contours of play. The importance of play as a therapy for people, especially children, to help integrate a broad range of elements, physical, emotional, psychological, has been identified by experts in the field. Play has been identified as a way emotionally disturbed children can begin to relate once more to a world against which they spend much time defending themselves (Bettelheim, 1950). A more recent case study described by Wilson, Kendrick and Ryan showed how play therapy might work with children with emotional difficulties while many diverse approaches have been outlined in Schaefer's work (Schaefer, 2011). The flexibility of play, displaying what Winnicott once called 'an inner world of imaginative liveliness' (Winnicott, 2000, p. 79) enables both children and adults to accommodate themselves to the world at different rates and in both regressive and progressive ways. Following a trauma, such as the death of a close carer, a child can regress into more assimilative patterns of learning and the same is true of adults. These therapies show that Piaget was wrong to limit symbolic play to the early years although he was right, or so Gadamer thought, to link play to patterns of assimilation to the world (Gadamer, 2004, p. 102). But the point at issue is that play is ambivalent, sometimes displaying the qualities of an inner psychic world, sometimes displaying the initial features of a world into which a child has barely ventured. To learn, using play, the learner must paradoxically set aside something very dear to its own psychic make-up, namely, its own sense of mastery in order paradoxically to regain it later but from a new perspective. And it is in the 'game of mastery' that the postmodern challenge can be glimpsed.

Mastery as the purpose of play

A 4-year-old, let us call her Jenny, picks up a pot from her play cooker and using the silvery bottom, she approaches me to look into my eyes. 'Look in here', she says. I pretend to look in, she then turns the pot around in her hand, and then I recognize that this is the doctor whom she visited the previous week and who used a similar flat instrument to look into her ears. She holds the device up to my ear and utters a meaningless (to me) string of sounds. Then I say 'Am I okay doctor?' and she replies 'yes'. She is happy with this and begins to repeat the game. The child has just repeated a previously experienced drama and is reproducing it at this moment because I am sitting at my desk and this has reminded her of the visit to the doctor. To make sense of this visit and gain 'mastery' over it, to assimilate its strangeness by repetition and rehearsal, Jenny has invented this game. During her visit to the doctor's surgery, the doctor asked her to look ahead while she shone a light into her eyes and then she examined her throat and ears. In Jenny's mind, the doctor had used an object similar to the miniature silver pot, she had established a coherency in this behaviour and was currently celebrating it triumphantly in her play. Her symbolic reproduction of the event gave meaning both to the behaviour of the doctor before and my current behaviour sitting at the desk. Quite logically she wanted to confront this new experience of noticing me at the desk using an old memory of the doctor sitting behind a desk and coming around the desk to examine her. She experienced assimilation by responding to the surrounding circumstances in a highly patterned way. Her play enabled her to assimilate the reality of what it must be like for grown-up daddies to work from behind a desk even though this understanding was bounded by her own strictly bordered experience. She felt happy, enjoyed the game and the sense of mastery it brought.

I am persuaded by Piaget's argument that a phase of apparent adaptation – the child is mother cooking dinner on her play cooker or the child is the doctor examining my eyes and ears – is in reality a form of 'pure assimilation'.

Frightening elements are censored and removed and the experience of the strangeness and fear of the original situation is replaced by a softer and more pleasurable mood. Jenny assimilates the experience but on her own terms, hence it is 'pure' and she does this to enable her to grow in confidence about an observed or remembered sequence of actions. In future, the memory of the game will give the child confidence to face the doctor again. If children are not able to keep reality at a distance in this way, then there are serious issues with adaptation. Expect the child to prepare the dinner in reality and the enjoyment of play, its essential ingredient, disappears, replaced by stress and the drawn look one finds on children's faces afflicted by being orphaned in war or in famine. There is no doubt that a high level of symbolic play builds up children to enable them to face the world with confidence and when the psychic furniture is ready to support a further stage, this further stage will offer the child a greater sense of participation in the real world. Play then as properly understood is not the establishment of a world cut off in itself but describes rather the ambiguity of the child's relations with a potentially frightening world which has been made safe and can be experienced in a masterly fashion.

So, what do we learn from Piaget? If the first phase of play is reflexive and the second is symbolic, the third phase of play is the increase in representationalism in symbolic play. The third phase enables the child both to relax when confronted with stimuli and to engage in a much more precisely observed manner even if still relating to objects in an egotistical way. With precision in the objective world comes precision in the subjective world, even if this precision is always somewhat illusory. The development of certain subjective schemas at this phase heightens the power of assimilation in the child. Now the child is able to match these schemas on her own terms with new situations (Jean Piaget, 1951, p. 93) which then appear and are clearly understood in the light of earlier assimilations. Everything is understood, even if unrealistically but this, I would argue, is true at all ages. Indeed from the ages of 4 to 7, ludic symbolism games lose their importance (Jean Piaget, 1951, p. 135) as children cease to be satisfied by ludic distortion and prefer more realistic representations in their games (the cup serving as a bus in a bus game needs to be replaced by a model bus or the bus game does not make sense).

The dynamic structure of assimilation and accommodation continues to operate when symbolic games give way to games with rules which alone, according to Piaget, survive beyond middle childhood (Jean Piaget, 1951, p. 142). The problem, however, is not cognitive understanding but the continually increasing ability to learn about reality through representations.

Eventually, Piaget contends, work takes the place of play (Jean Piaget, 1951, p. 147) and this view reflects the conventional belief that play along with the dynamic of 'pure' assimilation gradually disappears. It is in this context that the problem of mastery arises, for in traditional settings children were made aware of the Reality of the world and how it might impinge on them while in a world of modern technology, children create an entire bubble around themselves which they master much more quickly than the adults who in former times may have guided them. To learn about the real world, the child's magical sense of control must be set aside and yet magical control occasionally tries to make its return in play and in the normal power games, even adults enjoy. Adults too need to be wise enough to discern whether the power games they promote stem from some unreal sense of mastery over the world – the narcissistic attitude – the parent living out their sporting ambitions in the exploits of their son or daughter playing in the Under 10s – or whether this is part of the normal pattern of accommodation.

This feature indicates a word of caution. Traditionally the ambiguity of play meant that being 'lost' in concentration indicated that the child was aware that the game was not real and that the experience of mastery was artificial and only ever experienced as conditional. The child needed to observe the real world and learn from parents or those others who carried the weight of the world. The 4-year-old who gives her dolly a bottle assumes magical control over her own previous experience of being given a bottle. This is fun and safe. She explores the frontiers of a fondly remembered experience and adds to it the rigours of a limited but rationally narrow quality of thought. Like tipping her toes in a cold stream, the child withdraws her foot to have a look at it and check that all her toes are still there: she errs on the side of caution. With adolescents, mastery over the game takes the shape of knowing better than parents or adults and taking risks that are not really perceived as risks because of the youth's perceived control over the game. Parents, however, may be acutely aware of the risks – unwanted pregnancy, drug addiction, alcohol-related problems, self-confidence issues, compulsions, lack of discipline etc. In adulthood, these attempts at mastery have usually been abandoned due to the subtle recalibration of fantasy and reality that occurs in adolescence. But not always. The sobering thought is that we live in a culture where the use of ICT and the popularity of social networking contexts may continually postpone this equilibration by downplaying experiences of vulnerability in favour of immediate experiences of artificial mastery. Ironically the game adolescents play on computers in closed environments may well have the effect of lessening the learning effects of play.

Play in a postmodern setting

All in all, we can see play as a kind of focusing of a lens on life where a boundary is brought more or less into focus. Adolescents will understandably want to lose these external controls in order to gain mastery over them according to their own insights and understandings. In a sense they will be tempted by mastery itself to take short-cuts. In the absence of total mastery, they will enjoy allowing ideas to wander about, connecting what they know across the media, picking at other fields of knowledge, and generally savouring experiences of disgruntlement, daring, rebellion and arcane individualism. Access to a potential infinity of information through the web gives any iPad user the sense of mastery over information. The complexity and variety of information itself might hide its reality as a way of toying with information without the need for commitment or any ultimate management of findings. It is an unreal kind of mastery, whose Achilles' heel may not be apparent. Practical implications can be held at bay. In other words, teenagers who lack a playful disposition but enjoy the experience of mastery, might end up with boxed ideas and strictly rehearsed sets of actions, endlessly repeated but soon forgotten. They cast these ideas off when they are done with them or consign them to half-remembered entries on some wayward blog. This is because ideas that have never had a vaporous genesis in historical learning become constrained and limited by the experience of mastery which traditionally has been the step before learning.

Our conclusion has to be that children need play. Adults need play. Humans in general need play because play is important for thinking and being, for meaning-making (Vygotsky) and for accommodation to the world (Piaget). Traditionally children used play to gain mastery over the world, first by gaining certain powers over it but later by being confident enough to take on its challenges. Play therefore was never simply a type of recreation or leisure time activity but its serious side remained constantly alive. For reasons connecting play to strategies of learning about self and world, it could be viewed as a social practice because play describes the intimate process of how animals find their place in social groups. The use of a refined human language simply highlights elements of play in a refined semiotic field. Plans, scenarios are thought out in advance and thought through on the basis of angles of approach and perspectives on problem issues. All kinds of thinking involve playing with thoughts. So it is not entirely true to say that play is separate from work unless that work is marked by such a set of very tight routines that thinking is discouraged or made impossible.

These situations are rare even in factories, although joyless societies do exist and in these societies thinking is difficult if not impossible to achieve. The three features of play sketched out here culminate in an understanding of how play helps humans to relate across worlds and to learn from them. Rather awkwardly, however, some of play's postmodern manifestations increase the extent of the illusory grip of mastery by which contemporary culture has come to imagine itself. A different challenge is posed now if the adolescent is invited to come apart into a separate world of make-believe, for now mastery is presented as the reality. This invitation has had a significant and distorted bearing on the traditional function of play which was to help learners find a pathway from a humble yet masterful beginning into the real world.

Note

1   R. McKeon (ed.) (2001). *The Basic Works of Aristotle*. New York: Modern Library.

3

Empowering the Child in Postmodernity

Most writers . . . appear to conceive man to be situated in nature as a kingdom within a kingdom; for they believe that he disturbs rather than follows nature's order, that he has absolute control over his actions, and that he is determined solely by himself.

Spinoza, *Ethics*, Introduction to Part III, translated by R. H. M. Elwes

Introduction

How often have we heard it said that a particular child has great 'potential'. The presumption is that children are individuals endowed with some potential which can be developed by proper parenting and education. Empowerment in such a context seems to mean bringing a quality, talent or disposition from potency to act. Whatever importance can be attributed to the child's surroundings and to the care it is able to command, this linear grammar, represented in terms of an inside capacity meeting an amenable outside environment, seems to anchor education in a great nature/nurture debate. It might be a different matter if empowerment were not located in the child but rather in the environment in a more fundamental sense. Here no assumption is made about talent residing in the child nor is any linear geometry favoured plotting internal elements to external elements. This time there is a 'pre-mentalist' context where there has yet to be established any distinction between subject and object, talent and environment. If children were empowered in this pre-mentalist sense, learning would base itself on key emotional conditions by which the child would learn some key issues about its own identity along with issues about the world as it appears. This chapter sets out to explore this second scenario in more detail.

Buber's problem

Indeed considerations of this latter kind may have motivated Martin Buber to criticize the title he had been given to speak on at a conference in 1926, preferring to refer the reality of the child backwards to another set of conditions, no doubt religiously based in his case, but effective nonetheless in exposing the superficiality of educational debate at the time. When Buber was asked to speak about 'educating the powers of the child' at that Heidelberg Conference in 1926 using the title, *Rede über das Erzieherische* (Talk on the Educable), he baulked at the notion of 'power' and the notion of 'development'. He had the foresight perhaps to question the notion of singularity as applied to the child and to focus instead on childhood itself as a world event. He could barely conceal his own dislike of the individualism concealed in the title of his talk, preferring to speak on a more specific level about the renewal of childhood itself (1961, p. 109). For him the individual child was to be addressed from the perspective of childhood itself, a seemingly more abstract position and meaning in some sense that the world precedes the child and that the child comes into being already as part of a world.

At each moment of any child's life, Buber believed, a question about the ongoing humanity of the world comes into play. Perhaps it does so in a concealed kind of way. Perhaps our attention has been drawn away from it because of our focus on the individual child but any concern for the ongoing renewal of humankind has to depend in a critical way on these manifestations in the child. For Buber, it is through the child that the world renews itself. For him, there could be no resting on laurels, no time spent on personal development in the face of this more urgent question about the world's survival and ultimate destiny! In fact the world seemed for him to be the centre, not the child. Was Buber a dreamer to think these things? Had he become lost in abstraction? Educators looked on perplexed.

He had certainly shocked the organizers of the conference by claiming that the issue of individual development mattered much less than this general question about the renewal of the human world. Imagine claiming that personal development was fundamentally irrelevant to the educational process, not to mention the idea of 'powers'.

And yet Buber pointed out that some assumption underlies the idea that individuals, each singularly endowed with basic powers, are only waiting for the proper dialectic between an inside and outside in order to develop. The notion of talented individuals simply waiting for the right set of circumstances to arise overlooks a number of important points. The first is that the energy coming from within must be sufficiently strong to withstand any setback and still maintain itself as a creative outpouring – Buber calls this the 'originator instinct' (p. 111). Buber does not dismiss this instinct but simply suggests that it may be more superficial than is sometimes supposed, for where does the instinct to be original come from? The originator is not simply the *homo faber*, the producer of goods, the agent of *poiesis*, the executive manipulator of the shapeless manifold. How could we say that the child by the very fact of its own singularity can shape the world? Has the child the energy or the disposition to do so, that is, to participate as a producer of the world collective? Buber is reluctant to support this conclusion because no historical line of action can be traced back to an original moment, a moment when an 'originator instinct' manifests itself in the child. All evidence seems to point to something further back than this. Even if it is reasonable to think of the child as taking on responsibility for its own actions in play or work, the energy for creativity in the child occurs prior to all mental 'I' states. There is some reality before any 'I' word, such as the more fundamental basic word as 'I-thou' in which an entire world is implicated. So he suggests that an 'instinct for communion' effectively embeds the child in a world. To imagine how this might be true, perhaps a different scenario of 'non-human' empowerment might make a case for Buber's observation.

The talent to be a dog

When stories emerged from the Ukraine in the early 1990s about a young girl of 8 years of age who had been discovered living as a dog on a run-down farm, the question was asked about what ingredients are required to make a child human in the first place. It appears that Oxana Malaya had been raised by dogs ever since her alcoholic parents abandoned her at the age of 2–3, that she had slept in kennels with dogs and had eaten and behaved as a dog for about six years, running on all fours, eating raw food and barking instead of speaking. The interesting feature of this discovery was that it did not rely on second-hand reports and that Russian television was quickly on the scene ready to transmit pictorial images of a real live 'feral' child. It is evident looking at these tapes that this child earnestly desired to be a dog and learned many of the skills and behaviours that would be consistent with being a dog. All the ingredients at her disposal were called upon to help her become a dog. Oxana's hands and feet had been genetically programmed as hominid but she set out to use them as canine feet. Her physical sense had not been defined by what her legs and arms could do but by what she believed herself to be. Her limbs had learned to operate in very minute detail the way dog limbs operate. She had felt empowered to be a dog.

Let us critique for a moment the individualist basis for all talk of talent, which would locate the talent in the potentiality of the child, and promote the idea that the happiness of the child is understandable in terms of the child's individual's project to be self-fulfilled. If we begin from the collectivist basis, then talk of talent becomes a function of the potentiality of the group rather than the individual and the recognition by the group of the individual's place. An individual in this latter case only has talent in function of the recognition achieved for it within the group. The group has its own collective logic and value system and its own way of measuring achievement. In the company of dogs, achievement is set by the phylogenetic code appropriate to dogs, and in the company of humans, achievement is set and talent identified by the phylogenetic code of humans. Added to this in the human setting is an impressive array of cultural codes and values which intervene to present the complexity of human company. 'Talented' dogs such as pack 'alphas' appear in relation to group visibility patterns. Human visibility patterns are more complex. There is evidence therefore that belonging to a collective is not specific to the human species, since it is shared by monkeys and dogs, wolves and birds among other animals. The collective imperative to seek out affection and form an identity in animal surroundings cannot form the basis of a particularly human specific rationale for action but points to a pre-mentalist context as the source of human action, whatever the cultural manifestation of that action or its ultimate 'humanness'.

So the paradox lies in the fact that in order to become visible as a human, individuals need to be empowered by emotional ties that are basically animal in origin and are subsequently inflected by cultural markers. Even years later, having been rescued and re-educated and survived, where many do not survive, Oxana still preferred the company of dogs and expressed in human language her feeling that she was never happier than when in the company of dogs. Despite what others might say and what her physique might say after she had been 'rescued' from the dogs, she had formed a bond with dogs that was essential to her. If anything, she was the ugly duckling who, because she had found recognition as a duckling at a sensitive age, preferred to be an ugly duckling than a beautiful swan.

Buber again

Returning then to Buber for a moment, it is possible to imagine what 'world' might mean if the originator instinct is subservient to something else. As Buber gets behind the notion of talent, it is clear that the 'instinct for communion' is what enables the child 'to receive and imagine the world' (p. 116) and in so doing the child is happy to allow itself to be shaped by a world held in communion with others, and to shape this world in turn. He is more a player within the world than its originator and, within this world, he can take multiple perspectives. There are limits to this, however. Buber uses traditional constructivist language to imply an 'originator instinct' at work: 'Empathy means, if anything, to glide with one's own feeling into the dynamic structure of an object, a pillar or a crystal or the branch of a tree, or even of an animal or a man, and as it were to trace it from within . . .' (p. 124). For Buber, the 'I' is already compromised by its possible appearance in one of two worlds, the world of 'I-Thou' and the world of 'I-It', each allowing events to appear separated by an important paradigm shift. The significance of this to our argument is that Buber's 'world' does not originate in the 'I' but rather the reverse, the 'I' originates in the world.

To think of education as responding to some lack in the individual, tracing a linear move from potency to act, suggests in contrast that emptiness is the key starting point of all learning. However, to begin from the opposite position and consider that education starts from a fullness, a type of empowerment, then I think we are close to Buber's meaning. Buber was able to avoid elaborating on education expressed as desire, desire for knowledge, desire for fulfilment, desire for some future state of human flourishing by speaking about paradigm shifts between two quite different worlds, the world of 'I-Thou', the world of 'I-It'. Education in such a scenario would describe the move from more to less, from some kind of general empowerment to some kind of particularity. Education would then become the work of precision. And the anchor point would not be the self and all the developmental language centring on the 'I' but rather the world. I think back to Winnicott's position that children begin from a position of 'omnipotence' or 'false' belief about themselves and only gradually accept the lessons of vulnerability, particularity as they mature. They move from fullness to precision, from infinity to finitude.

Psychopathology: Managing the emptiness and fullness of being

Empowerment in the sense given here carries some drawbacks. For instance, human reason may not be able to relate well to its own empowerment since the latter is by definition, pre-mental, pre-linguistic, pre-phenomenological. Indeed this complication stems from the fact that reason may not be a good judge of its own empowerment. Theodor Adorno may have had a point when he wrote that reason manifests a certain psychopathology and that it has the power to twist itself beyond recognition into rationalizations and distorted world views. Psychopathology announces itself in continual attempts to sustain illusions about the self and about the world when these are not accessible to rational critique. Lacan defined the *Imaginary* in terms of a field of thinking stemming from the child's 'mirror stage' image, an image of self that forms at about six months, which is relatively 'stable' but 'ideal' and that gives rise to countless ruminations and cogitations about a self which does not exist. If the *Imaginary* becomes the dominant source of reflection and reflection's playground, then all is not well for the person. A noisy mental state might mean that Reality in the Lacanian sense cannot break through and indeed might become overwhelming, if it ever did. Lacan spoke of the moment that a human child began to play with its own mirror image in a manner that showed qualitative advances over the chimpanzee who quickly 'exhausts' the value of the image (1966, p. 89). For Lacan, this playful attitude of the child involves much fantasy and a long-term commitment to the fiction of the self, to a game of switching and swapping that is only afterwards exposed to the precision demands of social and educational contexts.[1] For this reason, much like Winnicott, Lacan believed that it is paradoxically healthy for a bogus fullness to accompany children throughout their development.

Winnicott's theory points to a bio-emotional beginning that accompanies the child, transferring on occasion to objects and events that offer a pay-back in terms of security and support. For Winnicott, the self is basically a feeling, communicated to the child by its environment and while the transitional object is not a mirror, it operates in a similar way by bolstering the illusion of an original 'omnipotence'. The theory suggests that some children, while feeding at mother's breast, develop the habit of grasping an object like the end of a blanket, a soft toy, a teddy bear. Soon they transfer the warm feeling of security, nourishment, omnipotence into these objects or gestures without quite knowing what is happening. An identified smell is also essential. A soother presented becomes a substitute breast and is associated with warm feelings despite the lack of nourishment. Winnicott explains how these objects and indeed routines gradually allow some children to begin to relate with confidence to the world of cultural objects, already softening these objects by their disposition and security, as engendered usually by the mother. They are the mother to some extent, each object appearing as a presentation of that undifferentiated association the child has with mother. They are symbolic in Lacan's sense in that they retain the fiction generated by this emotional support. They stem from a 'world' in Buber's sense because they crystallize the elements of an entire world around what is to be learned. For Winnicott, these things 'are evidence that things are going well in the child's emotional development, and that memories of relationships are beginning to be built up' (2000, p. 168). They are evidence of a child in a communicative mode, relating to the world around it as best it can but essentially from a position of omnipotence. No one really wants to grow out of this type of 'fiction' but, as the child develops, there is an ontogenetic and a phylogenetic progression also, meaning that there is a development in this particular individual (ontogenetic) and a development in the renewal of the human race (phylogenetic) (see Gay, 1983, p. 380).

Good enough parents are able to communicate the impression that the world is exactly the way the child imagines it to be so that he or she can master it completely. Psychopathology depends on supporting the illusion at all times. Indeed from this fantasy children can muster up the confidence to handle setbacks and inputs from the world which do not seem to fit the idealized patterns, events that can therefore be talked down as exceptional or unusual. Slowly, however, the outside world needs to make its impact and skilled carers can mediate the move from the self-confidence based on the illusion of omnipotence to the self-confidence based on the discovery of personal reality. Gradually gifted into the world by means of this more moderate kind of self-confidence, the child can take on whatever the world brings and there are reminders of transitional objects along the way to help with this, which allow momentary lapses back into illusion. The cuddly toy, which you always had, accompanies you to college or finds itself beside your bed when you go to a strange place.[2] It is more than a lucky charm, although less than a transitional object; it is a sign that it is safe to reach out into a strange world with your mother or special friend beside you to ease your transition into the unknown. Now it might seem a bit far-fetched to suggest that ideas too can perform a soothing function but it is nevertheless particularly important when teaching children to be aware that criticism of self ought to be muffled, if not avoided. Otherwise to ask a child to shift a familiar idea in which she has taken refuge and sought comfort, perhaps for several years, is to ask her to step out into the outside world without shield or spear.

This invitation needs to be made gently and in a context where ideas can be retained for a time as quasi-transitional objects within the psychic landscape. The challenge for educators is to achieve this critical sense and give permission to explore ideas without damaging the child's security or sense of emotional integrity, hence, essentially without treading on the child's dreams.

Much depends on which one of these models, filling the emptiness or limiting the fullness, is used as a basis for the educator's understanding of 'empowerment'. If we think of the child as a reservoir of potential, and we judge the child's surrounding circumstances to be hostile to the development of these potentials, we tend to think of the problems as coming from outside. There is an outside set of oppressive circumstances or an absence of support. And we can wrongly imagine that the child is likely to be unfulfilled and therefore unhappy when things don't go quite right, when resources are absent, when desires are left unfulfilled. On the other hand, it is interesting to see how the move from fullness to precision can be made.

Learning perspective

The mother's ability to distance herself while acknowledging acute feelings in the child becomes the key in the child's ability to develop, pointing to what Fonagy and Target call 'a higher order strategy of affect regulation' (1997, p. 696). The child learns to develop a grammar of the emotions. Emotions are expressed by means of a language that enables the child to develop subtle human patterns of association. The problem for the feral child is that the animal or animals mediating this emotion are not human, do not possess any subtleties of language which might permit non-isomorphic representation or other dispositions like sympathy or empathy that can teach the child how to cope with strong negative emotions. So in a curious way, the maltreated child who may become withdrawn from the world suffers in a similar way to the feral child. The human child, acting in human contexts, may well have to face patterns of maladaptive behaviour by parents, due perhaps to aggression, the mental illness of caregivers, marital conflict or overt violence or abuse, thus resulting in a muted array of emotional cues. The feral child has simpler but equally deep-reaching problems because all species-specific indicators of identity have been lost and the net effect may be that the child has been 'disempowered' and is unable to become human.

Not only Harlow (Harlow and Zimmermann, 1958, 1959), but Winnicott also mentioned the importance of the mother's holding of a baby – common to most primates – as a way of mediating strong emotions. Skin touch communicates comfort and security to the baby, answering its basic emotional needs and creating the basis for the child's emerging sense of world and self. There is a move from an undifferentiated inter-subjectivity where the child feels part of a greater whole, a pre-individual state, to a sense of the particularity of the self. Judging by these elements, it is clear that Oxana Malaya did not become a dog simply because of some potency in her to become one but rather because being an individual dog followed on emotionally from being part of a collective life-world. Her sense of agency, however, would not be aided by the subtleties of human language. She would not be directly addressed or named. She would not learn to handle strong emotions, especially negative ones, except by conforming to the system of the life-world, obeying the alpha of the pack, for instance, or taking her place in the queue at feeding time. By contrast human children under normal circumstances develop a grammar of the emotions which enable them to develop more subtle human patterns of association.

If alarm is sounded by one, it is felt by all. Some commentators on child development point to the stage in an infant's development that could be roughly described as pre-mentalist. Before breaking into higher language, language 2, an infant 'is not required to represent the thoughts or feelings of the caregiver' (Fonagy and Target, 1997, p. 682). Nor does it have any experience of a persistent I-state but presumes itself to be the centre. Thus the totality of an entire world over which the collective has complete control, due to the careful response of caregivers is behind the I-state. Gradually the child uses the responses it receives from carers to formulate a primitive teleology. These pre-mentalist clues soon act coherently in order to elicit a response and the child is able to establish in a pre-mentalist way that discomforts can be removed and replaced by comforts, that bad situations can change – nappy rash can be eased etc. Time is experienced in this pre-mentalist way, much as it is for chimpanzees and the representational mapping of experience, psychologists suggest, begins to occur between 6 and 18 months (Fonagy and Target, 1997, p. 682).

Recognition

We seem to be far from Buber here but the issue of empowerment is still to the fore. Buber's hunch that empowerment is a feature underlying all talk of development seems to be borne out by these psychological studies. An emotional 'set' is used as a basis for learning, however this is established. On the other hand, some theorists of mental states like Noam Chomsky postulate what Fonagy and Target call 'an innate (learning) mechanism with a specific location in the brain' (1997, p. 681). Our argument here is that mental states are not located in the brain or even in the individual as a potential of the individual. Instead mental states are located in the collective which is mediated through the emotions and only thereafter through the language used by *ratio* or reason. The reason this is largely ignored is the fact that the language used to describe primitive states is usually post-mentalist, and so a feature of the cultural language of humans (language 2). But there are commentators who have tried to identify this primitive state using other terms.

Axel Honneth follows Adorno to say that humans learn to be human by imitating other human beings and this sets the issue of imitation at the centre of behaviour (2005, p. 33). Honneth further contends that imitation has become critical to the development of self. This is a paradox, of course, because imitation is a kind of copying and generally thought to oppose the sense of individualism often thought to underlie the sense of self. The key thought is that talents or 'powers' do not reside in the individual self but derive from the empowerment from which the child has benefitted.

We can make sense of this if we begin with a totalized social fabric, implying that imitation is not simply copying but is a way of taking perspective on what the carer is doing. The love of the carer for the child should provide the child with an emotional filter which communicates confidence and enables the child to identify the outside world of objects as objects that are safe to be near. The child, like any animal imitates first the relation between a trusted adult and objects and people in the environment of the carer. An entire grammar of objects needs to be learned that the child only notices because he or she has received 'permission' to see them. The child's emotional life is the starting point for this learning. Oxana Malaya adapted to her environment by becoming a speechless communicator and by learning to use the range of semiotic behaviours established to communicate between members of the group. By extension with this, young humans in a consumer society learn the semiotic systems of exchange and positioning by shopping, dressing in approved ways and talking about approved things – shops, clothes, shopping-centres, bargain, colours, fashions etc. Much to everyone's consternation, the same logic applies to both cases.

Honneth also follows Winnicott's careful tracing of a mother's graduated de-adaptation from immediate affective states. He agrees that it is here that a cognitive differentiation between self and environment begins to become possible and a strategic 'relative dependence' eventually crystallizes in the psychic life of the child. A tantrum cry might be used by the child to test her ability to control the environment and to deny the 'objectivity' of the mother, but in normal circumstances, this attempt fails due to the skill of the mother to ease the tantrum by soothing noises and words. Indeed the child's loss of power to fill the emotional environment is the key to its development as an individual. While transitional objects might accompany the child to keep the fantasy of omnipotence alive – Teddy Bears, blankets, dollies – these all announce an eventual defeat. As Honneth explains it, there is a paradox in being alone which comes about 'out of a basic confidence in the care of a loved one' (1996, p. 103) which means that the continuity of the mother's care is central to the ability of a child to learn independently. This emotional security not only prefigures the child's psychological independence but also operates critically behind the child's learning independence, that is, learning for itself.

Handling vulnerability

Indeed Honneth's theory of recognition opens up the very centre of empowerment hinted at earlier, for empowerment, on his theory, is not located in the child as an individual 'power' but is rather a function of the supporting environment. It is a mistake therefore to educate children as if they were the originators of their own world, and so Buber was right to say that the instinct for communion is much more primordial. Educational empowerment makes itself more precise only after the exit of the child from the 'omnipotence' of early childhood. A loved child can open up by means of a kind of empowerment that predicts some kind of stability in later life but there is nothing automatic about this process. The key word Honneth uses here is vulnerability because, if we are to take Winnicott and other object relations theorists at their word, we need to recognize the 'specific vulnerability of humans resulting from the internal interdependence of individualization and recognition . . .' (p. 131).

This vulnerability, however, also extends to higher primates and other animals. It is not a specifically human feature nor does it lead naturally to specifically human ways of life. And yet it is the desire for recognition that continues to prompt humans to behave in culturally normative ways, facilitated perhaps by the accidental circumstances of their lives. Other ways of life are also open but there are reasons why they have not become generalized. There can be honour among thieves, solidarity among the perpetrators of genocide, mutual valorization by porn stars, convivial secrecy in a group grooming children for sex, camaraderie among soldiers who kidnap child soldiers, smiles and gifts offered by cults to attract new members, secret handshakes to promote cliques and power, circles that promote ritualist conformity. Humans and non-human primates need esteem as adults because esteem is a function of adult identity. It is a more fundamental need than the need for life itself. Against this background, it is up to society to determine in the case of children under what conditions they consider themselves valued – initially within a family, provided that family structure is supportive and provides the child with self-confidence but in the absence of this perhaps due to how children are supported. A good teacher surfs on this grammar of recognition, bestowing on children the confidence to grapple with things that are still out of reach.

Conclusion

So this then is the general picture. On the one hand, the superficial picture centres on the individual child. The child is thought to have resources that are still only potential and require principally only proper conditions for development. The surrounding world then can be vetted to determine whether it provides a suitable space for the flourishing of these elements. The child can be thought of as lacking in fulfilment even though there can be a debate about whether the natural resources of the child are properties or 'powers' or 'potencies' already in the child's possession and remaining there independent of the nurture provided or whether they are a function of the interaction between child and world. Outside circumstances, whether supportive or inhibiting, need to be carefully evaluated if the aim is to bolster a potential simply waiting for development in the individual child. On this reading, the business of the educator then is to remove the obstacles to desire and to the actualization of the child's potential. However, Buber's work points to the overall context in which the child operates that is generally not due to a property *in the individual child* but rather due to the way the child is constituted by the 'I-thou' world of relations to which it is bound. Here a completely different approach and model comes into play and if we follow Winnicott and Lacan, the challenge for the educator is to introduce some level of reality into what is a primordial happy place. The child is only too happy to stay in a blissful state of omniscience where security can be presumed. It is the move away from the comfort zone that poses the difficulty. Educators therefore need to move with refined emotional sensitivity when they concern themselves with the child's development from this perspective. Even though educators recognize when 'defensive postures' inhibit learning in children and adolescents, they need to be patient. The soother may need to be sucked for a little while longer as there is an ultimate trade-off between the admission of vulnerability and learning even in the postmodern context.

Following this 'collectivist' hypothesis means that the other more common hypothesis needs to be set aside, namely, the presumption that 'powers' are a function of some a priori potency in the child. Along with this we need to abandon the idea that education should follow the deficit model of desire and fulfilment. We need rather to think of empowerment as an a posteriori feature of a child's development, a historically generated set of circumstances that could disappear quite quickly from human affairs but is expressed in the emotions if it exists at all. Children that function well emotionally can identify positively with the pre-individual life of animals. They are then paradoxically empowered to learn in a human sense because of this animal association. It is here that some features of attachment theory become relevant to human identity and learning.

Notes

1 '. . . cette forme situe l'instance du moi, dès avant sa détermination sociale, dans une ligne de fiction, à jamais irréductible pour le seul individu . . .' J. Lacan (1966). *Ecrits 1* (Vol. 1). Paris: Editions du Seuil.
2 Some research has shown that the retention of transitional objects beyond a certain age is a significant predicator of mental illness. One might note that it is the mental illness which causes the retention of the transitional object and not vice versa.

Part II

Appearances

4

The Global Child

Nature passes so gradually from inanimate to animate things, that from their continuity, their boundary and the mean between them is indistinct.
Aristotle, *History of Animals*, VIII, 1, 588b 5, translated by R. Cresswell

Introduction

The globality described here is not the same as globalization, even though globality is linked to globalization at the deep-rooted cultural level. Some educators have recently thematized the effects of globalization on education (Burbules and Torres, 2000; Edwards and Usher, 2008) and the dangers of a cognitive colonization by economic forces have also been identified and explored (Zembylas and Vrasidas, 2005, p. 81). It has been a shock to learn that Burger King has opened academies in 14 US cities (Burbules and Torres, 2000, p. 8) and to recognize how the creeping privatization of education has affected public service education. It has been a shock to notice the focus on 'rational organization and management theories' imported from business models (Burbules and Torres, 2000, p. 18) and to see the traction that these constructions seem to have in state policies on education. It is a shock to see the extent to which the economics of the Western world encourages the privatization of provision and a state-level abrogation of responsibility for education. Edwards and Usher focus on 'the spatiality of globalising processes' (Edwards and Usher, 2008, p. 2). They expose the dis-location inherent in postmodern locations, the phenomenon of children being positioned as different in order to be set aside, as marginal, as relatively unresourced, as expendable (Edwards and Usher, 2008, p. 10). These themes blend in with what I want to explore here.

Parents in caring for their children know that they are not dealing with beings whose insides are already developed and so they must operate on behalf of the child. Parents need to create the substance which will eventually respond to their gaze. They know that lingering fantasy leads to emptiness and they are careful about the Reality that attempts to take its place. Who is the fairest of them all – the child is, of course, and, in a sense, that is the way things always have to be. It is these words that establish the child on the map. Unlike children raised in poor orphanages who never hear anyone say that they are the fairest of them all, this knowledge delivered by the praise of parents, teachers, supporters enables the child to learn by reasserting its centrality in the world. This is a knowledge that creates as it teaches; it is ontogenetic as much as epistemological; it etches out a place on the landscape, enabling the child's being to take root in a historical moment.

The mirror does not initially need to speak very complex words because the signs and gestures of language 1 will do, although where there is the capacity for language 2, the normal cultural language also speaks a human word, the word 'you', as Buber suggested. For the child to feel good about itself, this 'you' needs to be filled with positive feelings and positive gestures. The importance of this can be realized when examples of a different kind of upbringing come to the fore, children uprooted and raised in less than ideal circumstances, perhaps by street gangs, pimps, primers, self-appointed generals in children's armies, drug addicts, mental cases and abusive minders. Whether good or bad, these are the talking mirrors into which a child gazes to ask, mirror, mirror on the wall, who is the fairest of them all? The empowerment imperative will oblige these children to believe what they hear – they are 'good' killers, they are 'good' rapists, they are 'good' robbers, they are 'good' little papa girls. The imperative impels them to seek the esteem of those they are with, for the good or ill of society in general. So where does that leave our global child?

Parents also know that the mirror on the wall often tells necessary lies. Humans view themselves initially based on a very imprecise and under-observed illusion about our own bodies and beings, an image of the bottle being half-full rather than half-empty, a self that remains essentially imaginary – Lacan's *Imaginaire*. The child at the mirror stage (6–8 months) forms a sudden if imprecise 'imaginary' insight into its own body and into itself. One commentator referred to this insight as 'a caricature, at best a holding device for an ego that would never be fully complete' (Brown, 2008, p. 407). For Lacan, this imaginary ego does two important things. It first of all distinguishes the human from the animal and second, it more or less ties the human ego to a world of make-believe where reality – the Real if you prefer – would only encroach on occasion, and often with challenging results. Under normal circumstances the child could remain shrouded in its own psychological veil. And indeed this veil may well operate even more dramatically in teenage situations when more serious relationships are in play. Teenagers often 'discover' areas of their faces that they have been looking at for years without seeing them carefully. They look for years but they do not see. There is a dramatic change when a pimple turns up or when their lives suddenly enable them to 'see' the pimple. Luckily this does not remain an 'end of the world' experience for the individual.

There is a plausibility in Lacan's account. Human life is generally guided by some kind of fantasy that is held in place for emotional reasons and there are always problems in contacting Reality. Humans may need to live by some degree of mitigated fantasy in order to cope with an initial incapacity to handle the outside world. Children usually imagine themselves powerful in their play when in fact they are fragile. Indeed they seem to gain in power when they gain in an awareness of fragility. This is good for the film industry, good for partial self-presentations in blogging and social networking, good for myth, but not good for the transition from fantasy self to real self, the basic journey of adolescence. Someone who needs to learn about themselves is largely incapable of releasing themselves from subjugation to their own circular authority, Buber's 'instinct for communion'. Teenagers are still quite vulnerable to the need for recognition. And yet with gentle education their fantasy world proceeds to find expression in words, in language, in what Lacan in general calls the Symbolic and which Brown glosses as 'the ideological apparatus that surrounds and engulfs me' (Brown, 2008, p. 409). Under such terms I am the author of my own life, the one who sustains my own illusions, the primary reason why, as a teenager, I am scandalized by a pimple that appears on my face. Ultimately, however, it is Reality which begins to enter the scene and provide me with the stability required.

In summary, mirrors normally need to be anchored in the locality and to be indicative as a tool of esteem and recognition. Second they need to be in a position to enable us to access the Real. It is of no value to be told that we are the fairest of them all when in Reality we notice a pimple on our nose. Our education depends on the ability to let the messages of Reality in to operate as an agent of change. We now need to ask what happens to these 'friendly' mirrors when the forces of globality intervene to attract the postmodern child into becoming a refugee.

As an experiment we could inquire about globality in the sense of an exchange in cultural mirrors. There have been many examples of this in assimilationist policies and programmes in various places. I propose to look at one example which shows cultural assimilation between one world and another and how the displacement of mirrors can negatively affect child well-being and learning. This manifestation of globality has been clearly discredited and happily abandoned but it may still be present in subtler forms. Second there is globality as characterized by Giorgio Agamben's notion of a 'refugee', which may be a useful construct in describing the status of young surfers on the internet today. What might it be like to abandon the cloistered seclusion of an early living space and to become exposed to influences of every sort? Children are now more than ever exposed to the 'you' that someone who does not know them has spoken. This is the challenge posed by globality in postmodern spaces.

Globality mark 1: Pure assimilation

American Indian parents expected much for their sons and daughters when they sent them away from the reservation to a boarding school. They hoped that they would return with a trade and would be educated. Hence they were prepared in some cases to put up with separation from their children for four years or more, generally without any visits, since the distances involved, sometimes two days by train, the expense involved in travel, made visits impossible. It was effectively a form of dislocation. Brenda J. Child's collection of letters from parents to school superintendents and principals and their responses offers a sobering reminder of the white policy of assimilation, which underlay these attempts to educate Indian children up to the 1940s. Comments among these letters show how homesickness played a double role, often afflicting parents as they watched their children go away not to return for some years and almost always afflicting the children who had become the target of a disrespectful policy which, from 1870s to the 1930s, operated to change the children's mirrors from red to white. Before that, of course, the picture had been even darker for Indian tribes, rather encapsulated by President Andrew Jackson's comment, 'What good man would prefer a country covered with forests and ranged by a few thousand savages to our extensive republic, studded with cities, towns and prosperous farms . . .' (as cited in Pearce, 2001, p. 57).

Education was not a friendly force in these children's lives. Poor Indian children were sometimes forcefully removed from parents in order to be 'globalized' by means of an artificially constructed life in white man's boarding schools. Others came to State boarding schools in the hope of finding a trade, not realizing that once they entered the school they became to all intents and purposes incarcerated for a period of years. Native Americans used the term 'lonesome' to describe the feelings of homesick children and parents. Parents were 'lonesome' after their children and children were 'lonesome' after parents, wider family and tribal lands and customs. They were not foolish enough to think that education was entirely value free or positive towards Indian values but Indian poverty and cultural disarray were no friends in the daily struggle to raise children either. And everywhere there were the long-term marks of poverty and hopelessness. As Child remarks:

> When families could not earn an adequate living on the reservation or in the city, they often enrolled children in boarding schools as a temporary or long-time solution to some of their most pressing problems. Parents expected that in boarding school, basic needs would be met in the form of food, clothing, a rudimentary education, and the opportunity to learn a trade. Even modest expectations on the part of parents were sometimes disappointed. (1998, p. 24)

Child recounts the hopes of Indian parents who thought that, despite the poverty afflicting entire nations, their children would survive the experience of education in the white man's schools. They hoped that their children would return with their cultural identities still intact and with a trade, but they often lost out on both counts. First they found that their child came home without any viable trade, having been apprenticed to old servile trades like saddle-making for boys and dress-making for girls. The situation improved in the 1930s (p. 80 ff.). Second they found that they now had been indoctrinated against things Indian and had been left with a confusing set of mirrors speaking to them about their identities. In many cases, children only learned how to feel bad about themselves. In some cases, they returned home after four, five, six or seven years, having mixed in a pan-Indian environment for so long and having been obliged to speak English on a daily basis, without any adequate grasp of their own mother tongue or customs and, while their families accepted them, their tribes often did not. They were alien children and the children of an alien culture which they could not recognize. The tribes often saw them as lost causes:

> Sun Elk was one of the first boys from Taos Pueblo in New Mexico to attend Carlisle during the 1880s. After seven years of boarding school, Sun Elk had

grown clumsy with the Tiwa language. He was virtually ignored by all but
his family after his return to Taos, and the governor of the Pueblo rebuffed
him for not learning 'the things that Indian boys should learn'. (p. 97)

Few white teachers understood the dramatic impact of children losing their own
mother language since they judged speaking English as a step up in civilized
behaviour. To be 'lonesome' in contexts where one had become a refugee,
separated artificially from family and tribe, to have to face sickness and disease
on one's own, that described the sorry lot of these newly assimilated children.
To the governors of Carlisle, Haskell, Flandreau or Pipestone, 'lonesome' feelings
by children were only to be expected and would soon be overcome as the child
matured. Parents too initially underestimated the effect of this homesickness on
the overall ability of their children to learn and work. Yet some worried when they
knew about it, for homesickness often heralded a loss of the will to live. Parents
were unfortunately up against a total misunderstanding of the significance to
Indian children of their own culture as well as utter dismissal of Indian ways, both
evidenced in the comment of H. B. Peairs, Assistant Superintendent of Haskell in
1896, and later its Governor who suggested that Indian children learn nothing at
home (Bureau of Indian Affairs Annual Reports 1896, p. 63 as quoted in p. 74).

Notwithstanding the irony of these remarks, for Indian children often learned
nothing of value in these Boarding Schools, their education failed to fill these
children with any degree of self-confidence because they failed to act as mirrors
telling them who they were. Not only dislocated, they were also disempowered.
Nor did these mirrors enable the children to achieve the tribal status that Indian
children in previous generations had achieved. The mirrors presented never said
to any individual child – you are the fairest of them all. Indeed the feeling of being
alien accompanied these children in everything they did while at school and this
same feeling travelled back with them to the reservations. They attempted to
learn the white man's trades in order to survive into the next generation but they
returned often without the will to succeed.

Globality mark II: The global refugee

Hannah Arendt used the term 'refugee' in an article published in *The Menorah
Journal* in 1943, entitled 'We refugees'. It soon became plain that the title referred
not only to the *Shoah* against Jews but to all people living at the present time.
She was making the claim that a new historical consciousness had arisen and

that the widespread experience of population displacement during the war years had created the impression among the peoples of Europe that they were in fact 'refugees' in their own place (Agamben, 1995, p. 114). For Arendt, the inevitable decline in the nation-state structure following the war, together with the opening up of borders and the free flow not only of information but of peoples and workers, have combined to increase this impression. In the immediate aftermath of the war, people were less inclined to identify exclusively with one location but saw themselves as migrant workers or travellers. Giorgio Agamben applied Hannah Arendt's insight into the nature of the modern refugee to the notion of *bios* or life in its cultural manifestation. This could be a good thing, of course, but if locality and local citizenship are not the central governing idea determining the rights of people, would *bios* be in a position to do this any better? Would the fact that a human being was human carry any weight? Being a 'refugee' opened huge numbers of people to dangers because generalized war in the 1940s pointed to the reality of millions of lives left in the hands of armies. Refugees, the responsibility of no one in times of generalized emergency, could be allowed to die. Having abandoned all categories of esteem bound to a single locality or collective, Agamben asks on what basis can we presume the esteem which we all require to live in groups?

Along these lines, Agamben gives a brief history of the problem of refugees in Europe, distinguishing between stateless persons and refugees, for populations can be rendered stateless on a temporary basis or even within a state even if they are native to the place. The 1935 Nuremberg laws segregated Germans into full citizens and others (Agamben, 1995, p. 115). The presence of 'refugees' within the same territory initially promoted fears that they could be banished and this soon turned into the fear that they could be exterminated. This phenomenon, the phenomenon of the camps, became, in Agamben's view, the leitmotif of the (post)modern state which now asks questions about the extent of responsibility of any government for the lives of those who dwell in its locality, switching from a concern for the lives of everyone to a concern for the lives only of a documented few.

There may be implications of this for multicultural classrooms where there is a majority and a norm set to cater for the majority while in the midst of this majority stand another group or groups. But this is not the problem posed by globality in this second sense. The problem arises when the child configures himself or herself as a world citizen first of all, a global being who has more freedom from the local context, rules, regulations, systems but also less responsibility for it. There is evidence that the postmodern child may be attracted to this type of status. To be a citizen of the world, after all, means that one can range across borders, perhaps across languages, without having to show a passport but who is there to take care of this traveller? Or is care even a proper word to use? This is not simply a political question, although it is asked by political philosophers. It is an educational question because today's youthful citizen communicates with the whole world, travels via the internet across borders and jurisdictions and finds itself curiously resentful of borders, censorship, age-limits, including the limitations imposed by local laws, local customs. Such a world citizen links itself to the mindset of a 'refugee' with virtual citizenship status (and none) which he can cling to on the grounds of a common claim to be part of some greater wave of humanity and to enjoy the protection of various cross-border agencies. Here too there is the experience of leading two separate lives, one spent floating across what is still largely a commonage, an information superhighway containing everything including Government secrets, the other relying on local resources for support.

Agamben has described the new post-war refugee status of all peoples, not only children as a 'devastating experiment', particularly since it involves the wholesale abolition of rank as a cohesive, locally managed, social force. Henceforth rank will be managed on a worldwide basis. An experiment has taken place which, in Agamben's words, 'disarticulates and empties institutions and beliefs, ideologies and religions, identities and communities all throughout the planet, so as then to rehash and reinstate their definitively nullified form' (Agamben, 2000, p. 110).

Just what effect this new state of affairs has on citizenship education is difficult to tell. Where once human identity could make a claim to be a citizen of a place, now the same identity can claim to be free and relatively unencumbered by any need for citizenship or by any responsibility either. This is the époque of a new globality but the Faustian bargain is the same as always. Young people presume liberation but remain vulnerable to the fantasy profiles presented to them and supported less and less by the local economy of praise that every cultural group uses to make possible the emergence of the individual from childhood.

The point of inquiry is first to note the balance which has been achieved between two separate logics of government – the local and the global – and to note that the creation of a 'refugee status' is implied in attempts both to bypass the local and to privatize the provision of access to knowledge. Leaving aside the effect of this on adults, the point at issue here is how this ambivalent model of governance applies to the area of self-governance in children and in particular how children are learning to apply this pattern to themselves, to the development and management of their freedom as learners with immediate access to unlimited information on the internet and the continuing promise that they are entering a world of novelty orientated towards the future and under the protection of forces that are as yet undefined.

Educational effects of mark II globality

This state of affairs leads to a number of speculative points. Old institutions and old cultural spaces have been seriously compromised because of a political trend to accept a straight swop between the status of refugee and the normal cultural and institutional supports, which seem narrow-minded, partial, local and dated. The problem is that granting a new kind of educational refugee status on learners breaches the empowerment circle that they ultimately need. As refugees, they have become 'neo-subjects', marked by the trimmings of global power, but with no real connection. They are happy with this new social apparatus, as indicated by Agamben, but they have not weighed up the implications of this disconnection from human animal roots. As global beings, they are known to be users of technology, surfers, students, commuters, workers, holiday makers, stag party-goers, music fans, museum tourists, art gallery visitors, street protestors, volunteers, members of cults exposed to influences that come from nowhere. They have opted to cling to the arbitrary apparatuses of refugees, the experience of 'being outside and yet belonging' (2005, p. 35) because it gives them the impression of having plenipotentiary powers without destiny or responsibility, like a kind of game. This is not imposed from above but rather selected as a preference – to live not under the guidance of a dictatorship but in 'a space devoid of law, a zone of anomie, in which all legal determinations . . . are deactivated' (p. 50).

There may be good reasons for opting for the global if it enables the neglected child to relativize his negative circumstances and find a compass that might offer other possibilities. Indeed new technologies of education could develop a sense of global connection that permits him to plot a course around traditionally insurmountable local obstacles. If so, the child looks into the mirror and asks, who is the fairest of them all? and receives a global answer. This curious parallelism of messages (local and global) would enhance the child's range of potential self-concepts. But any trend to supplant local supports by means of state or internationally funded bodies, orphanages or schools, which claim to be able to manage the futures of children and rear them as they should be reared, is at risk of dismantling the normal and natural empowerment of the historical collective.

Local praise

Once this emptying of status occurs in the mind of the child, he or she may be offered the rights of a 'refugee' in return for some sense of liberation from history and locality. We have seen how an emptying occurred which turned Indian children into refugees, attending boarding school pupils while being artificially separated from a home. But contemporary practitioners note how linked praise is to local conditions, especially the way it adds a positive reinforcement to activities and practices (Conroy et al., 2009; Hester et al., 2009; Nelson et al., 2010). Apart from the wisdom of incorporating skilful praise in classroom interactions – skilful, that is, not haphazard, empty or indiscriminate, that it should be linked to a particular practice, that it should take place without much time delay, that it should be consistently applied in situations and across the sample populations (Wheatley et al., 2009), the effect of praise on the recognition of individuals is also significant. Of course, some dangers have also been highlighted (see Dweck, 2007) but in general once the praise is systematic (Sugai and Horner, 2006) and signals a positive feedback loop (Conroy et al., 2009; Partin et al., 2010), then praise can enhance the relationship between teacher and child. In vacuum situations from which praise has been expelled, on the other hand, children may well seek notice in other ways, as most teachers know. But every child needs to be in touch with local roots for those connections that empower them and keep them going at moments of stress and discouragement. This is what our human animal nature tells us. Otherwise globality will do to them what it did to the Native American peoples in the boarding school.

    Studies of praise show that it is the immediate and the local that works best to open up the child to learning and indeed to open up the learner to a self-confident engagement with learning at any age. In situations of racial colonization such as the attempt by a white culture to civilize the red culture, the defeated child was treated as part of a global concern that was quite indifferent to the expressions of esteem to which all children, indeed all the higher primates and most social animals are sensitive. The problem is that artificially engineered 'global' children cannot find any direction. If their place and language of origin had ceased to have the power to set them on a pedestal, they had found nothing in its place. The sense of loss and disconnection led these children to symptoms of chronic emptiness, mental health problems, addictions, depression and the sense of being worthless. To be educated in this environment, they needed to show that they had severed any deep connections between themselves and their local centres of cultural empowerment in their own family home. Teachers evidently held on to kids over the summer holidays to make sure that they did not lapse back into Indian customs and values as far as possible. Many Indian children preferred to cling to their red mirrors nevertheless. Their difficulty lay in the fact that their cultural memories were afflicted, compromised, not yet well enough developed. Not only had the pre-linguistic arena out of which all praise originates become dulled, but the cultural language (language 2) had become seriously compromised. And it was the absence of praise that had become a significant predictor of the negative educational outcomes of these children, as contemporary research is now showing.

Conclusion

In the old days Bebra stood proudly on the frontier between West Germany and East Germany, between the BRD and the DDR. Frontier towns gleaned their prestige in part from the fact that they stood bright and colourful next to 'no-man's land' and the occupied territories across the Wall. To leave Bebra station in West Germany and head eastwards in the direction of Eisenach was dramatic, if not traumatic. The American GIs who stood on the platform making sure none of their own soldiers boarded the Spartan train, ignored us students as we passed. As the train took off we passed after several miles into 'no man's land', a land suspended in time where the ground lay untilled and uncared for under the watchful eye of soldiers in gun towers. We felt eyes on us, telescope lenses, perhaps a sniper's rifle. Tension filled the carriage. We stopped and guards boarded the train with sniffer dogs and submachine guns. The door of our carriage flew open and the soldier shouted – *Ausweise* – we fumbled for our passports, fearing that the dollars we held would be confiscated and after some further chilling moments when the seats were upturned looking for drugs or pornography with an Alsatian looking at us in the eye, they withdrew and left us alone. Not far to go, we said. Not far. A trolley rolled by on the platform, Harry Potter style, selling sweets and drinks but no one purchased anything. Would dollars do? We were afraid to show that we had dollars in case they would be confiscated. No one had East German Marks. Some shouts and whistles later and we were on our way moving slowly across a desolate space which had not been tilled since the war, arriving at a station whose name I have forgotten but on whose platform stood what seemed to be hundreds of red army soldiers, each carrying identical briefcases and wearing sharp-looking hats. For a few moments, the traveller experienced the frightening illusion of being in a 'zone of absolute indeterminacy' (Agamben, 2005, p. 57) from which the rule of law had been excluded, an area governed not by *potestas* but by *auctoritas*. In 'no-man's land', the border guard could have said anything, done anything. Our lives were in his hands. What could be more terrible than this?

Nowadays in a united Germany 'no-man's land' has now engulfed the land around Bebra and its small twin town in the east whose name and reality have almost disappeared. These towns no longer show off the colourful uniforms of American GIs; no pensioner-pushed supermarket trolly squeeks its way along the platform of Gespunsart, nor is any visitor greeted by a wave of Red army officer hats and briefcases on the platform of Eisenach. No sober-looking carriages ghost over the border from *Frankfurt am Main* to *Frankfurt an der Oder*. An old mining town in Washington State would be more memorable than this 'no-man's land', its frontier obliterated, its ramshackle platform overgrown and deliberately neglected. Who is to say that this is not a metaphor for postmodern globality in the education context? Globality marks out the contours of an educational territory from which interest can suddenly withdraw, converting it into a wasteland. It is paved with good intentions, of course. It offers access to information without limit but also without any disciplinary poetics. It promises any time, any place access in return for something like the status of a refugee. It plays its tricks here; it weaves it web whenever young people drift out into an ill-defined world in the belief that the old order will somehow survive intact and be there when they get back.

5

Talent

We urge all this upon the lads, pointing out to them that they will not grow up to honour if they are rebellious and take no pains about themselves; but that if they take pains they may, perhaps, become worthy of the names which they bear.

Plato, *Laches,* 179d, translated by B. Jowett

Introduction

We have seen in our account how empowerment underlies all mentalist states and manifestations of the 'I' and this under-layer of support (whether positive or negative) might be thought to 'transcend' whatever the individual can do or say. The 'transcendence' is unlike its normal manifestation in the 'outside' world but it is now characterized by manifestations emitted from the 'plane of immanence' (Deleuze and Guattari, 1994) and characterized by eruptions of originality. The individual in its own name now feels empowered to manifest its often 'until then' unspeakable connection with the world of reality as distinct from the world of illusion. This explains why great artists 'speak' to so many people for they represent the 'reality' they have glimpsed and which is only available to humans through the empowerment which makes sight of it possible. There are of course, besides great art, those manifestations of kitch that proclaim the painful experience of not yet having understood anything about the reality of the world, but it is only of passing interest to see how far people still project make-believe constructions that soon disappear as time passes on. It is the talent for reality that interests me here.

The breakthrough of some transcendent elements has long roots in the history of ideas and it is sometimes metaphorically represented in tales of Muses, gods, guardian angels, daimons and the ubiquitous fairy godmother who is always on hand in an emergency. The sense of a transcendent support is expressed often in terms of an accompanying spirit who is there from the beginning and stands intact despite one's own historical experiences. In this spirit, there is an ancient view that genius operates as a separable being, accompanying a person since birth. This was the Roman view and in this vein Giorgio Agamben notes that in Roman lore, *genius* was the Roman god charged with the task of accompanying each person from the moment of birth (2007, p. 9). This would make genius timeless since it would be there from the beginning much as the Muses were always thought to accompany those inspired to creative action in Ancient Greek mythology. The Muses stood ready to inspire the poet or the musician with some creative thought. Along these lines, it is easy to think of talent as something we are born with which stands outside history and accompanies us like our own private Muse.

The association of the term 'talent' with a quantity of money is another metaphor of accompaniment drawn from the ancient world. It is perhaps due to the Roman word *talentum* meaning 'balance, weight, sum of money' and it is used rather famously in the biblical parable of talents (Mt. 25. 14–30; Lk. 19.12–25). Even Lacan's theory can be thought to imply an accompanying imaginary self which represents our historical selves on occasion and sometimes causes trouble when we struggle with failure or a set of non-ideal circumstances. The problem, however, is whether this accompanying self is historical, that is, changing or unhistorical, that is, unchanging. And both models have appeared in children's literature.

In children's stories, some pristine fairy godmother is always at hand to point the way forward and to serve as a gentle guide as to what children might become. It is as if a statement of the individual's potential is immediately intuitively obvious to the child. Sometimes this separable guide is also a companion reflecting the spiritual condition of the possessor. Hence Dorian Grey's picture hanging in the loft, for instance, or Philip Pullman's *daimon* which assumes the moral traits of the character to which it is attached, are historical beings subject to the vagaries of a life history whereas J. K. Rowling's Dobby retains his own independence of mind, fortunately enough. A writer like Elizabeth Gilbert has pondered on the topic of inspiration, linking it to terms that suggest the classical world view of a guiding spirit, a Muse standing ready to inspire with great thoughts, which suddenly and without warning take a grip on the artist and compel him or her to write, sketch, create in some way.[1] Inspiration, for her, comes from elsewhere, something like an accompanying Muse, standing outside history.

Medieval Latin in contrast attempted to banish the notion of an accompanying spirit or Muse by linking talent to a discourse of desire. Having a talent then becomes something like a psychological attitude, an 'inclination, leaning, will, desire' which brought the notion of a talent inside the psyche as a species of psychic need so that it became properly historical. If talent belongs to the historical circumstances of life, then it is much more vulnerable and cannot be separated. The nature/nurture debate now comes into full swing because our talent is thought to evolve in tandem with our life chances and the nurturing placed at our disposal. It might be reasonable to suggest that there are certain critical phases in life (such as in language development, for instance) which can be passed through and lost forever without proper care. These potentialities because they are historical always remain irremediably lost. Oxana Malaya was lucky enough, so they say, to have lived with human contact for her initial two years before being abandoned to the dogs. A musical talent might be thought to lie in wait for recognition and development and if a certain phase of life passes, so too does the talent. The ability to curve one's hand around the bow of a violin diminishes with age. There is also the thought that talent can be taken to refer to forces which come from the outside inwards, becoming some kind of chronicle of a response to elements that impact on the individual. In this sense many potential concert pianists moulder undeveloped and undiscovered in the barrios of Brazil or behind the barricades of the West Bank. If talent is a function of the individual's response to what is put in front of him then of course one would expect to find more concert pianists in Paris, London or New York and the circumstances of life would be thought to be critical to the emergence of any talent. The point is that whatever the circumstances, it seems that talent on this reading is always a historical event.

More modern metaphors

Another way of using the 'accompanying/non-accompanying' metaphor in a more modern idiom is to debate about whether intelligence should best be understood as a fluid or a crystal. Fixed ability accounts might point to a feature that is, impervious to historical decay. Therefore this child has an ability that is measured either by an instrument designed to measure a fixed ability such as an IQ measure, SAT, a Mensa test or even some scoring on a supposed multiple range of intelligences (Gardner, 1983). The 'givenness' of these talents points to their unhistorical character, the fact that they lie dormant, whatever happens. Sternberg, on the other hand, stresses fluid abilities like the adaptability to new situations and the estimation of cultural supports for certain adaptability practices. On this view, the flux and fluid nature of abilities is a better measure of intelligence. All learning then becomes vulnerable to the particularities of culture both as a combination of elements that localize the child and also determine its historical progress.

Most psychologists seem to prefer the fluid description over the fixed or crystallized abilities (Sternberg, 2002). Sternberg in an American-based study found that Latino parents valued social experiences more than Asian or Anglo parents did (Sternberg and Davidson, 2005), a thought reflected in other educators (Rolón, 2003). Hence performance abilities manifest themselves not only as individualized phenomena but also as a function of cultural variables that need to be noted and counted as part of the assessment task. Billy Charles, we are told, was 'an avid and extremely talented hunter, fisherman, and trapper' (Barone, 1992, p. 144) but he pretty much had to drop out of school due to generally poor academic performance. One reason Bobby felt he had to drop out was the way talent, ability, giftedness had already been crystallized in a form that was alien to Bobby. Insistence on the presentation of his talents according to the curriculum in hand resulted in that alienation widening and the student's disaffection from the system deepening. The outcome might have been different if his talents had been allowed to interweave or if the student's general abilities had been allowed to register on the assessment radar and this might have occurred better if the standards measuring ability had been fluid enough to accommodate those attributes for which Bobby was already positively known and admired in his community. Fluidity might have enabled contact to be made between his current curriculum and some of the complex forms of esteem offered by a local context.

The situation is not a simple choice between the 'unhistorical' talent and the 'historical' talent because our examples point to a regime that may be pre-historical. Talent in this sense points further back towards an empowerment network that needs to be presupposed first, thus a certain unhistorical framing of a person's talent and here we are right back to the 'accompanying' metaphor. Children can explore with confidence even in play when a parent is in the background (Bruner, 1983). Other examples show similar outcomes. MacKinnon studied a number of highly creative architects and found that certain events in their childhood and in the manner of their upbringing were critical to their eventual creativity (MacKinnon, 1964).

The reference here is to critical incidents, key moments, which permit this support to be glimpsed rather than the steady outflowing of some innate ability.

Similarly E. P. Torrance from 1959 to his death in 2003 announced his famous instrument for testing creative thinking at the University of Minnesota because he noticed 'potentialities that might otherwise go unnoticed – especially in children from culturally diverse and lower socioeconomic backgrounds' (as cited in Cramond, Matthews-Morgan, Bandalos and Zuo, 2005). There seems to be reference here to some hidden field of support or empowerment as if their self-confidence acts like a pluripotent cell, morphing into whatever is required at the time. Creative people, challenged by disorder, have the courage to reveal themselves, accept that there are different perspectives on the same subject and shape the world mindful of the grammar of multiple perspective (Givens, 1962, pp. 298–9). The last thing they need is surveillance and worry about competition evaluation (Zeidner and Schleyer, 1999), the pressure that follows the offer of excessive rewards including subtle ways of putting children in competition with one other and effectively cutting them off from cooperative learning possibilities. They are thwarted by over-control and strategies designed to put pressure on their every move (Goleman, Kaufman and Ray, 1992). Instead creativity should be marked by fluency, flexibility and originality where obstacles to these processes are not exacerbated by schools and school systems. In other words, gifted children are empowered to be creative in several environments, provided that measurement and competition are withdrawn, even if concerns have been expressed in the United States that creativity is on the wane since the early 1990s (Bronson and Merriman, 2010).

So, independent of the particular nature of talent or creativity in the child, I am still puzzled whether a child's talent derives from his pre-historical good fortune in having been empowered or whether he has benefited more critically from cultural supports, for it seems that a culture that thwarts genius can have a singularly devastating effect. My question is whether a child's creativity would be able to survive a succession of bad teaching experiences, assuming that the child has been positively empowered. How dependent is the child on the proper conditions to survive as a talented and creative individual? In a sense I am interested in what Carl Rogers once referred to as creative environments where the child is able to grasp the historical moment, whatever its shape. But this means linking talent to a particular kind of engagement. Talent expresses a particular relation to time or, as Nietzsche might say, to history. This means that talent is less a quality, possession, talent in the biblical sense, or even a capacity that might unfold over time with proper education that accompanies a person throughout life than it is a 'plastic' power. The result is that gifted students who come in contact with a very good Physics teacher in one school might construct themselves as Physics students for the rest of their lives while the same students animated differently in another school might become French or History students. The plasticity of talent is very often unpredictable in learner behaviour. For this reason it seems probable that talent is not hemmed in by surface 'ifs' 'buts' or 'maybes'. Talent manifests itself without equivocation in a particular context, even though in Berlin it might more likely manifest itself in the skills of piano playing than in the Amazonian jungle where similar capacity might manifest itself in skilful hunting. I have a suspicion that human creativity is much more fragile than is generally supposed and also much more versatile since it is associated with the ability to grasp the present moment.

Plato, talent and the time-now

In a certain way, this critical timeliness was recognized in the ancient world, although perhaps not in these terms. When in Plato's *Laches* two parents, Lysimachus and Melesias come to see Laches and Nicias, two well-known Athenian generals, they speak about their concern for their teenage sons. Both Lysimachus and Melesias are relatively speaking nonentities, unlike their illustrious forbears after whom their sons are named, Thucydides, an opponent of the great general Pericles and Aristides, a famous leader during the Persian war. They express their worry about how their boys will turn out. They don't want them to be as anonymous as themselves and they know that their sons must manifest courage and manliness on the battle field if they are to achieve the respect of others and build up reputations worthy of their illustrious ancestors. They want their sons to achieve more respect than they had achieved and because reputations are made in the heat of battle, they want to know how to help their sons give a good account of themselves. They worry because they cannot control this time-now appearance of their sons but they know that both the lives of their sons and certainly their reputations will depend on their actions in the time-now context of battle, for any fighter who held his ground in battle would be more likely to survive (*Laches,* 182b). Warriors respected courage as manifestation of the divine on the battlefield. We know this from Alcibiades' glowing account of the bravery of Socrates in defeat when on one occasion he turned and saved Alcibiades' life and on another stood his ground and did not run away, an action that saved not only his own life but also that of his companions.

What kind of education would teach them the virtue of courage in the heat of battle? Plato explains that neither Nicias nor Laches, two generals to whom this question is initially addressed, can find any clear answers to this question. Nor indeed can Socrates who attempts nonetheless to discount some easy answers. Nicias mentions the need for physical training, training in weaponry and the science of tactics (*Laches*, 182c). The combination of this knowledge will 'give a man a finer-looking appearance at the very moment when he needs to have it, and when he will appear more frightening to the enemy, because of the way he looks' (*Laches*, 182d). Laches himself is somewhat bemused by these comments, for even though he can see their logic, his experience tells him that 'not a single practitioner in the art of fighting in armour has ever become renowned in war' (*Laches*, 183c). For Plato the real question is whether the virtue of courage can be taught and how a teacher can be found who will make the boys' souls as good as possible (*Laches*, 186a). In another dialogue, such as in the *Gorgias*, he might have said that a clear understanding of what is entailed in the concept of 'courage' would help someone acquire it. But here the tone is sceptical. The issue is not easy to resolve for what it is that educates a person is not very easy to discern. Plato is actually trying to legislate for the *timeliness* of talent. A certain time lapse between learning what a thing is and performing it in the heat of battle is unavoidable. But what counts is its appearance in the moment of battle. The relation between talent and developed virtue would need to be replicated at a critical moment such as appearance on the battlefield. It could not be rehearsed in advance, for the terrors of battle can only be imagined by those who have never endured them. For this reason the sons of Lysimachus and Melesias need to become makers of history: they need to relate to the 'time-now' in a critical way and at a moment when something entirely new and unpredictable will appear, either their bravery or their cowardice. Who could teach them such a goodness of soul that would make this outcome likely? Socrates admits that he never learned it from sophists (*Laches*, 186c) but just happened to have this knowledge when pressed on the battlefield. Could he teach what he had not learned? What kind of an education would this be? It would involve at least living courageously on a daily basis and being courageous in many fields of activity. It would mean accepting what the physician recommends (*Laches*, 193a) and recognizing carefully the difference between foolish endurance on the battlefield and headless flight or between easy capitulation in argument and obdurate stubbornness.

Taking a step away from this dialogue and towards the reflections of the early Nietzsche, it is the issue of epic that is at stake. It seems that to understand epic performance, we must distinguish between two different senses of 'time-now' performance. One sense is historically 'thin', evident in talent shows when the time-now is predictable and supported by rehearsals, evident also in ritualized exams which have been well prepared and rehearsed in conventional scenarios centred on familiar thoughts and practices. The other sense is historically 'thick', occurring in a time-now *without direct preparation*, without direct prediction, where the resources suddenly manifest themselves that either help or hinder the ability to hold open this moment of appearance. Testing historically 'thin' talent can be well-predicted and practised by strategies of rehearsal and rote. Testing historically 'thick' talent refers us back to the formative basis of the talent, that is, its underlying empowerment, and to the manner in which the talent reinvigorates the quality of the person.

Historically thick action in the moment may also be what some appreciate as art, the art of some procedure which is celebrated as the very moment Proteus, that god of the deep, that god of many forms, suddenly but clearly makes its presence known and is captured in the shape of a singular event, a moment of inspired insight only immediately to change shape and slip from one's grasp. Could such a creative outcome feature in any educational system? If it did, it would herald the appearance of a creative talent in a timely fashion in whatever context, including the battlefield. These parents still search for that particular kind of education that might prepare their sons to manifest the art of being manly on the battlefield. This is the education they want their sons to achieve. And while there is no conclusion about the nature of courage in this dialogue, there is an odd passage (*Laches*, 198d) where the eponymous Socrates says of every art, including the art of courage, that it encompasses a form of knowledge about the past, about the present and about the future. Like experience, this broader vision predominates over the seer's insights that might be limited by a vision of the future only. When the time comes they want their sons to demonstrate bravery in the time-now sense that Nietzsche claims lies at the heart of genius.

Nietzsche on the uses of history

Nietzsche also helps us understand the timeliness of talent, its ability to hold the historical moment in its hands. From his perspective, Nietzsche defends genius (by which, roughly speaking, he means the timely presentation of any singular human being against the distortions of History (writ large) and so it seems on the face of it that history is the enemy and that there is an opposition between history and life) (1983, p. 97). It might be useful to distinguish between the freedom to appear historically, which is one of the outcomes of empowerment, and the freedom to appear in a timely manner, which bears the mark of creativity and is the great gift of human culture and education. Children who have been well supported can appear with a stable mental state 'I' but to appear in a timely fashion requires talent. Talent requires a certain way of relating to the passing of time and he preaches caution, not proposing, for instance, an 'unhistorical' relationship to time like cows in a field. The cows chew the cud happily, oblivious to time passing. As to knowledge, it might invest what is known with timeliness, renewing what is known and keeping it fresh while also respecting its historical thickness. As to being, it points to a certain timeliness that is manifest in the originality with which an individual engages with what happens in life.

Nietzsche argues that originality requires history and that it is the task of the genius 'to remint the universally known into something never heard of before' (p. 94). Nietzsche's historian is paradoxically very much a creative figure in the present and this is why he or she can be critical, can generate monuments that are noteworthy. As one commentator suggested, Nietzsche is presenting here a view of history *as pure art* (Pletsch, 1977, p. 39). Vague as it might seem, it is the art of living that enables the individual to link himself to current historical experience and represent the timeliness of life.

However, instead of this genius identity, children in the German schools of Nietzsche's acquaintance were taught to assume a feeble and vacant identity coloured by convention and jaded dreams about German greatness. It pained Nietzsche to see this kind of historical hijacking of new identities. He bristled at Hartmann's thought that this might be an age which 'no longer requires genius' (1983, p. 109) and he feared for children so caught up in the forward moves of history itself that no thought was given to their giftedness in the present. The denial of timeliness meant that the impact of history on identity had been down-played (p. 114) while an excess of history in his view had led to a number of distortions. Nietzsche lists out five of these (p. 83): a widening between the subject and object which damages creativity as if the individual has no important role to play; the illusion that one age is better than another; the hindering of instincts that help a person to mature; the development of an illusion that we are standing on the shoulders of the past; the strengthening of 'a dangerous mood of irony' or a 'dangerous mood of cynicism' in regard to events, treating them *as if there is no truth*. Nietzsche is opposed to this mood of free-floating emptiness, which he qualifies in several places as nihilism.

When the I is captured in its own egoistical sphere, generating its own sense of justice and spawning its own form of inauthentic art and religion, then the subject is disconnected from its historical moment of appearance and the 'world' is set at an 'objective' distance, becoming neutral, inhuman and excessively historical and scientific. The logical conditions for a 'scientism' is possible (although Nietzsche does not use the word). The idea, however, is clear as is its effect on the individual psyche which in turn might come to imagine himself as an 'objective' man, operating 'like a reluctant smooth lake whose surface is disturbed by no ripple of delight or sympathy' (p. 114). Instead of this 'unhistorical' attitude, Nietzsche advises another way of being a 'subject' which does not imply the widening gap between 'subject' and 'object ' (pp. 84–5), but invokes resonances with the Socratic tradition. Socrates once linked justice to the proper ordering of the human soul (see *Republic*, 443c–5b, also 592b, as referenced by Berkowitz, 2001, p. 19) and Nietzsche follows this advice in response to the Delphic temple's command of *gnothi seauton* (know thyself) which he reads as the command to seek truth 'not as cold, ineffectual knowledge, but as a regulating and punishing judge' (p. 88).

We need to remember that talent/genius/creativity as a concept requires two conditions. The first is the freedom to engage in the ongoing events of a life history and the second is the freedom to be timely and this latter demands education. However, instead of opting for the pain that inevitably follows on the experience of being alive, the young person, aided and abetted by elders, who should know better, opts instead for 'blind power' (p. 105) which Nietzsche describes as either the 'blind power of the factual' or the 'blind power of the actual' (p. 106). Why is this power blind? Why is it linked to death? Because, Nietzsche argues, it is ineffectual, it separates a person's capacity for knowledge from his capacity for action in the timely 'now' (p. 108). It refuses to allow the intersection between these two lines at a point where the past and the future meet.

This points back to Goethe's lament about the knowledge he experienced at school that did not invigorate him, did not open up to action but held him as its victim, as it were, caught under a spell by abstractions and a kind of promise that knowledge is timeless, mummified and dead. German education preferred to lead the young to follow a set of pre-set paths, weighing them down with abstract knowledge, history, culture, science. It induced them to absorb an entire volume of inert facts making them 'fainthearted' (p. 84). Meanwhile a similar experience, this time expressed in other terms, would see Dewey complain about rote-learning and mindlessness in his own school experience (Dewey, 1988). The failure to promote creative genius almost always follows the attempt to construe knowledge as a body of facts. Indeed the quiet, dispassionate ease of school-based learning is never implied by the Delphic command to engage in the process of self-knowledge as part of the learning process. Nietzsche concludes that we need knowledge to be of a certain kind and history to be of a certain kind in order for them to be creative and to serve life.

Authentic views of history

Nietzsche makes a distinction between what he calls three authentic uses of history. Proper use of history is made by whoever 'acts and strives' (monumental), 'preserves and reveres' (antiquarian), 'suffers and seeks deliverance' (critical). Each of these approaches is vulnerable to abuse. The problem with ambitious people who act and strive is that they can easily be 'gifted egoists and visionary scoundrels' (p. 71) who learn how to take refuge in some great era or personage of the past, so as to disguise 'their hatred of the great and the powerful of their own age . . .' (p. 72). Similarly the antiquarian runs the risk of narrowing his field of vision, to see the world in a manner that is 'much too close up and isolated' (p. 74). This narrowing of focus restricts his perception of the past and sets up a form of phenomenology which filters out anything new, like children in games who filter out complications to enable a game to form itself around some highly significant event that has been barely understood. This phenomenology uses history and culture as ready-made descriptors of identity and Nietzsche suspects that many teachers operate out of this type of phenomenology. Their eyes fix on some kind of mummified essence which is subsequently handed on anaemically in a vacant manner. Such false antiquarian knowledge effectively conceals the pain which accompanies creative knowledge. There is a lack of proportion in the vision obtained. A third error occurs when criticism becomes all-pervasive and ill-founded. Indeed Nietzsche anticipates Heidegger's notion of 'idle talk' when he criticizes the link between the babbling of critics and their refusal to support any values. This approach annoys Nietzsche because it signals a babbling culture which by definition does not value what it recognizes or criticizes. Indeed, Nietzsche complains about 'the precocious up-to-the-minute babbler about state, church and art . . . the insatiable stomach which nonetheless does not know what honest hunger and thirst are' (p. 117). A more resolute critical attitude would summon up everything before the tribunal of reason in an attempt to assess its value and would only tolerate what survived this work. Old educational and political institutions would crumble fast if subjected to such a pattern of critique, Nietzsche believed.

Creative genius

In a similar manner, Giorgio Agamben holds that all humans are caught in a poetic tension that spills over into life from time to time, a tension that points back to the primordial dualism between what is given and what we make of it, between genius and ego, between nature and culture. The superabundance of genius can spill over its natural borders and can lead to panic, driving some people mad, whereas a fraught ego can attempt to manage a person's life history too tightly and to afflict it with order and predictability at times when spontaneity is required. So, on the one hand, there is a tendency for the energy to burst forth uncontrollably – an idea, a piece of art, an un-choreographed dance, a spur of the moment song, while on the other hand, there is a tendency to bring everything under control, to prevent spontaneity and to frame every event against the constancy of character demanded by a predictable and ordered process. If a flash of genius arises that risks carrying everything away, it will be brought back and controlled; if ego becomes too restrictive, avenues will be found to make it less so. Good art requires this tension. Proteus is such a disturbing god to capture!

To counter this Protean nightmare, children and adults often enter into a stability pact with history. For short periods at least, they stop engaging in historical experience and instead pull aside from history into play. In play everything returns to zero no matter what happens: children's cartoons, adult routines, games that might be lost but can be started again, all these allow history to be denied. Time can be accepted as a recurrence of the old, an elaborate game that returns to zero at the start of each year with a new competition, a new league season, a new golf tournament, a new holiday, a new course, unhistorical games that forecast their own failure on a continuing basis. The sense of history can be dulled and the child can be induced into conventional thoughts and behaviours. Granted that there are sometimes normal, perhaps healthy, devices that promise escape from the struggle with time, convention itself can be a more unhealthy strategy of insulating oneself against the creative moment. Conventional manoeuvres in the classroom, like rote-learning, pre-guessing exam questions, crowding the curriculum, all play their part in taking up the time where something creative might otherwise have been possible (Goleman et al., 1992).

Conclusion

How relevant is Nietzsche's talk of creative genius to classrooms as we know them? We know that Torrance initially focused his interest on child creativity because he found that children, identified as having behaviour problems in schools, were often also very creative (Cramond et al., 2005, p. 290). This potential paradox has raised serious questions for the kind of education that any society promotes for its children. If we want a tried and tested, congested and fully formatted education system along with its transparent tests and measures then we may exclude precisely the type of timely engagement identified by Nietzsche as central to the human genius. How important is creativity to the living skill-set of people in the future who will need to survive in a society awash with images, demands, choices and distractions? As parents like Lysimachus and Melesias, we want to seek out educators who can prepare our sons and daughters to live timely lives.

Like Nietzsche, we want them to be living spirits who are not bounded by the ties and conventions of current market values. We do not want them to be separated from history, cocooned and divided into subgroups as consumers. We do not want them to be conventional thinkers in a globalized world, subject to the many mandates of globality that feature in postmodern environments. We need to teach them how to marshal the time and the quality of life they are lucky to have in order for them in turn to imprint the human spirit on the world and not to be deceived by the technologies of power that beguile people in their weaker moments. It would be sad, however, if they learned as a result of schooling, that it is unwise to take risks with an idea, a thought, a new expression and that it would be preferable in all circumstances to surrender to the cumulating censure of adult society and the norms set in place by peer culture. To have the courage to accept the new and not to be submerged in history, that is the challenge of creativity announced through Nietzsche's work.

Only something that appears in a timely manner, in the performance of some action has the power to escape general convention. In devaluing the significance of timeliness in classroom inquiry, in giving no time for it, educators, rather ironically, withhold permission from children to be new and creative. The emotional constraints, competitive pressures, frequent testing and time-stress environments, under which conditions school children are normally obliged to work, have a strong negative effect on creativity. They reveal the importance of respecting the emotional engagement in learning that Torrance also intimated. It is these holistic concerns that have been reiterated in later studies. Indeed some kind of combined cognitive and emotive response to time-now may be precisely what Nietzsche had in mind for any creative spirits brave enough to bear the burden of history on their shoulders.

Note

1   See www.ted.com/talks/elizabeth_gilbert_on_genius.html as accessed 4 September 2011.

6

Tactility

Tangible objects we perceive not by any action upon us of the medium, but concurrently with it, like the man who is struck through his shield. It is not that the shield was first struck and then passed on the blow but, as it happened, both were struck simultaneously.

Aristotle, *On the Soul*, ii, ii, 423b 15, translated by R. D. Hicks

Introduction

A dozen readers are in my library area at the moment. All except myself are of an undergraduate student age. Only two of us have no computers open in front of us; only three of us have books, only two with books open; only two of us bother writing with pens; only four of us have notepads close by. The students seem in general busy working on their laptops; they seem to be clicking rather than clunking and I can hear a ratchet sound as someone scrolls down noisily through information. Their body positions are curiously static, head stationary, hands forward, only a mouse identified as the area of locomotion, its sliding motions detected occasionally by a slight scrape as its encounters the roughness of a touchpad or a sudden slap as it is lifted and slammed down. By contrast my head is rolling and I notice the other student with a book and notebook open is busy switching to and fro from book to notepad and back again. The other students seem vaguely superior, their bodies comparatively static, with rigid postures and sudden, almost imperceptible darting movements led chiefly by finger and hand. About half the total number of students have ear phones connected. Some pan between mobile phones and the laptop screen.

For newly arriving students, wiring up is part of the preparatory ritual as the plugs and wires present the tactile evidence of being connected in an otherwise wireless environment. The tactility of feeling for the socket and plugging in is soon rewarded by contact lights and familiar jingles, which reverberate periodically around the room as other students announce their arrival. Tiny green lights illuminate to indicate that a contact is alive, signs that someone is 'on' and others in the same TeamSpeak session are absent or 'off'. The tactility of clicking, sliding the mouse briefly or the finger across a mouse pad, the tactile adjustment of the ear phones, all prepare for the chorus of clicking which sound like depressed cicadas on a rainy holiday. Clunking noises corresponding to keyboard use are rarer while fingers are poised over favourite keys, ready to push open new platforms, open up new worlds or reverse the journey, the adventure over, the risk lessened, the return to zero always held in reserve as an option, contact made, broken, made, broken. One click and the World Trade Center is down; another click and it is time for lunch: *toshibo ergo sum?*

Lessons from Aristotle

A combination of sense is evidently in use. Seeing is in use, hearing is in use, aided by ear phones, no taste, no smell but plenty of touch. If Aristotle could speak our language today, he might well say that there is evidence of motion in the soul occasioned by sensory stimuli, especially sight, hearing, touch. Learning, which is reflected in a kind of motility of the soul raises questions about the nature of the learner's executive control over the sensory input and while Aristotle thought of touch as the most blunt of senses, curiously it is the latter which has become singularly important in this library setting today.

Aristotle was once very concerned about the motility of the soul, meaning the way in which the soul moves. The soul is not an unmoved mover, for that quality is reserved for god alone. Even though many philosophers since Descartes have claimed that humans are unmoved movers, well capable of choosing and acting in some absolute, that is, unmoved executive manner, Aristotle repeats in various ways that the soul is not a self-moving number (*De anima*, 408b 30ff.).[1] This means that even though the soul can be moved, it is not a pure form or a totally active executive agent. It has a capacity to act but it is not itself a pure act. Like many of the Greeks, Aristotle thought of the connection with the body as a damper rather than an enhancement of action, even though his biological interests made him much more positively disposed to the body than others, like the cynics, for example. Aristotle nevertheless judged human action to be often hampered by moods and prone to be carried in various directions by the incontinent excesses of our sensory lives. A formal principle – the soul as a substance – would normally and after some moral training put a rational shape on all these moods and dispositions, reflecting the 'essential whatness' of who we are. We are not giraffes or snakes; we are humans but being human in this sense does not reveal how humans are to act in human ways.

Aristotle's analysis is interesting to reflect upon because it raises the important issue of executive action in the context of sensory stimuli. The soul is not a pure agent but rather a substance which has powers of various kinds, each power understood as a *dynamis* (energy), a *puissance*, a potential which might be enacted or not, a condition in which both potency and act participate equally. It is in this context that if we were to use the language of potency and act we would need to ask what moves the soul. Aristotle organizes these powers hierarchically and so suggests that there are nutritive powers common to all living beings, sensory powers that are only common to some beings and intellectual powers that are only found in humans (*De anima*, 415a 20). The problem is that these powers do not operate in a vacuum and indeed could hardly be said to exist at all without the biological condition that supports them.

In relation to sensation, Aristotle suggests that sensation moves the soul from outside, and that this movement from outside brings about a change of some kind in the inner operation of the soul although he thought it a mistake to follow the view of Democritus in considering the senses to induce a purely passive response (*De anima* 417a 5). For Aristotle there are no discretely differentiated arenas of inside and outside and for this reason there is no discretely passive element in the senses (a receptor, if you like) and another discretely active element (the thing itself or the agent), although some empiricist philosophers came close to proposing this model following Descartes. Aristotle's position is happily equivocal compared to these more literal models. He suggests that the senses are both active and passive together. It is hunger, for instance, that formulates the need to eat but it is the agent who must formulate the thought and design the plan to eat. Sensation, on Aristotle's view, requires stimulus from outside in order to become active but neither the outside stimulus nor the inside intention is adequate on their own to sense objects. It might be a different matter when it comes to intellectual activity where people seem to be freer to conjure up thought patterns and engage in learning with greater independence from the context. For some sensation to occur, on the other hand, the context contributes more vitally to the success of the operation. The obvious example is that there has to be some light in order to see anything, as Aristotle explains.

Why is this relevant to our topic? Because quite simply the sensation of touch behaves rather peculiarly according to Aristotle and, as a result, Aristotle relegates it to the bottom of the list of senses. Of all the senses it is closest to the life of plants, according to Aristotle's understanding of the way plants operate. Normally it is possible to divide sensation into the five senses, each of which requires a different 'medium' or outside set of conditions to operate. In the case of seeing, Aristotle engages in a lengthy discussion about the importance of 'light' as a condition for the visibility of objects. This condition combines with the object itself to become the stimulus to the eyes and induce the act of seeing. The same holds also for sound and smell, for if sounds, sights or smells are brought into immediate contact with the sensory organ, no sensation will be produced (419a 30). Taste is located in the tongue and requires different objects in order to become operational. Touch is rather peculiar because we might locate it in the hands but then we can touch using various parts of the body and we can be touched in many places. Hence touch is less locatable in a specific organ and more diffuse and furthermore it requires contiguity of elements or immediacy in order to become operational. Touch is a feature of the sensory lives of most animals, even insects. Touch in its basic meaning enables a being to be 'in touch' in a manner that is less discrete than smelling, hearing or seeing.

Now the issue at hand is that a new kind of tactility has announced itself, a tactility aided by machines, a tactility which expresses itself in clicks, clunks, wipes and ratcheting finger movements. But this new tactility approximates more to what Aristotle meant by an intellectual rather than a sensory operation. This is strange because to see *in an intellectual sense* does not require a medium and hence it is not a kind of sensation or perception and does not require for its operation any kind of sensory continuum. The intellect can think up something and immediately 'see' it in an intellectual way. Touching, however, always seems to require, well, touching and yet our students can be 'in touch' in a disembodied way by having their phones switched on or their team-speak lights on. They apparently present a disembodied profile when they use touch-based technologies and they need to be in permanent contact with machines. Otherwise they begin to feel unwell, 'out of touch', uneasy. Touch in Aristotle's system abandons the need for a medium in the moment of touch and becomes an immediate sense. This is both a strength and a weakness. Not only when we shake hands or touch do we feel physical connection in some reciprocal manner but we can use touch to enable us to extend our intentionality through the instruments we use, pointing a stick forward and dragging it along the ground, for instance, or choosing to feel the vibration as we wish either at the tip of the stick or in the hand. This example could be taken from Aristotle (423b 15) or from Merleau-Ponty. The absence of a medium (422a 10) and the contiguity of objects linked by touch ensures that attention can shift from hand to pavement as one moves the stick across it. The information about the nature of the surface over which the stick travels is interpreted by hand and brain but the contact is immediate and the discrimination between here and there is only made after the event. In what way therefore do these machines enable our researchers to touch the objects they find?

Being in touch

In contemporary culture, there is evidence that not only children but adults too have become more touch-based in their living habits. Being in touch, keeping in touch, getting in touch operate as more than simple metaphors; they have become mandatory requirements in our postmodern appetite for connection. Individual agency might not be a strong feature of such a state of affairs. Young people might simply be 'in touch' only partially initiating contact and partially receiving it, slowing down agentic states that might promote discoveries that children need on their way to developing their own identities.

My claim is based on the physiological fact that the initial action of touching seems to fade into insignificance once one finds oneself 'in touch'. Interwoven by connections, it is not 'I' who am in touch with 'you' but rather 'we' who are in touch with each other and as part of an in-touch system there is no longer a strong executive sense of an 'I' and a 'you'. In addition no one is clear why there should be a contemporary appetite for this kind of connection because the social rhetoric still supports illusions about individual expression and individual life and the operation of recognizable communication practices in complex societies. It may be that agency is only a presumed feature of this new tactile culture, that someone somewhere is able to come up with an original idea, but if touch moves from being transitive to being intransitive, this means that the intransitive nature of touch blurs all borders, not only the border between 'I' and 'you' already mentioned, but the border separating humans from machines. Just as two fingers touching can be considered to be connected without the agency being apparent except for some shared sense of agency due to the diffuse character of touch itself so we may find ourselves witnessing a world of connection where any element can be deemed to be the beginning point or the destination point of the communication. There need not be any agency anywhere and there need not be an original thought anywhere either. Indeed when this happens any point is replaceable by any other as origin or destiny. This is the secret of the matrix: there is no particular entry point and no particular exit point, for the logic is circular and all identities are the same. And if there are no definite borders between me and you, then there might be no definite borders either between me as animal and me as machine. Not only biological discourses but also mechanical discourses can come to describe my essence as part of this matrix of connections.

In keeping with these student behaviours, statistical studies concerning the use of computers in schools or at home confirm this trend. Drawing on Lankshear et al. (Lankshear, Peters and Knobel, 2000), Somekh et al. found in their 2002 study that 10–12-year-olds spent 3 times as much time on their computers as they did in school while by age 16, this proportion had risen to 4 times (Somekh and Mavers, 2003, p. 413). Further studies tell the same story. Belgian figures note that 91.2% of primary school children surf the internet at home while there has been an increase in internet use of 342.2% from 2000 to 2011 (Valcke, De Wever, Van Keer, and Schellens, 2011). A study of Korean schoolchildren from 2007 also indicates internet use by school-goers of 92.8% (Sook-Yung and Young-Gil, 2007). Computers have become part of a new literacy affecting children as young as 5 or 6 but how does this affect their learning patterns?

With renewed vigour and meaning, touch is the sense which nowadays opens up all sentient learners to intellectual information and insight but it does so outside the traditional borders of the disciplines where animal and machine and human all have definite places. My claim is that connectivity in this new sense has become the privileged human gateway to knowledge, authenticity and power but has set aside the polarity features normally summed up in words like agency, identity, 'I', 'you', 'subject', 'object'. I now need to develop this argument further. In this chapter I need to blend two important concepts – the concept of being in touch or tactility with Deleuze and Guattari's notion of the 'rhizome' as elaborated in *A Thousand Plateaus*.

Ways of being in touch

We can be in touch in three ways. There is first what might be called a total connection, a connection that betokens a form of touching which excludes separation. When a tick senses the body of a mammal at 37 degrees and drops onto it, it immediately penetrates the skin and sucks inward even when its stomach is removed. The tick does not relate in any way to the environment but operates without reflection and in a total fashion within the environment. These features of a life governed by touch are somewhat alien to human experience which is open to a wider compendium of senses and are enhanced by the human search for pleasure. But the total connectivity evident in the life of the tick should issue a silent warning about the dangers of touch as a primordial sense. Touch, because of its immediacy can return all action to one unlimited world and it is the perception of one world only that is dangerous to humans.

A second possibility is to suggest a radical break between worlds which nonetheless might be 'in touch' under certain circumstances. For instance, according to von Uexküll, a potentially infinite distance is announced between the spider and the fly, each insect governed by its own meaning markers within its own 'functional circle' or *Funkstionskreis*. These insects lead separate lives which are coincidentally in contact with other Umwelten or environments. The fly does not recognize the spider or see the web nor does the spider hunt the fly. The *Umwelt* or environment of each insect just happens to coincide to the obvious benefit of the spider. Agamben concludes in this anti-Darwinian way saying that 'the fly, the dragonfly, and the bee that we observe flying next to us on a sunny day do not move in the same world as the one in which we observe them, nor do they share with us – or with each other – the same time and the same place' (2004, p. 40).

This story points to a third kind of distance, a distance that includes gaps or mediation, a distance represented by philosophers as the theory of 'world'. As Deleuze says, 'mediators are fundamental' for without this distance, there is 'no critical falsification of established ideas' (1992, p. 285). This critical distance is also related to the appetite in human beings for politics, as Aristotle insightfully remarked. Although the use of click-it technology carries with it the danger of becoming absorbed in a totalizing environment of contact, humans who claim to be in touch with the world as a result of this technology should be more open rather than less open to the world but the patterns of touch are subtle and we need to be wary. Since touch itself is not very discriminating, being-in-touch might signify total connection (the tick), while at other moments, some kind of coincidental connection might happen (spider and fly), while at other times there is a pattern of successive contact and break-off that nonetheless never returns to the exact same coordinates.

Educators and those who cherish the incipient steps to independence of any child need to ask more specifically about the kind of touch involved in the tactility which expresses itself in clicks, clunks, wipes and ratcheting finger movements. If we speak of computers as a medium then there is a gap between finger and machine just as there would be a distance between my two fingers if I drew them apart. But the variations in touch mean that one needs to be critical of the quality of contact and even more, the quality of the agency emerging from that contact. Information may operate simultaneously in two ways both outward and inward, without any notable originator, a two-way movement without sense of origin engendering a rapid-fire feedback system. Similarly an in-touch student may not be aware of any distance signalling active agency and passive response but might instead be drawn upward into a web of connection where no differentiations occur. Instead of vulnerable connections, some virtual reality mode of contact may be preferred and this becomes operational by means of the apparently godlike selection of web-pages and information, control, choice, judgement and the manipulations of ideas, including a loss of the sense of what plagiarized material might mean, not to mention borrowed notions, phony thoughts and imposters who can conceal the constant inward rush of uncritical claims.

Rhizomatic knowledge and its bodily implications

Most people think of knowledge as a tree-like reality, having its roots embedded in the earth and from this image we derive the logical consequent images of knowledge as a 'root and branch' affair. There is a 'discipline' to knowledge and a 'discipline' to identity. It is a very old thought, extending back as far as the sculptor Socrates, that to study within a particular discipline or to exercise a particular craft changes the soul. As a practitioner of the art, I become formed and shaped by its values and traditions. Similarly as I study the discipline area, I need its limitation and its general profile to become shaped in turn by the knowledge that I form. As I study its teaching and practise its norms, I become first its learner and then its teacher. All disciplines offer this payback, not only professional ones but also trades and crafts. The discipline forms my identity and I develop a disciplined identity. Knowledge in a disciplinary sense is tree-like. Teachers use this concept constantly in the way they organize material for teaching. The tree plots a point and fixes an order (Deleuze and Guattari, 1987 (1980), p. 7), an order which is then followed according to fairly conventional rules.

By contrast, a rhizome follows no such structure but reflects more accurately what my clicking and clunking friends are doing. They are opening pages willy-nilly, following hunches, attacking information which is not pre-arranged according to some preconceived linearity. The clicks can be concatenated into a series but this does not constitute a disciplinary reading. They might be reading what a nuclear scientist has blogged as part of their preparation for writing an essay on Madame Bovary. And the research seems to be broken up by pleasurable detours. There are no borders, branches or tree-like structures. Instead knowledge has become rhizomatic. This term stems from Deleuze and Guattari's famous use in *A Thousand Plateaus*. Explained simply, a rhizome is a type of root which is not embedded in the earth but rather turns around itself, as if it were totally bound up within its own system. Deleuze defines it as a taproot with a 'multiple, lateral, and circular system of ramification' (Deleuze and Guattari, 1987 (1980), p. 5) and this quality enables knowledge formed in this way to become a totally connected system boasting all the tactile associations that this connectivity brings. Educators have noticed this pattern also. David Buckingham notes how 'to the distress of many adults, children's media culture is increasingly distinguished by a kind of pleasurable anarchy and sensuality' (Buckingham, 2007, p. 81). He is right. The pleasurable anarchy and sensuality of surfing the net frightens those who believe in knowledge as discipline with its twin advantages of forming the subject in the discipline as well as shaping the discipline itself. The case for considering the normative benefits of discipline runs up against the non-normative but more pleasurable benefits of rhizomatic research.

The anarchic learning journey might not be totally removed from Dewey's idea that all true educational knowledge promotes the continuity of experience but it is a continuity that Dewey never imagined. Dewey never considered that this continuity might not be tree-like. In *Experience and Education*, he explains the proper functioning of subject-matter (content knowledge), rules and regulations (governing behaviour) and general school organization (1988, p. 28). Understood in its traditional sense, subject-matter could be taken as a body of material, clearly defined and taken up by a teacher as a package to be handed on. Similarly rules, originating outside the learner's circle of influence could be handed down, as it were, from on high on an authoritarian basis, becoming a demand that learners learned to obey. School organization could then find its place in the division of the day into timeslots and activities occurring in dedicated spaces. Set against these traditional approaches, Dewey proposed radical but not rhizomatic changes which treated knowledge as the pragmatic outcome of a process of learning rather than a body of eternal truths to be handed down. Dewey's pragmatic approach opened up subject-matter to the vagaries of human experience, particularly a child's human experience. Subject-matter, he argued, should more properly engage the educative experience of the learner (and he gave some rules for defining what educative as distinct from 'miseducative' experience might be (p. 25). Rules too should be transformed, arising in a democratic sense as a collective consensus enabling an activity to take place and reach its objectives, while schools could be organized around structures responsive to the interest of learners. Similarly the kind of radical shift Dewey envisaged in his progressive method might be taken to support some kind of rhizomatic learning in schools, even though the resulting model would be quite different from anything Dewey imagined.

Under rhizomatic rules, the subject-matter (knowledge) our library students engage with is certainly not fixed or contained in authoritative textbooks supported by some Local Authority, District or Curriculum Board. Nor are the rules of engagement filtered through socially approved authorities (Ito referenced in Buckingham, 2007, p. 77) but neither is it democratically structured. In keeping with a progressive approach, the general organization of learning is not apparently governed by any regime, any panoptic power, any surveillance operation promoting the docility of bodies. Yet the bodies are docile because they respond to the demands of contact. They remain curiously passive, immobile, except for the swiping of fingers and the depression of keys. Slouched in chairs, the body becomes quite inactive and the freedom that surfers experience is exposed frequently to the unsuspected surveillance of software that picks up on their moods and passing appetites and then relays this information back in the form of distractions and sales pitches. Sometimes this information is random. In such circumstances, there may not be the traditional structures to protest against because many of the real players are invisible and automated and there is a false sense of invulnerability, indeed even a kind of bodiless sensuality that will attract its dramatic expression in movies like *Limitless, Inception, The Source Code, Avatar*. Basic embodiment becomes a troubled thought.

Rhizomatic knowledge and standards

It is somewhat ironic that while subject-knowledge (information) has moved out of anyone's control due to access to web-based information at any time of the day or night, school organization has become more preoccupied with inspection, transparency, accountability, metrics. Strong competition for third level places, an increase in student costs, a tightening in the time available for inquiry in school curricula and the onset of round the clock assessment squeezes the organizational spaces of schools and makes them relatively unpalatable and unpleasurable learning environments. Have we seen the return of what is now being called 'educational fundamentalism' (Kenway and Bullen, 2001) as some kind of supervenient response to an underlying disintegration of traditional learning patterns, as if high levels of stress can conceal the fact that the horse has bolted? I would like to know whether the clicking and clunking I hear in a third-level library indicates the resistance of an in-touch generation to the educational fundamentalism they want to reject or are they flies caught in a web of an in-touch environment? Computer software will offer them several possibilities, drill and skill products that promote the 'decontextualised practice of technological *skills*' (Watson, 2001; Somekh, 2004 as referenced in Buckingham 2007, p. 95), vivid exploration packages like GoogleEarth, construction games or Robinson Crusoe in new settings. But ultimately these programmes and games ceaselessly change the subject-matter, linking it now to this aspect, now to that, making it relatively disordered and liberated from regimes of control and even from social norms and customs. The access to information is certainly non-linear (Buckingham, 2007, p. 77), meaning that the information is already there in a stream waiting to be tapped but not part of a social world.

Web-navigators then become 'hyperreaders' (Callister and Burbules, 2004), as surfers hop across levels and media, YouTube videos, Google, Facebook or Twitter notices and various Team-speak fora. There is a syntax of jumps, jerks, attractions, distractions, pop-ups (if not disabled), ads, attractions and marginal distractions designed to get you to click sideways while the surfer has to refocus and de-focus constantly to resist interruptions from email and take an independent track that follows no strict order in a manner that might replicate a tree of learning. It is helpful to see each of these pages or windows as layered platforms with rhetorical enticements subtly placed to prompt jumps from one layer to another and to entice the surfer away in order to follow some more sensuous path. Inquiry is now subtly invested in these sensuous asides. This activity is governed by the syntax of the instant feedback to a finger click or finger-slide signifying executive freedom and lord of all one surveys. The infotainment characteristic of this way of learning marks it off from exploration of an arboreal presentation of knowledge, as the platform and indeed interaction pattern switches radically from link to link, touching base as part of a unique chain that no outsider could rationally comprehend. Buckingham sums up this complexity:

> In most children's leisure-time experiences, computers are much more than devices for information retrieval; they convey images and fantasies, provide opportunities for imaginative self-expression and play, and serve as a medium through which intimate personal relationships are conducted. (2007, p. 151)

Knowledge has changed if it is required to do all these things at the same time. One has to pity teachers, even progressive ones, who are trying to compete in this environment, for if they follow the linearity of tree-learning they become comparatively dull and the motivators for learning come from elsewhere. Where knowledge is not exclusive to rules of organization or cognitive moral or political norms but is also open to intimate fantasy play and new forms of immediate self-expression, there is no time for a reflective quality to be introduced. Learners are drawn to the tactile quality of information like tics to a mammal's body with no particular entry or exit points. Compared to the excitement of a sensuous anarchic experience, school-based learning seems dark and dreary, separate from the familiar landscape of *Facebook* buddy pages.

Using the rhizome

Rhizomatic learning can be found in an interesting initiative in art education commented upon by Brent Wilson. Wilson noted how some teachers attempted to incorporate rhizomatic learning into their classrooms. Wilson analyses the *manga/dojinshi* phenomenon in comic book art, which has in recent years spread from Japan to Taiwan, Hong Kong, Korea and the Chinese mainland and the United States (Wilson, 2003). This art form involves the multiplication of micro-stories into an overall unending comic book story where 'the disappearance of one part is of no particular consequence because it will be replaced or supplemented by other parts' (p. 222). All individual input is eminently substitutable, indicating that the average players write their own prints/pictures to this virtual world in response to the broad guidelines suggested for the characters. Their contributions for a moment can become central to the never-ending action and also eminently deletable. While they can achieve instant acclaim by having their images published as part of the totality, they do not have to bear any responsibility for carrying the story forward and can withdraw at any moment without recrimination. They can also be jettisoned without recrimination as one of the authors. They are in a sense both reader and writer at the same time, having achieved a status of being that is both hyperreal and empty. Their storylines and imagination operate like rhizomes which can tolerate being broken off from the totality because the story can immediately branch in another direction, if they wish:

> In exploring manga/dojinshi one quickly discovers that there is no hierarchy. It's all surface and one can enter the surface of the dojinshi subculture and its millions of images from any place and move anywhere. (Wilson, 2003, p. 23)

Should anything be done to save traditional learning with its tree-like structure, its beginnings and endings, its learning outcomes, its hierarchies of authority, its measures of performance, its standardized codes in the national interest when set against this mindset of a circular, displaceable and replaceable rhizome? Or should one even try?

Wilson suggests three possible solutions: either downplay the importance of this rhizomatic development by restricting it to the register of popular culture and keep school-based knowledge the way it is; or add elements from rhizomatic culture to the more traditionally structured curriculum by means of some kind of delicate interweave; or finally, abandon the structured curriculum in favour of 'the vast rhizomatic realm of popular visual culture' (p. 222). While the first option is doggedly defensive and ultimately reactionary, it is favoured by most teachers. Wilson's solution is to try to blend tree-structured curriculum to a rhizomatic curriculum by shifting 'the locus of pedagogy from the formal art classroom to a space between the school and the realms of contemporary art' (p. 225). This solution acknowledges Buckingham's 'digital divide' separating school from home where the average middle-class home is much better equipped and offers much more surfing opportunity to learners. It recognizes Somekh et al.'s findings of children's facility with computer technology and supports. A playful interchange between these domains might respect what is of value in each domain. Homework might then become the actual *work* destined to take place either in school or at home supported by the context of a home environment (exposing once more the inequalities of home circumstance). These work spaces would characterize the rich rhizomatic cadenzes of popular culture while the school could limit itself to more traditional arboreal tasks. A certain parallelism might be instituted in art production in order to acknowledge the very different contexts governing the products of those newly educated in art.

Now this idea is interesting as a possible solution to what is emerging as two forms of knowledge, rhizomatic and arboreal. This distinction applies to subject-matter and would need to be explored further for its effects on rule making and school organization, two other key features of education noted by Dewey. It may be that the rhizomatic learner soon becomes the rhizomatic worker and this compromises the social engagement of the learner in the institutions where she learns. Not a learner only, but a teacher also; not a receiver of facts only but a generator of facts also. The entire authority structure of learning would shift from expert-based to a more democratic sharing but this would happen in a manner that Dewey did not envisage. Dewey believed, perhaps naively, that human societies, even commercial enterprises, would hold themselves together democratically only by acknowledging the key importance of each individual's contribution to the objectives of the institution as a whole. In a rhizomatic environment, however, individual contributions are dispensable.

It is clear that rhizomatic structures could support institutions in a democratic sense if they could formulate learning plans on a piece by piece basis where teacher and learner roles would be constantly interchanged. Teachers might become editors of material and consultants to be used on an ad hoc basis as learners grappled with a potentially infinite amount of data. Students could become leaders of projects geared to their success and general effectiveness in negotiating the media available. However, one is at a loss to know how sustainable such a model might be or what effect it would have on other social structures. And the effect on schools as we know them would be profound. And yet according to the balance normally built in to such systems rhizomatic learning might well prepare participants to be substituted in any order at any time. It might prepare the learner for a logic of disruption even if, as things stand, jumps, breaks and re-links are no basis for undue concern since they present as normal actions as applied to subject-matter, rules or school organization in rhizomatic systems.

Conclusion

These studies point to a sea-change in the nature of learning for school pupils as a result of the culture of being in touch. Despite the potentially infinite inflow of knowledge, learning might be gapped and thus vulnerable in unpredictable ways as speed takes over and as the solidity of outcomes are not tested for. At a future time younger people will know more and learn with more speed and will appear to be precociously superior in knowledge to their traditional companions until one day the solidity of this knowledge is tested hopefully with positive results. Rhizomatics does not test for solidity but only for connection that can instantly be snuffed out and cancelled.

In the meantime, my student companions are getting ready to leave. As they pack their wires away and zip their laptops into handy cases, they are ready for the rest of the evening but not without switching on their phones to check out their contacts as they leave. The matrix never closes down. The Borg always require a gentle handshake for the sake of reassuring everyone that the system is still working, that we are all still 'in touch'. Tactile culture knows no other way.

Note

1   J. M. Cooper (ed.) (1997). *Plato: Complete Works*. Indianapolis/Cambridge: Hackett.

7

Visibility

No more Latin, no more French, no more sitting on the old hard bench. Kick up tables, kick up chairs, kick old . . . down the stairs.

Anonymous

Introduction

Few of us had any inclination to kick Master O' Malley down the stairs but we sang the song with gusto nonetheless. These, however, were more innocent times. Appearing as ourselves simply meant putting on summer gear instead of the school uniform and sleeping in late. To break free of school rules and declare our freedom as we left the school building could be represented visibly in T-shirts and sneakers or runners, as we called them. Had we simply exchanged one set of permissions for another? The thought that the issue of our 'visibility' might be related to permissions, 'rules of appearance', 'regimes of truth' and codes determining which permissions are appropriate would have seemed absurd. No, the school uniform, that was slavery, the T-shirt, that was freedom. We were free and that was all there was to it.

Many years later I listen to a group of teenagers describing the experience of heading to a class party. They all feel hyper and happy and excited; there is a great buzz, a great sense of freedom. The stimulation is 'unreal'. But the situation today seems more complicated somehow: how to dress, what to wear as make-up, what eau-de-cologne or perfume is 'cool', what drink to order, what pills to take or not to take, how to move on the dance floor. Indeed the rules of appearance built in to these occasions are picked up as social imperatives by these teenagers only too happy for the chance to fit it. They feel bound by the rules of the technology pre-determining their appearance. For Foucault the appropriate clothes would be evidence of the 'subjection' of these teenagers to a hidden code governing the technology of the body, a type of disciplinary culture inscribed in bodily behaviours from which not even a holiday T-shirt could represent escape. We might, in Douglas Kellner's words, think of these clothes as evidence of freedom whereas in reality they would only ever be 'the operations of power, particularly as they target the body to produce knowledge and subjectivity' (Best and Kellner, 1991, p. 46).

Almost all commentators agree that the perceived self-liberation of the child from parental control represents the key struggle for independence. For many of us growing up in a traditional society, the breaks with the adult world seemed relatively easy because childhood itself was relatively invisible. However, in a consumer culture, childhood seems to have become very visible and to be tied in within the lattice work of adult society so that when children put on the brand name shirt of their choosing – the recent rebels in Libya also wore brand-named shirts (2010) – the effect may not be to achieve any independence from the adult world but rather only to declare ownership over a particular social space and to claim recognition by another set of rules. This may be because every area of appearance has already been targeted by market forces. In the United States, the market in children's clothes has been estimated in 2010 to be valued at about $110 billion and the population of the 13–19-year-olds age has been predicted to be around 35 million individuals (Ebenkamp, 1998, p. 22). In such circumstances, individual appearance is always seriously compromised behind the demand to be always 'cool'.

In the United States, retailers like Kmart or Wallmart work hard to attract customers from the brand shops by studying what teenagers consider to be 'cool' about places to buy 'cool' things. The concern to be 'cool', is an artificial construction in itself and it respects no national borders. Grimstad et al., for instance, cite a 13-year-old Norwegian girl, saying, 'If you don't follow fashion, you wear like, sorta childish clothes' (Grimstad Klepp and Storm-Mathison, 2005, p. 323). The liberation sought is not a liberation from the adult world but a liberation from an earlier, quite visible, childish world and the choice between following the functionality rules, which their parents might use (a warm coat, gloves etc.) and following their peer group's inclinations is all part of a guided move managed by several layered consumer markets. This means that many teenagers have accepted brands as their preferred way of casting off the permissions of school only to mire themselves in further compromises, their step by step gradual disentanglement from the influence of parents now simply a step by step further entanglement in the subtly concealed consumer rules of childhood appearance.

Moreover such a set of circumstances has prompted the critical school of Giroux and Aronowitz (Aronowitz and Giroux, 1985; Giroux, 1992) to wonder whether any resistance is possible and indeed what kind of education might support that resistance. These writers go to much trouble to argue that the subtle refinements of a modern capitalist society point continually to intractable difficulties for children who still stand in need of liberation. Similarly many parents are also unhappy if their own children are not developing a critical independence from all such influences. They look for the availability of the right critical education for their children so that they can learn to be themselves. Many would certainly be dismayed if society did not value the child's singularity. So they play the game that most people play and encourage their children to conform to what is required. If a young person eventually learns how to declare its independence and to become indifferent to the brand name culture, they worry that she or he is becoming odd. They worry if their child is becoming 'invisible'.

I would like to note three perspectives on the appearance of children that now need some discussion. The first is the discourse of freedom where children use visibility – normally clothes – as a way of breaking away, resisting if you like, uniforms and what goes with it in schools. The second is the discourse of consumer appearance which represents liberation in an ambivalent manner due to the complicit nature of brand-name culture. But the third issue is rather ironic and is the core issue underscoring this chapter. This is the possibility of the radical disappearance of the child in a culture of extensive visibility where all appearance is codified and managed. To believe Žižek, a child's visibility today is more a function of his power to 'appear to appear' (Zizek, 2009, p. 29). This is a more tenuous claim to visibility, the claim to a kind of 'cool' appearance that is ephemeral, vaporous, non-committal. In the world of rules and permissions, appearance in this non-committed sense could have been interpreted as freedom of a sort. In a mode of 'tenuous' appearance, the picture is not quite so clear.

Foucault's visible subject

Foucault's work is already quite well known. I want to concentrate here on the need to recognize that two discourses are taking place simultaneously in Foucault's work – a discourse detailing the subjection of human being to social and academic categories – and a discourse promising some kind of liberation from these. Commentators of Foucault sometimes wonder whether emancipation is manifested well enough in Foucault's account to succeed or whether Foucault's vivid description of human enslavement actually prevails over accounts of liberation. In his later work, Foucault advocates the possibility of finding a reality in ourselves that is not circumscribed by institutions, cultures and structures, indeed by 'rules of appearance'. He holds out hope that a reality can be identified, nourished and cared for by parrhesiac (confessional) practices, such as were common in Epicurean and Stoic practices. But in the earlier text, *Discipline and Punish*, he operates as a post-structural researcher, which Best and Kellner sum up as the attempt to present the 'historical formation of soul, body, subject within various disciplinary matrices of power that operate in institutions such as prisons, schools, hospitals and workshops' (Best and Kellner, 1991, p. 47).

Given that Foucault's aim is to promise liberation not subjection, despite the detailed descriptions of normative slavery embedded in the institutions he identifies: clinics, schools, prisons, he is also concerned not to underplay 'a history of the different modes by which in our culture, human beings are made subjects' (Foucault in Dreyfus and Rabinow, 1982, p. 208). This aim is consistent with his underlying belief that freedom of some kind is still possible. Given that Foucault argued against structuralism's view of the way the very structures of societal organization and thought had come to achieve dominance, he struggled to spell out the detail of human liberation and seemed drawn to vivid pictures of subjection and imprisonment. The signs of a soldier, with which Foucault begins his chapter 'Docile bodies' in *Discipline and Punish* offers evidence of a public shaping. The seventeenth-century soldier was visible from afar and had become capable of being shaped like a constructed machine, demonstrating the 'automatism of habit' (Foucault, 1979, p. 135). What is exercised on the body is some kind of 'subtle coercion' and a body is docile when it 'may be subjected, used, transformed and improved' (Foucault, 1979, p. 136). Set against this military frame and its implied control mechanisms – the scale of the control which incorporated a fine eye for what detailed changes needed to be made, the object of control which analysed movement, gestures, attitudes in a general economy and the modality of control – whether the supervision should be constant or sporadic, these were the means and methods of disciplining the military body. If the body of the soldier could be disciplined in this way, then could the body of a mental patient or a child be similarly disciplined? Foucault is willing to extrapolate further from this context and to call all these bodily measures 'disciplines' through which a certain 'domination' can be exercised (Foucault, 1979, p. 137). This domination is relatively new because its intention is to produce subjected and practiced bodies, 'docile bodies' (Foucault, 1979, p. 138) and to install in public life a new micro-physics of power. This same 'economy of visibility' could extend its influence more broadly by means of generalized examination (Foucault, 1979, p. 187) and it is this theme which raises the temperature of most educationalists. But how could the humble examination have become so heavily embroiled in a general pattern of bio-political domination and incarceration?

Foucault's account of the panoptic strategy of an examination, which works to subjectify individuals in enclosed spaces such as workshops, factories and school settings, offers a further insight to daily practices in the classroom. It also shows how the appearance of the bodies of people is governed by applying certain rules of appearance. What makes Foucault's analysis persuasive are his insights into the spatial distributions that become operable in this economy of the body. Where spaces are defined, rules for the behaviour of people in those spaces are also defined. Foucault is concerned to point out the coercive nature of these rules. When children become free they manoeuvre outside the memorized rhythms of school life – all of which indicate that they had been 'doing time'. The weekly ranking in a school, class captains, row captains, test leaders and the weekly or even daily re-distribution of places based on new assessments, new perspectives, new controls – all these could at last be cast aside. As Foucault explains:

> Discipline . . . individualizes bodies by a location that does not give them a fixed position, but distributes them and circulates them in a network of relations. (p. 146)

Ranking now indicates a different understanding of time. Indeed ranking has become not only the 'place one occupies in a classification' (Foucault, 1979, p. 145) but also a temporal function of the ordered subject in a rank. When combined with the panoptic effects of the test, this leads to the paradoxical conclusion that tests are permanent, not results. This continually communicates the message to the young person that while the code is permanent, ranked individuals are only as good as their last test and therefore not really permanently graded. Relatively speaking, it is the test instrument that is permanent, not the child. At time t1, for instance, candidate M was to be ranked first in the classification but this was never meant to hold for time t2 so that, despite M's success, he or she is presented as a potential failure, subject to the vagaries of time, form and performance variables. Alternately, he might be considered a success, no matter what the result but this is rare. It is the sense of failure or potential failure that seems to dominate. So someone could equally argue that time t2 allows for candidate N to step up and be ranked in first position. But the fact that esteem in either case is only temporary, even achieving an A is not entirely good news.

The esteem operating in animal societies where a more permanent kind of ranking prevails, requires that animal leaders are usually visible and permanent. This may be because an animal group's survival depends on the continual functioning of authority lines within a group. Competition for food means that only one heron survives in the nest. In other cases juveniles manage to survive provided they are not put to the test. Although Foucault does not mention chimpanzees in his analysis, his analysis of ranking points to the problem I have just mentioned. For Foucault, two ranking systems, each claiming to code visibility in society offer themselves. In each case the ranking system 'creates' the individual.

In the first, more traditional example, the creation of the individual is marked out only by those who exercise power at a higher level and so children need to learn how to fulfil the requirements that will bring them to achieve the status offered. Several children can 'come of age' at the same time and without being in competition with each other. Foucault calls this the 'ascending pattern of individualisation' (Foucault, 1979, p. 193), which is roughly equivalent to the permanent status achieved by individuals in an animal group. Success is occasional, organic and operates without a code. Where there is an 'ascending pattern' there can be a matching 'ascending order' of visibility. The social visibility is marked by ceremonies that distinguish a higher visibility individual from lower visibility individuals according to a permanent ranking system. This occurs in coming of age rituals, military ceremonies, promotions, graduations and special honours ceremonies where the deeds of anybody can be enshrined in monuments that leave a legacy for future ages. In such cases, individuals have been granted a future perfect status (they will have been great).

Rank is invariably marked in human societies by increased visualization. In these social visibility networks, the ordinary individual is relatively invisible, the juvenile and the child certainly invisible – children are seen but not heard, but they can aspire to be famous some day in their own time. Disciplines in the old regime of ascending visibility become the publicly ritualized means for the presentation of individuals.

On the other hand, a descending order of individualization becomes exact and unrelenting, casting a 'scientifico-disciplinarian' veil over all disciplines

(Foucault, 1979, p. 193). This kind of visibility is not in any sense plotted back to an ancient map or generalized categories that commemorate even as they celebrate. Rather it results in the epiphany of a 'secret singularity' which has now become only instantaneously visible before disappearing immediately. It is the unique appearance of the individual that now seems important under the scientifico-disciplinarian regime. The child has now appeared not as a potential doctor, lawyer or teacher but rather primarily as themselves, individuals who must show that they are still up to standard, momentary holders of a role soon to be set aside when proven incompetent or made redundant by an accident of economic circumstance. The child is presented with a pattern of visibility focused on his own singularity – no more a classification like a soldier, plumber, sailor, policeman, but a ranked *individual*. This social experiment says to the child: You are only as good as your last lesson, your last essay, your last drawing, your last spelling test. This disciplinary regime offers a 'descending pattern of individualization' from which there is apparently no escape. Like seeping water, it penetrates every grain of wood or stone and exposes every crack to extreme attention. It says that your ranking is more demanding and yet less believable because it is impermanent. Under this rubric you need to pass continually through the narrow gates of competitive assessment to achieve visibility. And you are entirely alone in doing so. Observers only need to look at the stress on children's faces or to note their ever earlier interest in binge drinking or drug-taking to see some of the negative consequences of these manoeuvres. As Foucault explains:

> In a system of discipline, the child is more individualized than the adult, the patient more than the healthy man, the madman and the delinquent more than the normal and the non-delinquent . . . The moment that saw the transition from historic-ritual mechanisms for the formation of individuality to the scientific-disciplinary mechanisms, when the normal took over from the ancestral, and measurement from status . . . is the moment when a new technology of power and a new political anatomy of the body were implemented. (Foucault, 1979, p. 193)

This moment is here already. Children are now understood as 'subjects' in a descending order of ranking which makes them visible in many of the things they do and don't do. School-going childhood is then to be understood as the end point of a whole series of normalizing judgements that are built up on the basis of generalized surveillance techniques:

> It is the examination which, by combining hierarchical surveillance and normalizing judgement, assures the great disciplinary functions of

> distribution and classification . . . the fabrication of cellular, organic, genetic
> and combinatory individuality. (Foucault, 1979, p. 192)

Given the pervasiveness of this 'descending order', Foucault suggests that he wants
to begin to examine the patterns of resistance to 'subjectification' in human affairs
but yet his description of disciplinary culture makes this unlikely in *Discipline
and Punish*. Foucault scholars may disagree. They may point to his call at the end
of the text when he speaks of the apparatus of carceral mechanisms set in place
by the new order of discipline (Foucault, 1979, p. 306) and how wherever there
is a trend to increase these powers, there can also be the trend to decrease them.
But the picture remains bleak. By taking 'the forms of resistance against different
forms of power as a starting point' (Foucault, 1979, p. 211), he proposes a new
post-structural path to liberation that begins from existing structures. However,
human freedom has become a seriously compromised notion, split between
the contradictory aspirations of becoming visible (on condition of accepting
the rules of appearance) and becoming invisible by resisting its most insidious
mechanisms of dominance. As Foucault developed his analysis, he was obliged
to recognize how irrevocably compromised the experience of liberation had
become. How in the use of enclosed spaces is it possible to resist the dedication
of space to particular purposes?

In general I have two minor concerns with Foucault's account here. First,
although Foucault may be right about both the formal and informal operation
of carceral discipline on mass society, his analysis in other respects glosses
over the contextual setting for some of the examples of oppression he cites. He
takes no account of the subtle tactical manoeuvres used by humans to resist the
ranking systems of carceral societies, as Michel de Certeau would later outline
by means of his theory of tactical and strategic action (De Certeau, 1984). For
this reason, his account does not explain how experiences of dominance in his
terms continue to exist in schools, hospitals and factories without precipitating
reflection, reaction, even rebellion. Anyone who visits schools on a regular
basis has to be struck by the wide variety of atmospheres that govern school
institutions. Sometimes it is not the particularly well-resourced schools that are
happy and warm; sometimes it is not the frugally resourced schools that are
sad and backward. Sometimes a superficial visitor may note that the conditions
are less than ideal while the staff makes up for the difference. There are subtle
resistances in these locations which need to be acknowledged and which mitigate
the judgement that 'the school became a machine for learning' (Foucault, 1979,
p. 165) for such intensification (and we would have to call it 'intensification'

as Foucault presents it) would be quite simply unsustainable over time without the necessary counterbalances, which teachers, nurses, prison guards recognize as always having been required. Humans inevitably resist these intensifying mechanisms. They find them suffocating. Where discipline is too tough, as it was in Indian industrial schools or in the Victorian reform schools, 'subjects' invariably seek by means of truancy and even death to mollify the effects of these machine-like processes (Humphries, 1981). Resistance might be weak, but it is real and significant nonetheless.

The second concern is that sometimes these resistances could be evident by playing off classification and ranking, negating the 'subjectification' effect of each by the other. Indeed sometimes a wider context casts a different light on practices. Consider the many harsh regime schools, which promised children and their parents an exit from poverty. We have already mentioned (CHAPTER 1) how in relation to the De la Salle school, in defiance of the writing guilds, the skill of writing was introduced free of charge to the poor. In this case, careful attention to the detail of writing would have been doggedly embraced by pupils as a resistance to the hegemony of the Guilds. It is therefore impossible, taking this wider context into account, to read the temporal elaboration of actions NOT as an example of the imposition of an outside power demanding obedience, in the mechanical manner Foucault suggests (Foucault, 1979, p. 152). Such exactitude and precision of bodily movement might in contrast have been tolerated by the poorer classes if it held out the hope of breaking through the glass ceilings operative in French society at the time. Hence the precise disciplining of the body in this case signalled liberation rather than subjectification.

Similarly while Foucault suggests that discipline 'is an art of rank' (Foucault, 1979, p. 146) and correctly notes the negative effects of the fluctuations built into contemporary forms of ranking, this overlooks the possibility that members might step in and out of classification as a mode of resistance. Accordingly, the imposition of a classification and the establishment of a rank are two quite distinct operations. He speaks of the 'classificatory eye of the master' whereas classification might also have been seen as a way of resisting ranking in certain circumstances. The child, who is an expert 'fisherman' might use knowledge of this to lessen the pain of being ranked at the bottom of the maths class, having switched his identity from the classification of 'mathematician' to one of 'fisherman'. A child's stamp collection can make up for equations going wrong. In this sense the 'subjectified' child, already subjected to tests of literacy and numeracy, language and culture, loyalty and citizenship, can seek refuge from cellular forms of identity and hence 'resist' these by opting to shift classification and wear brand-name clothes outside school, or participate in a club or establish herself as part of a network which then guarantees them some kind of permanence of status in contrast to the nomadic constructions of neo-disciplinary ranking practices.

There is a psychological need then to belong to a classification as distinct from a rank and to accept the rules of appearance appropriate in such a context, especially as classifications can be self-selective and do not necessarily involve ongoing evaluation. There does not have to be any ranked way of being a Manchester United fan, or any ranked way to attend a concert or declare oneself a fan of x or y, or any ranked way of looking at a tennis match or wearing a particular brand of sneakers. Belonging to a classification is still a privately or group-managed practice that resists the rigorous ranking of a disciplinary system even if attempts can be made to subject every classification to the ranking mindset. What these switches of classification demonstrate is the manner in which the very same ranking logic can be resisted. In opposition to the ranking ambitions to make visible 'the place one occupies in a classification' (Foucault, 1979, p. 145), resistance to the ranking is brought about by a switch from one classification to another and by choosing one's participation in a non-ranked manner so that race, religion, nationalism, political party allegiance, even extreme party allegiance, club membership all present possibilities of refuge. Of course each of these classifications can in turn be troubled by the same disciplinary-ranking structures that originally required escape from them as fans try to distinguish between first-class fans and second-class fans etc. But this move can be resisted more easily as the degree of 'buy-in' that any individual accepts is always quite relative. It is no wonder that over-stressed accountants in suits from Monday to Friday take refuge in ribald chants at football matches on Saturday afternoons. For them to belong to a classification (football fan) allows them a form of permanent visibility which is preferred as a resistance to the ranking mechanisms which hold practices from Monday to Friday under constant temporal surveillance.

Foucault is right to indicate that resistance is required because the finitude of human beings cannot abide the exhaustive (infinite) pretensions of ranking mechanisms, especially their temporal elaboration. Human beings, even postmodern ones, prefer to define themselves in relation to the temporal space of a lifetime in keeping with the medieval advice that the whole is worth more than the part. In Foucault's words, 'The disciplinary methods reversed this relation, lowered the threshold of describable individuality and made of this description a means of control and a method of domination. It is no longer "a monument for future memory, but a document for possible use"' (Foucault, 1979, p. 191). Where resistance is strong, on the other hand, attention is directed away from those elements that can be used as comparators in any ranking system and towards the benefits of more generalized classifications. That allows for a pattern of stable equality quite different from the unstable equality characteristic of micro-managed ranking. Ironically it may be that, by wearing the logo T-shirt, the ranking is mitigated and humans return to taking their own place in a more general classification. In this way a stable visibility is possible similar to the one enjoyed currently by chimpanzees.

Despite these minor objections, Foucault has made a valuable contribution to our understanding of the two main kinds of disciplinary discourse, first the traditional 'ascending' order and second the new 'descending' disciplinary order. This analysis makes a key contribution to understanding the present problem which is to seek out the rules that enable children to be visible today while resisting forms of 'subjectification'. We are still asking about the visibility of children, their prospects for appearance as themselves and the possible contribution of education to this proposed appearance. It would be a disappointment if we too as educators opted to define our children entirely by means of a ranking technique. If educators stand *in loco parentis*, they must surely want to resist this perpetual ranking of children of all ages for some of the reasons outlined here.

The disciplinary culture analysed by Foucault warns about the danger of opening every area to surveillance. In the case of children who often need darkness and staying out of the limelight to develop and move through learning difficulties, the less said and the less seen is often better. In an environment when everything is changing, it may be best not to shine a torch on the painful detail of growing up. And yet the descending disciplinary attitude is relentless and continually seeks to 'improve things' by measuring everything. Children have found a way to escape from these torchlight strategies and have jumped instead into the fully visible theatres of talent contests, X-factors, Facebook walls, Twitter accounts and 24-hour-a-day mobile phone contact. It is quite possible that they have chosen to be totally visible in a last ditch attempt to resist the ranking of society and manage their own appearance. But there are dangers in this strategy, which educators know only too well, because a total visible world will not enable them to appear either. Maybe they have jumped from the frying pan into the fire.

Baudrillard's visible subject

Baudrillard suggests that in a hyperreal environment, visibility may be easy but meaningless. Vanity, vanity, all is vanity, as the *Book of Ecclesiastes* says, or as Baudrillard translates from the Hebrew, simulacrum (Poster, 1988, p. 166): simulacrum, simulacrum, all is simulacrum. All practices bear the resemblance of 'real' actions when they are in fact only engagement in a type of mimicry which affects everyone. We are at the moment unsure of the rules of appearance because what we see is often not what we get. And we see rather a lot. Does visibility under such circumstances then mean a form of non-appearance?

In a rather remarkable image described in *Simulations*, Baudrillard speaks about the fragments of a map which once covered an entire territory but now remains in tatters (J. Baudrillard, 1983, p. 1), a mere remnant of its former glory as a one-to-one representation of reality. The fragments of this map are stitched together, the gaps are filled out imaginatively and an entire fictitious map is reassembled to represent a world that has disappeared. Baudrillard argues that contemporary culture represents 'reality' as pastiche, a patchwork derived from out-of-date symbolic systems which have lost their original points of reference and simply maintain themselves in a relative system of relations. Hence the situation for postmodern culture is even more extreme than Foucault's reflections on power might suggest. There is no law or set of conditions plotting the appearance of objects in postmodern culture: their meaning is a volatile thing. Each simulacrum draws to itself the layered meaning of a complex pattern of associations, part representative of a disappeared world, part imagined coherence of the map itself, part the wilful delusion that all is the same as before. In any event, as Baudrillard says, this map of fragments effectively precedes the encounter with the world and intervenes as a psychological medium between the viewer and the 'outside' world. This position is very reminiscent of Lacan's mirror and points to the possibility that in our culture we may be imprisoned in our own unreal subjectivities, given over to wishful thinking and still incapable of recognizing the encounters which might make us more Real.

Baudrillard's point is that Borges' empire, which presented itself as the map of the totally known world, no longer represents the totality of any real world. A culture made up of fragments, lacks the correlation with other parts. Moreover isolated bits of a relatively incoherent patchwork achieve dominance in the society of the spectacle, achieving a status identified by Baudrillard as *hyperreal* and promulgated in a kind of game that simulates difference, what he calls 'the simulated generation of difference'. When a simulacrum produces a total environment, it creates a supersaturated positivity that allows no space for perspective taking, not to mention resistance or, dare one use the word, rebellion. Instead the youth loses himself in a kind of exaggerated vertigo (1983, p. 31) which has lost traces of any geometric reference points, including linearity and the switches occasioned by dialectical engagement. This state of affairs should be worrying to educators who are presented with kids who seem to be entirely independent while actually being bound up by the hidden rules of simulated belonging. Not only the parent's but the teacher's basic instincts have been 'unhinged by simulation' and cut loose in such a manner that 'all determination evaporates, every act terminates at the end of the cycle having benefited everyone and been scattered in all directions' (p. 31).

Supersaturation leads to the trend among people, including young people, to locate their identity in a hyperreal environment marked out by the commodities which have a fixed currency for a time in popular culture. This is not the disciplinary power of ranking as indicated by Foucault which insists on making the singular visible but rather an entirely surreal event. Hence what is exposed is the attraction of the supersaturated forms of appearance such as the brands which allow them to achieve a density as beings which might otherwise evade them. Because they wear *Adidas* or *Nike* for a time, they can appear as themselves. This supersaturation comes at a price because the ritualization of supersaturated life – Big Brother House, paparazzi servicing the cult of personality, the venal parade of nonentities, the fashion latest, the conveyor belt of incontrovertible statistics which claim to map everything of value, all become the guides to personal appearance. Fascinated by these maps, the micro-politics of 'reality' is overlooked. Instead it is you who have won the right to claim your identity as part of this supersaturated reality. You are drawn in by means of a 'circular seduction where you can detect easily the unconscious desire of no longer being visible at all' (p. 143). You are then invited to disappear also. There would be a way of mapping appearance back to 'reality' if only the map contained any features of a map that might describe 'reality' but the new logic of mapping and representation precludes this. Instead this new system has now opted for self-referencing symbols. Appearance is now governed by the display of a brand in a move that Baudrillard describes as displacing the sign by means of the 'indeterminacy of the code' (Poster, 1988, p. 127). The indeterminacy means that those children who invest their public appearance in codes have engaged in a process that is guaranteed to make them both visible and invisible:

> Everyone seeks their look. Since it is no longer possible to base any claim on one's own existence, there is nothing for it but to perform an appearing act without concerning oneself with being – or even with being seen. So it is not: 'I exist, I am here!' But rather: 'I am visible, I am an image – look! Look!' (2005, p. 23)

Hence the very means of liberation referred to earlier in our comments on Foucault – the switch from being bound by temporal ranking to being liberated by losing oneself in a new classification of ill-defined ranking has now been replaced by a peculiar kind of liberation where no one can be noticed at all. This returns us to the paradox of visibility, for it is precisely when the child or young person is visible in these supersaturated ways that they lose their own visibility in the normal sense.

This same idea recurs frequently in Baudrillard who is also famous for suggesting that 'power does not exist' (1987, p. 58). Hyperreality allows children to appear only in a total manner like ghosts who pass through one another, each one claiming control over the total space. The child who takes its identity cues from this hyperreal space, is thereby prevented from operating as a public agent bumping up against opponents, which might require plurality, reflection, argument, even a tolerance for idiosyncrasy. Instead he must confine its appearance to the rules of list-being, a general order governed by seduction (p. 44) from which the very grammar of critical engagement has been excluded. One hopes that Baudrillard might be exaggerating when he writes, 'there is no longer any critical space, a space where subject and object are respectively present, but a paradoxical space, a space where subject and object have respectively disappeared' (1996, p. 80). But the problem with the simulacrum is exactly as Baudrillard describes it, for it is not representative of anything. If you reach out your hand, you find that nothing is there and furthermore you find that the representative power of a simulacrum has been lost. The culture of the simulacrum holds out no promise of an encounter with anything. One wonders how, under such conditions, any personal growth can enter the life of the child. Perhaps it can happen by accident but then there are many distractions to keep the child fascinated by the fast-acting movement operating within a supersaturated environment.

List-being

Combining our comments on Foucault's analysis of classification with Baudrillard's concept of the hyperreal, we need to ask whether it makes sense to say that visibility is a mode of appearance. It could mean that the appearance that is really valued is a hidden kind of thing, the appearance under a classification or membership of a list – the *Nike* list, the *Nokia* list, the *Apple* list. But in which sense? In the sense of the exhaustive visualization matching the exhaustive individualization of Foucault's ranking or in the sense of the vacant generalization of the hyperreal? Hakanen (Hakanen, 2002) has suggested that the singularity which bore the brunt of Foucault's descending order of discipline, has been mercifully defracted by a kind of list-being. Rather than being subjected to the tough ranking of school, I bark out my riddle 'No more Latin, no more French etc . . .' but now rather than go home and put on a T-shirt to mark my freedom, I have to think which brand I can put on and which list I am on if I appear at the street corner. The space in which I appear has already been prearranged by a commercial field of forces. Huckleberry Finn is no more. In these circumstances, children can be tempted to see themselves, as Lacan's mirror suggests, as entirely whole beings, defined by the list, ready-made and finished off even before they start, imaginary whole persons not immersed in history or vulnerable to time or circumstance, not hampered by poverty, neglect or ignorance, or limited by sickness or disability but rather as an already finished performer, an agent for *Adidas* or *Nike*, a crusader-participant in the world of commerce, a loyalty card holder, a *list-being*. Is this not Foucault's 'ascending' order of discipline by another name, each trying to buy in to the list that they can afford and thus despite its modern-day resonances simply returning to old aristocratic principles?

Was it not the same for teenagers in Western societies before? Certainly. But the point is that *list-being* children have other pressures to contend with. For these children, brand names are presented by the world of fashion as part of a ready-made spectacle that defines itself as an alternative both to parental culture and to liberation culture. Lists for some have come to define the space of their public visibility. They are the wearers of Liverpool scarves, Gucci handbags or Wrangler shoes while the society of the spectacle, as Guy Debord noted, 'empties and nullifies every real identity' (Debord, 1983, p. 95). Guy Debord once advised that 'Everyone must magically identify with this absolute celebrity – or disappear' (Debord, 1983, p. 64). For these reasons, Debord rather darkly linked the spectacle to the 'autonomous movement of the non-living' (Debord, 1983, p. 2) an entire *Weltanschauung* that is all too evident in the recalibration of public life in terms of transparent lists. The spectacle is a type of total circle; what is in the circle is good and what is good is in the circle or, in Debord's words, 'that which appears is good, that which is good appears' (Debord, 1983, p. 12). Such a lack of differentiation in the absence of other features leads to major questions about personal identity.

Conclusion

Are there any implications for education? We would have to believe that Baudrillard's insistence on the predominance of make-believe in contemporary life signals a rejection of the discourse of liberation as an educational ideal. Baudrillard did not win many supporters among sociologists for suggesting that society had disappeared, for this was surely his most highly exaggerated claim. And yet Baudrillard's controversial position is that the simulation of an action is now necessary because there is no society into which a child can be introduced. Children now enter a world of 'as if' and they resonate with this world since it reminds them of their own play. They learn about 'as if' people without alarm – 'as if' bankers, 'as if' regulators, 'as if' politicians, 'as if' clergy, 'as if' police, 'as if' schoolteachers. They learn to engage with systems 'as if' they and the system are 'real'. The problem for real politicians, real bankers, real solicitors, real schoolteachers is to counter the play-acting of jokers and messers. The problem for Baudrillard is the prevalence of non-society over society and the culture of suspicion which prevalues the hyperreal, symbolic order over symbolic representation. To simulate in this context is not simply to 'feign to have what one hasn't' (Poster, 1988, p. 167) as it might have been in a traditional society. It has now become a way of life. To feign to have what one hasn't has been a rule of life for X-factor winners. Hyperreal children suddenly emerge without effort onto the world stage due perhaps to the purchase of a new pair of sneakers. They do not proclaim power in Foucault's sense, which can then be challenged, undermined, supported, as the case may be but rather an acquiescence of some kind before the power/powerlessness of the spectacle.

Meanwhile 16-year-olds in a local second-level community school are spending part of their transition year pretending to be stars. They have been broken into groups in music class and are busy setting up promotional videos of their talent and work. This activity is no doubt good for their confidence and it builds up a number of skills of potential use in the world outside school. The learning seems to belong to the doing of the thing, to the actual engagement in a process of mimicry. The aim is to produce videos that are on an effortless par with the best there is. They make use of the talent at hand and display sufficient technical quality to attract some hits on *YouTube*. The ability to 'look cool' is important, if not central. As I watch a number of these videos I am struck by their sameness and brand-like quality as if caricature has entered the agency of these young people, an avatar-like quality which has induced them into replication rather than action. It is only my impression, of course. No doubt others will say that what I am seeing is no different from the traditional imitation by a teenager of his parents on the farm or working in the local shop. But somehow I suspect that the scale of imitation in the case of these videos has gone quite beyond traditional limits. Not only are values imitated but so also are tones and styles and ways of being. The performances are curiously stylized, indicating perhaps that their imagination has also been colonized by the normalizing gaze of a media-savvy music industry. They seem to have been left without the agency to act otherwise, teenagers whose individual resistance in the name of self is radically in doubt, its place having been taken by the vacuous appearances legitimated by our age.

8

Invisibility

By emotion I mean the modifications of the body, whereby the active power of the said body is increased or diminished, aided or constrained, and also the ideas of such modifications.

Spinoza, *Ethics*, Part III, Definitions, translated by R. H. M. Elwes

Introduction

Foucault's examination of panoptic spaces in schools has reminded everyone of one way to make children visible. A model of visibility created and governed by discipline whether this follows the structures of an ascending order or the structures of a descending order, as Foucault explains, makes children visible by shining a light on them in various ways. The traditional link between discipline and children has made this form of visibility quite predictable in postmodern settings. Children either give the impression of being perfectly corralled in fixed exercises designed to test their performance levels or else they are liberated to aim at imitating certain exemplars that appear to them in the media or elsewhere. In contrast, a sceptical Baudrillard has spoken about excessive visibility, an obscenity of images that no longer have any symbolic grip and this causes problems for the young who want to appear, want to be visible in predictable ways and yet find themselves lost in a hyperreal environment where symbols are in constant flux. Baudrillard argues that this excessive visibility even causes a kind of invisibility: so many symbols that visibility is no longer credible.

As we now begin to look at the issue of invisibility, the same kind of curious paradox begins to surface. The human body is relatively invisible not only to the child but to adults also, despite being often adorned with all the symbols of cultural visibility. Do clothes make the body visible or is it nudity that makes the body visible? Do we not have our English Gardens in Munich or our nudist beeches or Baywatch television programmes to show off in statuesque magnificence the profile of the youthful human body? The body, even the naked body, has always appeared as a cultural artefact, its contours studied carefully, its aesthetic appeal the object of painting, literature and sculpted pieces, its frightened presentation in beauty pageants sometimes alarming. Or is it our elegant fashions that warrant attention, as there seems to be an interplay between the conventions of visibility and our current culture of nudity. The problem, however, runs deeper than this because the invisible body lies waiting to erupt in peculiar ways. Sometimes neither nudity nor high fashion can manage to hide its frightening presentation. It bursts forth in laughter or in anxious screams or sometimes in silent bodily complaints. The invisible body erupts only occasionally into the world of visibility and when it does, the appearance is more than a momentary switch in the conventions of appearance. That is the subject of this chapter.

An examination of invisibility might then be justified on two counts. The first is the obvious fact that human beings are not naturally transparent to themselves in their composition or make-up. They live first and then reflect second, usually in a fragmentary fashion. The result is that the living part of their lives remains invisible, lived out before reflected upon, undergone for the most part in a spontaneous way before any clear ideas emerge to give it a rational shape. Aristotle was clear that action always contained within it a non-rational component, represented, for instance, by the involuntary beating of the heart, which seemed to move automatically and could quicken without rational control (see Aristotle's discussion on incontinence in *Nicomachean Ethics* 6, 1149b 25ff.). Indeed so unpredictable and ultimately dangerous were these bodily elements that many philosophers over the years tried to design systems that would bring them under rational control or at least prevent them from holding sway over the rational life. These philosophers pointed to a human need to control the body in view of its apparent similarity with animals, to calm the savage breast, as the poet William Congreve put it in 1697, to ease the short, brutish life complained about by Hobbes in 1652, in general, to save mankind from beckoning barbarism (Sloterdijk, 2009, p. 15).

The need to keep base instincts under control was generally considered to be a necessary qualification for administrators in the Roman context, even if this principle was often honoured more in the breach than in the observance. One remembers Tiberius in self-imposed internal exile on the isle of Capri, prey to paranoid fears where he could indulge his baser appetites out of the sight and knowledge of the Senate, or the earnest advice of Seneca to his brother Novatus to curb his anger and temper his disappointment at being passed over for appointment (Cooper and Procope, 1995). Accordingly, it was thought wise for humans to learn how to manage a host of hidden passions which could from time to time erupt to carry them ahead of themselves and in unexpected directions. The human ability to reflect on what was happening became an important resource in establishing rational coherence in life but the aim of making bodily life fully transparent has come into fashion now that it is theoretically imagined that robotic aids and ultimately cyborg-humans can be programmed to operate according to strict rational principles (see Hayles, 1996, p. 416). Can the involuntary aspect of life not then eventually be discarded? This continued lagging behind at the heart of action offers evidence that pre-human elements can still manifest themselves in the midst of human society. But will they one day be abandoned?

The second justification follows from Lacan's view that the human body remains potentially invisible for emotional reasons. This does not mean that our bodies are literally invisible to us but rather that they present themselves as intelligible only in certain ways, sometimes as originators of passions to be sensored and curbed, sometimes as the sources of inspiration which are thought to be commendable and representable in art. The body makes its presence felt, although it cannot be seen or even heard very well. It is as if the human reality folds back in layers. We cannot explain its features simply by using medical description unless we include psychiatric description. The model that our bodies are like Russian dolls arranged in layers with each layer identical to the last and therefore understandable in the same way is known not to apply. Subjected to trauma or illness, the body can slip backward into layers or presentations that are unspeakable, beginning either a healing or a dying process, which even medics cannot fully understand. It is 'touch and go'; it 'needs time' . . . the 'chances are' . . . bodily presentations like human actions are difficult to pin-point exactly.

Hannah Arendt used the broad stroke distinction between biological life and zoological life to explain the realm that can be spoken about and the one that cannot. She identified the *bios* with the cultural presentations of life that might be recognizable as human while the zoological life veered more towards animal life as such. Giorgio Agamben added a political element to this zoological life, arguing that if some device could be found to isolate 'bare life', the ground might be set for representing the murder of humans as a process of purification and improvement, a process that achieved notoriety in the camps of Auschwitz and the like (G. Agamben, 1998). Even under normal circumstances, it seems, the human body is only presentable because of the linguistic filters that have been put in place and when these break down, some rather extraordinary manifestations of bodily life occur.

   In keeping with these reflections, we might note two manifestations of invisibility in the life of the child. The first is that the child might well manifest a form of animality that is usually thought to have been excluded from human life on the grounds that humans are 'above' animals. The second is that childhood culture might currently be in the process of preparing itself unconsciously for a semi-machine-like existence where humans choose to evolve in more predictable ways with the aid of implanted devices or robotic parts. Imagine a future state where humans see themselves, not only enhanced by machine features, but identified as semi-machines or cyborgs. We may need to explore these two particular trends towards invisibility, in view of the way they manifest something essential about human being, the first a return to some underlying manifestations of bodily being, even touching on the immortality of animals (meaning that the imperative is for the species to survive rather than the individual), the second an outreach into incorporeality with the ultimate promise of longer life, even immortality as a machine or a collection of information. Each of these trends has a certain power within the child's current environment.

Descending into animal life

The first trend towards invisibility is the eruption of pre-linguistic patterns of animal life. This step is not without its problems because the human species has sought to separate itself from the animal over many millennia (Sloterdijk, 2009). One old gambit to avoid 'animal' status has been to suggest that humans are in fact gods that have entered into a human body temporarily and will pass on when the time comes, thus lessening the importance of bodily existence and thus of animality in the experience of humans. And yet the denial of the importance of embodiment obscures the human understanding of itself as do divisions between mind and body or, in other contexts, between soul and body or mind and brain etc. These have all led to the impossible discourse of modernity which has sought to create the world in the image of a rational system. No matter how it is measured or evaluated, the human reality is still animal in many respects and a realization of this connection must lead to new educational interests in embodiment studies. Programmes in healthy eating, healthy exercising, healthy living in general pretend to make visible what remains invisible and may well stir up features of embodiment that stubbornly resist any facile attempts to make them linguistically available.

For this reason it is perhaps best to start with this first sense of invisibility – the eruption of invisible forms of bodily being. This might be categorized as invisibility per se since to be in a bodily way is already a feature of the human reality and not a construct. Perhaps this is the very feature which Spinoza noticed and which he went to such great pains to articulate in the *Ethics*.

Animal bodies

Konrad Lorenz's most famous work, *King Solomon's Ring*, first published in German in 1949 details many encounters with animals at his house and gardens in the Austrian town of Altenberg. His successful attempt to raise mallard ducks saw him imitating mallard call-sounds, which infant mallard chicks did not have to learn, but which they recognized and followed easily, provided he crouched low to the ground and made movements mimicking a duck's waddle. Once he repeated this sound often enough and took a low enough posture to a group of orphaned mallards, they were happy to recognize him as mother and to follow him around the garden. Greylag geese were even less discriminating. Once the young geese saw him, they started following him as their mother. This lack of body-self awareness could be considered typical of certain animals and may also have saved the lives of human children on occasion. Lorenz leaves his most detailed chapter to the study of jackdaws which, over generations and interrupted by the war, lived at a cleverly constructed aviary at Altenberg. Initially it had been Jock, a jackdaw, which had formed a close attachment to the author and to his wider family and household:

> Birds reared in isolation from their kind do not generally know which species they belong to; that is to say, not only their social reactions but also their sexual desires are directed towards those beings with whom they have spent certain impressionable phases of their early youth. (Lorenz, 2002, p. 127)

Lorenz observed this lack of bodily self-awareness or 'invisibility' in the behaviour of several animals he raised – a goose which had been raised in the company of chickens and which sought to attract the dominant male cock, having spurned a gander introduced for the purpose, a peacock which had been raised with tortoises and which engaged in mating rituals with a tortoise, having remained completely detached from peahens, the two jackdaws which had been raised as orphans, one becoming attached to Lorenz's housekeeper and the other to himself, the latter insisting on pushing finely minced earthworms, mixed with jackdaw saliva, into his mouth as a gesture of friendship/courtship. These behaviours can be taken to be incongruous to humans who might wonder at the invisibility of a species member to its own bodily being. And yet the evidence suggests that without definite messages coming from the troop or group as to what a young chick is, that chick will not grow up with a congruent instinctive sense of body-self. Lorenz believed that all animals come to a sense of their own bodies through education, by which Lorenz meant the messages which the group or troop give it. If the animal happens to be in the wrong place or with the wrong group, then these messages will be 'wrong'. There is no reason to believe that humans are any different from jackdaws in this respect even though those who believe in the importance of human reason might be optimistic about the likelihood of any feral child thinking its way out of a situation in favour of human bodily being. They would, however, be wrong.

Lorenz shows that jackdaws learn the collective intentions and meanings of a flock by call sounds and behaviours. The 'fly away' call is accompanied by the flight of a bird off a branch and its testing to see if other birds are interested. If the individual has influence with the group, it might precipitate a general movement upward off the branches. The 'fly-away' call may well be repeated and imitated, in which case the remaining members find the call irresistible. The call to 'fly home' is similarly tested and executed later in the day while the warning aggravated call is precipitated by seeing any jackdaw or black object dying or dead or in the grip of another animal. Perhaps 'blackness' had been learned as a bodily identifier of jackdaws but in Lorenz's view it was due to the remnant of an instinct. Some fundamental instincts still remain. Indeed Lorenz recounts how his special friend, the jackdaw named Jock, suddenly swooped down to attack his hand one day as he held another bird, ready to put it into its cage. The action caused a painful gouge in the writer's hand, which he explained by saying that this attack had occurred as a basic instinctive response to any presentation of an inert black object. In some instinctive sense, the jackdaw might have recognized the black object as a sign of jackdaw life but for Lorenz this example represented one of the few unlearned behaviours of the jackdaw groups he studied. In general jackdaws needed to learn everything by observation in the company of other jackdaws. Even their body-sense is learned in this way since, if they are separated from other jackdaws, they become like those orphaned animals raised outside their own company and unable to recognize the symbolic life-calls of their own kind.

The ugly duckling

The evidence suggests that if the animal is beyond a certain stage of development before being introduced to other social contexts, it will not be able to unlearn these 'wrong' lessons. Does the same hold for children? Surely the brain power of human children would override these basic contexts of learning. In observed cases where the child has been raised in the company of dogs or monkeys during a critical period of development and then retrieved into human company, it will have difficulty in relating to a body-sense created for it by its newly rediscovered human society because it will already have identified itself in a bodily sense with the previous company of non-human animals. There are differences of degree, needless to say, which might explain why some feral children are more severely affected than others. This observed result is somewhat surprising because although we might have expected problems of adaptation to happen in the case of jackdaws and mallards, we would have thought that the child's brain power would prepare him to form a sense of bodily identity independent of his early company. Would he not recognize himself to be a swan among ducks? Apparently not. The strange fact is that even human intelligence cannot overcome a biological misfit entirely, even after many years have passed in the re-education of that human. As we have mentioned in the case of Oxana Malaya (CHAPTER 5), an early life led with dogs had a marked influence on her and she was reportedly never happier than when in the company of dogs. Similarly, in cases where children were kept in isolation (consider Genie, discovered in California in 1970), the management of human company became an insuperable difficulty and very much depended on the caring nature of the child's new environment. In animal groups, socializing is an extension of the normal bodily behaviours learned by juveniles in every group.

Jacob von Uexküll spoke of the hermeneutical implications of life forms which live in their own bubble worlds and which from time to time come in contact with other bubble worlds. He used the expression 'functional circle' (*Funkstionskreis*) to describe this bubble.[1] This view in itself proved somewhat controversial because it ran counter to the accepted Darwinian view that animals survive because they are best adapted to their particular environment and therefore most 'open' to change. If Von Uexküll's view were upheld, then one would have to say that at least certain animals survive almost by fortunate coincidence because animals in general, on his account, are unable to give flexible responses in situations. For Von Uexküll, animals share with each other and communicate only within fixed parameters and include serious blind-spots.

This curious limitation seems also to apply to humans operating at the zoological level. The *Umwelt* or 'environment' of the animals becomes the determining context for action. Within it are certain significance markers, markers that map the cognitive boundaries of their own meaningful space. Agamben speaks of 'the paradoxical coincidence of this reciprocal blindness' (Giorgio Agamben, 2004, p. 42). This blindness helps explain why children who descend (if descend is the right word) into a purely zoological level of experience find themselves operating within a closed 'world' or 'circle' in function of which a new identity as individuated autistic or psychotic subject is sometimes established. Moreover care strategies may not be able to break this down.

The patterns of action in this world are also odd, as if some level of autonomy has not yet been achieved. Consider if you will the bird which has just flown into the garden and is perched warily on the bird-bath. Now that the bird has landed, the environment has changed for the bird and a new set of actions are possible depending on what the bird finds meaningful – drinking from the water, taking a bath in the water, flying off. The bird checks for the slightest sign of danger but is not perturbed by the presence of other birds, provided they do not come too close or claim the territory of the bird-bath, in which case certain hierarchies seem to apply. Chaffinches seem particularly timid and yield ground to greenfinches every time; robins will fight with any bird no matter what size and jackdaws have a hierarchy. Near the fountain a rabbit hops about and the birds take no notice of its presence and vice versa. If a cat or a human suddenly appears, there is an instant response and the bird flies to safety. Even a sudden movement might startle the bird and cause it to take flight. This example might well reflect what one commentator, Ziser, has called zooscopic reflection (Ziser, 2007), meaning that the bird scopes the environment for meaning-markers and responds accordingly. The bird does not make choices about what it will do, although to look at it, it seems to be trying to decide whether to stay or whether to go. It is looking about, fidgeting, uneasy. It seems to live its life like this. It does not have autonomy but rather is governed by what von Uexküll calls, 'disinhibitors'. A 'disinhibitor' is something that launches an action without reflection or choice by not preventing it from taking place. For example, appealing bait presented to fish launches an action to strike at it. The animal is not exactly free to do otherwise. The bird at the bird-bath is not really free to flee the bird-bath or to stay but the merest gust of wind that signals danger and it is gone; similarly, the fish's 'world' has become very narrow when a lure is presented to it at feeding time.

The study of animal action perhaps suggests that it is one thing to be free but another thing to be 'autonomous', that animals, not restricted in cages, are still bounded by the instincts and inhibitions of the 'bubble-world' to which they are connected. Their world is not intellectual but mainly corporeal where self-identity is defined in terms of bodily coexistence with other similar beings. Animals are not free to break out of this 'bubble-world' because they are bounded to it ontologically as a space of action. Indeed this form of action indicates that this closed 'world' is not a 'world' at all in Heidegger's sense, for animals do not share each other's 'bubble' worlds, a fact that inspired Heidegger to speak later of animals being 'poor in world' (Heidegger, 1995) and Giorgio Agamben to characterize human life as 'open' by comparison (Giorgio Agamben, 2004). In contrast, humans, benefiting from the development of language, live in the world with 'other' beings and 'other' world views so their 'being-in-the-world' precipitates a form of action that is not simply governed by the release of inhibitors. Indeed human action contains the rudimentary ingredients of autonomy, that is, the ability to impose laws on oneself, meaning that individuals can, to some extent, accept or reject laws to impose on themselves. The child's 'no' is significant as the beginnings of this process. But why then does a member of the human species not eventually win out over the 'functional circles' of monkeys or dogs in certain kinds of circumstance? In the case of human children taken out of the sphere of human cultural presentation of the body through illness, trauma or the death of carers, loss of connection with the normal sphere of human culture seems to mean that they fall back instead on an alien *zoë* (i.e. form of zoological life) as their own. This indicates an imperative at work here, even if it is invisible. Human children prefer to remain dogs, if they are with dogs, ducklings, if they are with ducklings, for it is better to be an ugly duckling than nothing at all. The invisible body, apparently, works according to its own kind of logic.

Lessons from feral children

More evidence about the invisible body comes from the history of the feral child, a topic that has been plagued by tall stories and myths. This concept has been controversial ever since it was announced by Linnaeus in 1758. Indeed many commentators have since found the idea of humans raised by animals simply preposterous. There is evidence that the Amala and Kampala at the orphanage of Midnapore during the 1930s drew sufficient notoriety to the orphanage to enable it to be financially maintained. In this vein, earlier writers seemed to be justified in casting doubts on the idea of the feral child. Already nineteenth-century writers like E. B. Taylor had rejected the concept pointing to inadequate data and hearsay while others argued that congenital idiocy could explain the 'wild man' hypothesis.

Others, theoretically at least, saw these cases as reflecting an earlier stage in the development of *homo sapiens*. Ernst Haeckel in *The Riddle of the Universe* (1899), for instance, concluded that Dubois' Java man (*pithecanthropus erectus*) was a human ancestor without language. Could wild children, the wild boy of Aveyron, for instance (Itard, 1932), reflect an earlier stage of human development? These speculations may have been given new wind due more recently to the general acceptance of Darwin's theory of evolution, humans being 99% chimpanzee plus or minus some genes such as the Fox 2 gene for language. But the difference we are examining is the way the body manifests itself within the child who should be able to recognize itself as a human being among dogs but is apparently not able to do so.

Broadening the definition of 'feral'

Zingg counted up to 37 reported and documented cases in the literature of the 'wild child' phenomenon (Zingg, 1940) and recent documentaries have catalogued other cases. What is interesting is not whether these cases were genuine but how their bodily characteristics were described. Rather interestingly, Zingg had distinguished between cases of (i) children who had wandered away; (ii) children who were (allegedly) nurtured by animals; and lastly, (iii) children who were isolated by cruel, abusive or incompetent parents. These distinctions broadened the definition of the 'feral child' sufficiently to accommodate less extreme cases than children simply raised by wild animals. This moved the debate from the arena of the freak show to the arena of psychiatry. On the basis of Zingg's research, Sprehe (Sprehe, 1961) speculated that wild children lacked the social context that might make them human. His 'social animal' thesis presumed that animals do not socialize whereas the evidence from Lorenz and von Uexküll is that animals do indeed socialize but within very fixed circles of possibility or 'bubble' worlds. Sprehe missed signs of the zoological body at work because he overlooked pre-linguistic form of social organization. He had stumbled across but not noticed examples of the 'bubble' relations of animals which now manifested themselves in the new situations or contexts in which children found themselves. Nevertheless, Sprehe's study had merit for renewing Linnaeus' descriptive triad of *mutus* (mute or unable to speak human language or even to learn it), *tetrapedis* (of four legs, meaning that such children moved on all fours like dogs or wolves in preference to taking an upright stance) and *hirsutus*, meaning 'hairy' or, in this case, paradoxically the preference to remain naked and to grow bodily hair in response to the cold. It was these details that struck a chord with Bettelheim who worked with profoundly autistic children. On the one hand, 'feral' children had learned how to present themselves as bodily beings in imitation of the bodily behaviour of the animal collective which had sheltered them. On the other hand, this behaviour had manifested the eruption of the invisible body in the lives of these children.

As shocking as these conclusions might seem, Bruno Bettelheim analysed these links further when, as a sceptic of the feral child hypothesis, he first confronted Zingg's examples. Qualifying the feral children hypothesis as 'a widely held error', Bettelheim nonetheless mapped his own clinical experience of autism at the Sonia Shankman Orthogenic School of the University of Chicago to these reports (Bettelheim, 1959, p. 455). Identifying the experience of aloneness that 'shuts anything that comes to them from outside' and wants to 'maintain sameness' (p. 455) as the core symptom of infantile autism, Bettelheim speculated that the symptoms described as applying to the feral child were uncannily similar to symptoms he had come across. Bettelheim spoke of scales falling from his eyes as he read through Zingg's details. His sympathetic description of these children (Bettelheim, 1950) testifies to his extraordinary sympathy for children and his keen awareness of zoological presentations of the body. For Bettelheim, bodily symptoms supposedly indicative of wildness, were features of autistic behaviours also. Not only did severely autistic children want to cast off their clothes and eat alone out of their hands, there were other symptoms like (i) unrecognized defecation and urination; (ii) screams and howls replacing talk; (iii) raw food in preference to cooked food, accompanied often by sniffing, smelling or licking; (iv) biting others or self (underlining the importance of teeth for tearing and biting rather than the hands which can manipulate and share). To these can be added a total absence of laughter, as autistic children seldom if ever laugh, and there is an absence of libido.

For his own reasons, Bettelheim focused on the issue of care rather than the sudden eruption of an invisible body and its coincidental denial by mass society. He became embroiled in a debate about parenting and criticism directed against him, which disturbed him greatly. But unknowingly he had pointed to the manifestation of what Arendt called the zoological body. Unwisely he had exposed the denial of socially unacceptable manifestations of the body. So from Bettelheim's work we can take the sense that there are many psychiatric conditions that impair the human capacity to operate as members of the human world. Many are afflicted by the traits of living in a 'bubble' reality where the freedom to think autonomously and invent in the company of others does not seem to operate. These traits, though 'invisible' may be closer to human actions than we normally think.

The Milgram experiment

Another manifestation of this 'bubble-world' is the less extreme context of Stanley Milgram's 'obedience' experiment (Milgram, 1974b). Milgram's well-known experiment need not detain us too long but it significantly involved over a thousand subjects, opened up the real possibility that humans under certain conditions could lose their 'autonomy' and become more likely to obey the command of a trusted authority than listen to the voice of their own conscience. Coming on the back of the Eichmann trial, these results were alarming. The experiment asked for volunteers to help test the effect of punishment on learning. A 'teacher' was asked to administer punishment to a complicit 'learner' and to administer electric shocks in a graduated manner, beginning at 15 volts up to 450 volts in response to wrong answers. At 75 volts the 'learner' grunts to acknowledge the pain and from then on the reaction of the complicit 'learner' increases until at 285 volts the screams of pain are unbearable to hear. Will the 'teacher' give up in response either to the stress he or she feels or in response to the appeals of the 'student' enduring the pain? At each stage, the experimenter remains calm and reassures the 'teacher' and so the experiment continues. Milgram found this surprising:

> What is surprising is how far ordinary individuals will go in complying with the experimenter's instructions. Indeed, the results of the experiment are both surprising and dismaying. Despite the fact that many subjects experience stress, despite the fact that many protest to the experimenter, a substantial proportion continue to the last shock on the generator. (Milgram, 1974a, p. 604)

The most fundamental lesson Milgram draws from this experiment is the degree to which ordinary people, with no particular malice, will easily become executors of pain and possible death, meaning that even a taboo as deep as the prohibition to kill would be easily moved aside if set against the need to belong to the 'high-level' behaviour represented by the scientific experiment. Milgram suggests that 'teachers' wanted at all times to be reassured by the experimenter that they were fulfilling the task well, that their performance was commendable and he construed this to mean that the desire to submit to authority overrode all moral quandaries about the behaviour concerned. It might also be possible to say that 'invisible' features of the body had come into play and that the bodily instinct to be part of a team, group or troop, in this case, the experimental team, had overridden all other considerations. On this reading, it was not conscience that had been set aside in favour of obedience but rather autonomy that had been set aside in favour of conformity to smart behaviour in the 'bubble-world' of scientific experiments. One could argue that it was participation in 'high status' performance as a respected member of a team and a participant in the development of science that triggered this 'immanent' law of bodily togetherness. In summary, the invisibility of animal life manifests itself in the 'strange' behaviour of these 'teachers' who, without any training, had been prepared to become torturers for the sake of participation in the high status life of a scientist.

These three examples, the bodily sense of animals, the bodily sense of feral children, whether bogus or not, and the bodily sense of operatives in a high-order human activity are simply speculative pointers, flawed certainly, but important enough to point to an 'invisible sphere' which still plays a significant, though neglected, role in children's education. But another set of manifestations moves us in quite a different direction.

Rising into a machine

The second manifestation of this invisibility arises in the appetite to become a machine. This might be presented as the invisibility of the body *per accidens* since it is a deliberate attempt to bypass the organic limitations of the body and to replace these by means of a new form of (human) being.

This trend to become posthuman and to forge a new life form as a cyborg or a machine seems on the one hand plainly exaggerated. However educators now need to work out the implications of this trend. It begins first as a general acceptance that the ideal life is compatible with an enhancement by means of machines, iPads, tracking devices, information retrieval instruments and then that such extensions are something of an ideal, marking oneself out by its means from others in competitive settings. The normalization of organic enhancements such as implants and the creation of robotic aids leads in turn to pragmatic considerations of resources and political access rather than any return to the fundamental question of changes to the human identity across the new environment created by cybernetic machines. In the imagination of people a new form of cybernetic identity is possible. It may now be only aspirational, but it effectively empties previous social networks of their significance as forbears and predecessors. The mantra is: get back to the future.

Posthumanism

Posthumanism as a theory is driven by names like Max More, Ray Kurzweil, Kevin Kelly, Peter Sloterdijk, Keith Ansell Pearson while a critic like Katherine Hayles (Hayles, 1996), argues for a limitation to these approaches. This prospect is often suggested in fictional terms and described using fictional metaphors. But one practitioner in cyborg research, Professor Kevin Warwick at Reading University, presents himself as a cyborg. He wants to demonstrate the plausibility of implant technology. The hope that such implants can improve the quality of life of the physically or visually impaired offers a ready-made rationale for the further development of this work. Think of the advantage of not getting sick, not losing one's eyesight or hearing, not suffering from heart attacks or cancer. Indeed we might benefit from having bodies that are self-monitoring, self-regulating, fully rationalized systems of organic support. One might choose to become invisible by turning one's back on organic vulnerability, preferring to keep oneself monitored through a fully rationalized form of consciousness (represented, for example, by Star Trek's *Borg*) and moving gradually to break free of organic limitation in the move to becoming posthuman. The objective is to become invisible as a conduit of pure information which flows like a liquid across borders and systems without physical profile or entropic loss. In its more extreme forms, this approach might even redefine humans as cybernetic machines and if that were to happen even the deepest features of human embodiment would be affected. Bendle worries at the prospect of 'potentially . . . digitized quanta of information "living" within cybernetic systems' rather than 'embodied beings living within history' (Bendle, 2002, p. 46). This posthuman presentation of the human would certainly try to bypass the limitations placed on operations by physical elements. Humans are to become bionic in a way, bolstered by Enlightenment ideals that promote the improvement of the human condition and by belief in the inevitable forward progress of humanity. Adding to Hayles' view, Bendle can summarize the situation as follows:

> These notions facilitate the re-conception of human beings as essentially information that is only contingently embodied and therefore capable of

being 'uploaded' into 'super-intelligent' communication and information systems that know no limitations of time or space . . . (Bendle, 2002, p. 47)

The posthuman movement holds up limitless existence as an ideal, which would be frightening were it not so familiar to children used to science-fiction presentations. The sense of being able to disappear in a vaporous state (*Avatar*) becomes the end that justifies whatever means are required and various scenarios present themselves in science-fiction accounts of the future, including medication (think of the romanticization of drug-taking in *Limitless* or the *Hulk*), implants of various kinds (*Bionic Man, Bionic Woman, Iron Man*), gene mutations (*X-men*, superheroes) and the attempts made to harness dreams and the unconscious (*Inception*). The popularity of these representations of future life accumulate the necessary evidence to make these developments plausible at least in an imaginary sense.

The disappearance of the human body, as we now know it, into a cybernetic system may not be all negative if considered from a metaphysical point of view. Indeed Sloterdijk holds that the new relation between human and machine has effectively negated an older metaphysic opposing nature and culture, which he advises us to abandon (Sloterdijk, 2004). Indeed it is now appropriate to call in question not only the separation of nature from culture but also other dichotomies between self and world, human and machine which in cybernetic environments are no longer appropriate. Coining the term 'anthropo-technology', Sloterdijk wants to characterize this current age as one marked by cooperation between human and machine rather than domination (Sloterdijk, 2004, p. 19).

Simondon's transducers

A similar sense of connection is found in Gilbert Simondon's notion of transduction. Arguing for a stronger connection between human and machine, Gilbert Simondon questions the assumption that that there are separate living milieus, a milieu for humans, a milieu for animals, a milieu for plants and lately, a milieu for machines. He further questions the need to separate the realms of reason, sensation, nutrition and cybernetics, which are often taken to underlie these milieus. Transduction thus refers to a process or movement of individuation that incorporates various fields into the same experience. In the words of Dumouchel, it is a 'process – be it physical, biological, mental or social – in which an activity gradually sets itself in motion, propagating within a given area, through a structuration of the different zones of the area over which it operates' and ends up expressing some sense of organic individuation (Dumouchel, 1992, p. 313). This is a transparent system by means of which individuation goes deeper and wider into the environment of human action. It sets up conditions where the human 'bubble' can broaden and deepen and perhaps eventually disappear. Transduction theory suggests that machines are not totalities standing in their own space, evolving according to their own principles of efficiency, but rather cultural instruments intimately bound up with human taste and development. This seems both attractive and reasonable. Machines make bodily presentations more explicit as if they are companions rather than aliens to the human life form. Consider the way buildings have improved their insulation and energy footprint over the years; consider the way cars have become more ergonomic and economic; consider the way people improve their coronary health with the help of heart monitors on exercise machines. If we are prepared to allow this influence from culture to machine, we need also to allow the same influence from machine to culture. Tools and machines have become part of culture and part of human identity and human development.

Expressed in this way, things do not seem so bad. For humans to evolve they might need to develop closer links with the machines they invent. Explanations of individuation need therefore to include the world of technical objects within which human beings operate, for individuation 'not only brings the individual to light but also the individual-milieu dyad' (Dumouchel, 1992, p. 300). Dumouchel's commentary is also echoed in Sloterdijk's understanding of anthropo-technology. The way forward for a milieu containing machines is sometimes to be seen in the design of a new machine, so that machines do not derive their value from some human whim but rather achieve viability because of their contribution to a new human milieu. More accurately, there is a general transduction across the whole milieu which means a development anywhere can lead to a development everywhere. We cannot look at a car and say that it is a piece of metal organized in a particular way by its own principles. In reality, as well as being designed for efficiency, it is subject to the same cultural conditions of individuation that apply to living human beings. Hence the car conforms to current social values concerning climate change. Its efficiency in depleting current carbon resources is carefully monitored. Our health-enhancing machines help us exercise safely and they must be checked for their efficiency regularly since they help people make bio-critical decisions. Current access to information is relatively painless and efficient, permitting a higher level of expertise to be attained earlier and sooner.

Indeed an entire system of coherence comes to life in the temporal ontogenesis of the living being, which now involves the human interaction with machines more closely than at any other time in history. Simondon thinks of this process in genealogical terms as a discontinuous path of being towards individuation. Rather than becoming in the sense of a growing branch, 'beings "switch" from one state of being into another: individuation is either complete or it is not . . .' (Del Lucchese, 2009). So there is a constant feeling of being successively out of focus and in focus across the continuum of experience. Like a crystal which develops at its frontiers, extending and parting, 'growing' in multiple and unpredictable directions, the human world holds together as part of a superstructure, the past with the present, the material with the spiritual, the biological with the cybernetic. On this reading, children as living beings change laterally as a totality, their entire cellular and organizational structure changing with the passing of time. Included are all machine and technical elements in the environment. So when you exercise on a treadmill in the gym, you expect to see a read-out of heartbeat and a calorie counter and you feel that you need this type of feedback to know yourself properly. Similarly you can immediately cope with puzzlement and confusion by reaching for your iPad to google the problem so that instant access to information replaces, fumbles, guesses, pleas, requests, inquiries and negotiations, meaning that learning becomes a succession of meta-stable structures which advance erratically (Dumouchel, 1992, p. 304). We have moved from the organic to the crystalline:

> In a certain sense, it could be said that the only guiding principle is that of the conservation of being through becoming; this conservation exists through the exchanges between structure and operation, proceeding by quantum leaps through successive equilibriums. (Del Lucchese, 2009, p. 6)

Perhaps I can be more amenable then to the chorus of clicks and clunks that accompany me as I sit in a University library, for these machines, I can argue, are mere extensions of the intelligent research activity of these students and as such are helpers, enhancers in a common project of learning. These clicking and whirring noises curiously play a central role in the individuation process of learners who are no longer challenged by the abrupt intervention of an alien world of knowledge but are participants and co-creators of the fluctuations in the general system, aided significantly by friendly, democratic, easily accessible machines. Our students are not pained by the disciplinarity of knowledge because they experience the mollified routines of clicking and clunking. They are reassured by the gentle cadences of a shared world in which humans and machines are becoming one and the same reality. But they are more 'subject' than ever to the ideology of the Enlightenment and the view, now mediated through machines, that the world is better now than ever before.

These transductive beings can have a purpose in their combined action which is constantly to refocus the inquiry within a narrow band of plausible search parameters. Students can be motivated to allow themselves to be guided by the rubrics designed to achieve efficiency within the system. Steering well clear of vague ideas and based on a set of given connections which define the here and now, the transductive being moves from the pre-individual 'invisible' manifestations of being towards the transindividual twenty-first-century being, marked by general cybernetic energy. Like a focusing process that brings sharpness to an object provided the viewer also remains static, the main feature of transductive being is to reaffirm that we already exist as a connected species governed by the logic of being in touch. The novelty now is represented by that networked world which has an immediate impact on the child through interactive media connection. Who is to say whether this environment will have the power to influence the learner, generate puzzlement, push inquiry and research, despite its rhizomatic patterns? The challenge is how to live in the 'supersaturated' context of human life where individual substance has disappeared, indeed where the individual, not needing bodily location, has reinvented its own 'invisibility' as a form of information.

Conclusion

In summary, we have here two contrasting ways of disappearing and becoming invisible, two forms of disappearance that beckon to children today. The first way beckons them to lose themselves in the entrails of carbon-based organic life, to return to a form of collective being dedicated to mutual survival in a pre-human sense. This happens in various ways, sometimes manifesting itself in feral behaviour, eating disorders, promiscuity, bodily intoxication, binge drinking, collective orgies, as the attractions of the zoological collective draw close and the rules governing cultural life are set aside. Von Uexküll's study added to Lorenz shows how impossible it is for animals in general to set these kinds of rules aside because they are predestined, as it were, to lead their lives in 'bubble-worlds'. Humans can for a time at least play between the human and the pre-human as they experiment with their freedom and the zone of invisibility which keeps teaching children about their own mortality but in ways that seem irrational and pre-linguistic. And yet they can seldom deny this mortality without damage to the cultural construct of human life.

The second way beckons them to lose the human footprint in a general structure currently led by machine technology and to qualify this structure as a living environment enhanced by machines, reaching out beyond the footprint of the organic towards the panacea of life as information. To become invisible in the depths of bodily life or to become invisible through the clicks and clunks of electronic supported contacts, these are two plausible aspirations for the postmodern child to consider. The first is a familiar one which philosophers have claimed does not enhance the human cause. The second, however, involves the rise of the machine and is particular to this age because it does not simply involve an addition to human capacity, as a tool normally would, but rather a replacement for some of the organic frailties from which humans have suffered over the years but which has kept humankind human as a general rule.

Tactility has brought today's child closer to the posthuman by configuring him or her as a transducer in Simondon's sense. Whether this move will lead to a reinvestment by a new generation in patterns of bodily expression that are still fully organic but also historically human, that is the question which philosophers of childhood and philosophers of education cannot now avoid.

Note

1 'Die vershiedenen Funkstionskreise in ihrer Gesamtheit bestimmen einen Ausschnitt von Eigenshaften, die im Leben des Tieres Bedeutung haben' [Different functional circles in their totality determine a cross-section of properties, which have meaning in the life of the animal]. See Adolf Portmann, Introduction to Jacob von Uexküll's *Streifzüge durch die Umwelten von Tieren und Menschen*.

Part III

Education

9

Vapour Trails and Noise

Man is only a reed, the weakest in nature, but he is a thinking reed. There is no need for the whole universe to take up arms to crush him: a vapour, a drop of water is enough to kill him.

Blaise Pascal, Pensées, # 200

Introduction

In this chapter, I set out to write an apologia for philosophy in a postmodern setting and to steer its method between vagueness and dogmatism, two characteristic ways of thinking I have found in classrooms over the years, the first being easily understandable in children, the second somewhat frustrating in teenagers.

The term 'vapour' is a metaphor designed to describe a half-thought. Vapours are half-thoughts, conjured up to put a shape on impressions, feelings, notions. They are easily dissipated and the merest distraction blows them away, perhaps to be forgotten forever. This explains why an artist, a poet or a mathematician might suddenly scramble for a notebook to jot down some half-thought lest its vaporous state be incapable of withstanding the moment by moment winds of change. A vapour is much more intangible than a hypothesis, which is the concept sometimes used to describe an improperly tested scientific proposition. Moreover half-thought but scientific testable hypotheses are already sufficiently well crystallized to allow them to be expressed and tested and so they can boast of a solidity that vapours cannot boast of. Indeed vapours are the half-thoughts that need special care lest they dissipate completely. They can easily be wiped away by the polished concepts of adults who can easily present adult thoughts in place of the child's thoughts.

Matthew Lipman was always careful to advise that when flip charts or whiteboards were used to record the child's reaction to a text, that the words should be written down exactly (within reason) rather than 'taken up' and 'polished' by means of the superior linguistic control of the teacher. There was a sensitivity in this method to what I refer to here as 'vaporous thoughts', even if Lipman and his associates never made use of the term (Lipman and Sharp, 1978). Indeed when children in particular come within range of a new concept, they begin to lose their way in the confusion that is normal when things are strange and impenetrable. If they don't immediately dismiss their own half-thoughts as worthless, they may be tempted to present them as dogmatic conclusions to a non-existent process of reflection and research. In either case the vaporous thoughts dissipate.

This chapter is about this moment in the lives of learners and inquirers generally. Do learners allow themselves to learn? Or have they learned the ways of subterfuge to avoid this sense of vulnerability. This chapter will argue that philosophy in a special way encourages these vaporous moments by opening the space of learning, for it is when knowledge is opened in this way that the experience of wonder comes into play. The task of philosophy is to combine knowledge with wonder, to identify what is known as a stepping stone to some future discovery about the world or about the self. This does not contradict an education for exactitude or precision, which is the form of unpuzzled learning favoured in schools where neither question nor wonder intervene to disturb the onward predictability of the day's events. But it does set such learning in a different context. While the scientific instinct tends to favour exactitude and hard conceptualization, thus forcing learning down a narrow tunnel, new thinking in science owes its success to an ability to live with the vapours of thought. And while there is no doubt that every intellectual effort requires precision, my argument here is that educators in particular need to be acutely sensitive to the management of the opposite of this, namely, imprecision, if they are to encourage the type of 'outside the box' thinking that has marked humans off from the animal kingdom. This is a paradoxical objective because most teachers want their teenagers to be clear in thought and purpose. So how can this issue be resolved?

A challenge to the proposed nurture of vaporizing thought is posed by a version of philosophy that is mesmerized by science and indeed presents itself as an intellectual discipline boasting exact parameters. This is because children often raise questions that they are not only unable to answer but are also unable to *ask*, so when 'scientific' philosophy spends its energies reformulating the questions to suit the contours of an imagined disciplinary response, it often misses the fact that the child has not *asked* that question in the first place and so may not be enthralled by the answer given. This process in itself might present itself as logical and coherent and worthy of scientific attention. Deleuze and Guattari's suggestion that philosophy is 'the art of creating concepts' (Deleuze and Guattari, 1994), should not conceal their real meaning, namely that philosophy deals mostly with vapours. During the teenage years there seems to be an inverse relation between precision and self-confidence – the more precise the answer given, the less self-confident the answerer remains . . . usually.

Wonder and perplexity

Philosophy needs to wage what Wittgenstein in the *Philosophical Investigations*, paragraph 109 called 'a battle against the bewitchment of our intelligence by means of language' (see Murris, 2000, p. 266; Fisher, 2008, p. 99). This has sometimes been taken as the call to make half-thoughts clearer and more refined and to promote a way of thinking that would encourage learners to 'broach problems in more systematic and logical ways' (Fisher, p. 101) or steer them 'away from confused, contradictory and foolish thinking' (Conroy, p. 151) whereas what I argue here, echoing Murris (Murris, 2008b), is precisely the opposite. The bewitchment comes from clarity itself and from the refinements of language which only persuade questioners to cede inquiry to other authorities. And the reason this bewitchment is so strong has to do with the modern response to Plato's challenge that 'nothing imperfect is ever a good measure of anything' (*Republic* 504a as quoted in Nussbaum, 1990, p. 250). It is true that Plato disparaged myth makers in the *Republic*, but his position is clearly nuanced since he makes use of metaphor, story and even imaginary dialogues to communicate his ideas (for an interesting discussion, see Smith, 2011). It is perhaps more honest to acknowledge what Arendt has called in deference to Sophocles and Socrates the disturbing nature of thought itself:

> The consequence is that thinking inevitably has a destructive, undermining
> effect on all established criteria, values and measurements of good and evil,
> in short, on those customs and rules of conduct we treat of in morals and

ethics . . . Socrates seems to say . . . if the wind of thinking, which I shall now
stir in you, has shaken you from your sleep and made you fully awake and
alive, then you will see that you have nothing in your grasp but perplexities,
and the best we can do with them is share them with each other. (Arendt as
quoted in Vansieleghem, 2005, p. 27)

Combining the call for clarity with the call for expertise in its Greek sense
of *sophia* effectively eclipses the perplexity and wonder which accompanies
the questioning of the early child. Commentators have been slow to embrace
developmental categories when speaking of this issue due to misgivings about
Piaget or a general neoliberal belief in the equality of all beings at every stage
of life. But those who might care to examine the early teenage years will find
a different set of categorical obstacles to philosophical thinking which is not
helped by curiosity and the admission of needing to learn things but is rather
motivated by the need to look cool and to present oneself as having known
these things already. Focus on expertise alone risks overlooking completely the
dogmatic nature of teenage thinking, which is quick to banish uncertainty and
instead to claim minor clarity as its own invention.

Perplexity seems even further from the agenda in these cases. For Aristotle,
all teachable knowledge is based on experience (*Meta*, 981a 15) and this means
that human concepts find their genesis in a process of becoming. Teachers need
to nurture this sense of puzzlement (Pring, 2008, p. 19).They need to allow
children to raise the question they cannot yet ask in order to explore it for as long
as their patience will allow. Children often wait for permission to explore in this
way, which is why perhaps in the Lipman method, every effort is made to write
down what the children say on a flip chart. The experience of perplexity and
indeed the obstacles it creates to learning are different in children at different
ages. Very young children might well ask embarrassing questions like, why does
that man have a big nose? And everyone will recognize this question not to be
answerable in terms of genetic codes imprinted in this man's DNA that determine
the development of a big nose but rather to have been raised perhaps out of fear.
Why is it okay for that man to have a big nose? Who gave him permission to
have a big nose? What did this person do to deserve such a big nose? And could
it happen to me? Behind this, and also not yet asked, are questions about the
stability of being and change, the question of permanency in life and difference
and the issue of unpredictability, the fear of death, the fear that granddad might
die and what might prevent this happening. These are not the questions *asked*
but they are *raised* in an incoherent manner. The child still thinks magically but
nonetheless raises philosophical questions.

Raising and asking questions

Given the fact that most philosophical questions are unanswerable, they can nevertheless be asked with a greater or lesser degree of clarity. They are not bounded at either end by having a beginning or an ending but present themselves like a 'string of spaghetti' (Haynes and Murris, 2011, p. 292). Children chug along using concepts that generally have 'fuzzy meanings' (Murris, 2008a, p. 106) and this feature risks opening a Pandora's box that distinguishes philosophical from scientific questions.

Teenagers, however, can sometimes be dogmatic from the start. They tend to work back from answers. They don't see the point of raising questions at all. In these cases, the teacher's skill is needed to open up teenagers to the ground of questioning, to release them, as it were, from the bogus security of absolute knowledge into the vulnerability that characterizes human knowledge generally. They need to be motivated to experience wonder. The evidence that secondary school pupils respond sometimes with impatience to a request for them to think for themselves should sound a warning bell that their inquiries have not yet taken root. They can select puzzlement or google and they have chosen google. Their concern is to gather information from the stable world not to find out how best to adjust themselves to the world. Their culture favours information in the form of wikis, blogs, databases, web-pages, information sheets, blurbs and tweets formulated in an instant and instantly discarded. As a result, the teacher who keeps the question open stands in an awkward place – a place where pupils can find their own voice, provided they generate the courage and self-confidence to face life as a bonafide member of *homo sapiens*. How to do this becomes the problem. James Conroy suggests that the philosophical tradition can profitably be used in the classroom (Conroy, 2008, p. 150). It would be an appealing prospect for a skilful use of traditional texts to become the powerful way to open children to self-questioning. Yet it is a presumption on the part of the facilitator to claim to be able to shape the question too easily. There needs to be a sensitivity in the way philosophical questions are raised even using traditional texts because academic philosophy on its own, and here I agree with Haynes and Murris, 'does not necessarily provide the skills or the courage to engage and support others in philosophical conversations' (Haynes and Murris, 2011, p. 290). And there are two aspects to this, as I see it.

Two basic aspects

First there is a need to respect the *principle of child-centredness*. It is the child or the teenager who actually needs to raise questions and to do this, they need to feel that they have permission to pursue the question and to 'own' it. They then need to have the courage to pursue a question until it becomes clearer. Some kind of sociocultural condition needs to be in place before a child can *raise* a philosophical question and pursue it down a path where it can be *asked*. Would this condition not need to be fulfilled for all kinds of inquiry-based learning? Or is it particularly relevant where the form of learning is self-referential like philosophy? If teachers respond by enabling the child to *ask* a question they have not raised, then the child may be distracted from the question that is looking for roots in the child's own life and some other question will be asked instead and probably answered. Young children are easily distracted while older children are not easily eased out of the ports in which they have taken refuge. Respect for the original vaporous state of a question *raising* is needed and to show this, the teacher needs to open the space of inquiry and keep it open. Only in some cases – the successful cases – is there an admission of vulnerability. There is the 'I don't know' admission of Charmides, for instance, who is unable to answer for himself when Socrates questions him and who defers to his cousin, Critias. There is the puzzlement of Alcibiades who cannot figure out why Socrates does not find him irresistible but keeps remarking on the state of his soul. In these cases, there is a sufficient glimpse of the search to recognize the vaporous thoughts that had been set aside in the interest of defending dogmatic self-presentations. Then and only then, when the original vapours are recognized, does philosophy for the teenager begin.

In similar fashion, a perspective must be won before it can be built upon and defended. Before gaining perspective, however, vaporous views require an environment of support and an intellectual will on the part of some pedagogue to prevent any single authority from entering the fray as a dogmatism and 'answering' by means of a ready-made 'conceptual' scheme. There is always a tendency for teenagers to seek out this authority for defensive reasons and even though the old authorities of church and state may have been replaced by Facebook clubs, the instinct to attach to the dogmatic voice is still as strong as ever. How can these teenagers be prised from their dogmatic slumbers?

This second aspect is the concern to respect proper method in pursuing questions of a philosophical kind. Some writers, as we have seen, feel that participants need to have control over the scientific form of argument construction before they can engage in what might be recognized as philosophy. Michael Hand makes competence a clear requirement of philosophical discourse, claiming that '[t]o be competent in a form of inquiry is not just a matter of asking questions of a particular kind: it is a matter of answering questions of a particular kind by means of appropriate methods of investigation' (Hand, 2008, p. 5). This is a rather strong position and, on his own admission, less plausible than others which also insist on proper method, for it includes as a requirement the outcome of arriving at clear answers. This position could qualify the 'vaporous thoughts' of children as fuzzy, perhaps immature, and clearly at odds with true (scientific) philosophy. Indeed this position could suggest that the control of concepts is not only appropriate, even to beginners, but a requisite condition of philosophy (Kennedy and Kennedy, 2011, p. 269; White, 2011).

The wooliness of the approach I am suggesting here would disturb these writers. Quite understandably they fear that it is a betrayal of philosophy to promote woolly mindedness or this 'vapour' as Deleuze and Guattari call it. They are concerned that proper training be applied in order to make both teachers and children competent in the art of dialectic (White, 2011). Even Lipman favoured this kind of 'scientific' control as is evidenced clearly in his systematic texts for children like Harry Stottlemeier (see Lipman and Sharp, 1978; Lipman, 1984). The norm for philosophy would be to declare itself to be a logical science with strict rules. Indeed John White's argument is that these are the tools of the trade, and that without the ability to construct a coherent argument, the work of philosophy flounders because the tool-set is not quite in place. Children could profitably learn how arguments are constructed and how best to move logically from the beginning of an argument to its end. Along the way they can be shown how to gather evidence, make claims and explain the warrant of these claims so as to develop an entire justification for the opinions that follow.

Bewitched intelligence

On the other hand, an objector to this 'scientific' position could similarly say that the appropriation of language itself does not necessarily lead to philosophy either. Grammar, syntax, claims and arguments might be excellent skills to acquire but they are as much required in law courts as in philosophical treatises. What justification can be given for advocating mastery over a precise language and technique if it only leads to dialectical skill and not philosophy? Are we allowing ourselves to be bewitched by the need to be proficient in language itself and the requirements of logic (Fisher, 2008, p. 99) and have we thereby reconfigured philosophy less as the attempt to verbalize wonder and more as the attempt to defend opinions in a court of law? Furthermore, it would be unfortunate if, in its more exaggerated form, this science of logic became scientistic in its rationale, turning into a more instrumentalist and 'skill'-based behaviour which, however attractive to funders and policymakers looking for ways to improve test score averages in schools, would be an abuse of the philosophical method (Long, 2005; Vansieleghem, 2005). Indeed a scientistic trend may well resonate with young people of a certain age, particularly between the ages of 7 and 12, where to follow Kohlberg (Kohlberg, 1981) and Fowler (Fowler, 1995), children prefer to construct quite literalist meanings of the world. There is a swing from complete vacancy before the age of 7 roughly speaking to complete assurance at the age of 9. Philosophy does not seem very useful or even relevant in this type of context except as a 'tool' especially when the attitude of general inquiry seems to have ceded considerable ground to the colourful dogmatisms that have found endorsement in the child's life.

As most parents know, a natural attitude of inquiry soon changes into one of dogmatic knowledge where children lose themselves between nothing and everything, perhaps because they actually have come to believe that there are answers to every question or perhaps because they fear there might not be. Learners in middle childhood (ages 10–12) have to be motivated to set aside their dogmatic views and to embark on 'inquiry' once again because natural questioning seems largely out of place, slightly 'outgrown' by a child who is now careful not to ask 'childish' questions. Philosophers know that these children still need liberation from dogmatism but unfortunately they need this at precisely the time when pressure is mounting on them to conform to social pressures and to digest a large amount of facts for public examinations. One has to wonder whether a performance-focused curriculum in schools (see Masschelein, 2001; Smith 2010, 358) is an environment conducive to exploration in this sense and whether a strategy of constant comparison and surveillance by State agencies is the way forward. When teachers lack the time to design the activities that promote thought, vapours no longer form into notions, nor does anyone have the time for children to work through them. Only exceptional teachers are able to curtail the effect of these distractions under normal curriculum delivery conditions. These teachers try to avoid setting up a prescriptive context for learning characterized by what Iris Murdoch described as 'a special unambiguous plainness and hardness . . . an austere, unselfish, candid style' (Iris Murdoch, *Men of Ideas* NY 1979 as quoted in Nussbaum, 1990, p. 251). Here especially, Nussbaum notes the important role that philosophy plays in breaking down dogmatic habits of thought, the defensive rationalizations that suddenly rise up to defend the speaker against learning and change (Nussbaum, 1990, p. 254).

Judith Suissa in a recent piece uses Dewey to strike a mediating chord, stressing the fact 'that the essential function and significance of philosophy is as an intelligent, critical response to questions of meaning thrown up by human and cultural experience' (Suissa, 2008, p. 134). But the problem once again is to know what shape a 'critical, intelligent response' might take, especially if the child is attempting to grasp vapours and organize half-thoughts which have not attained a solid state. Even a pragmatic stance can end up casting its concepts too robustly especially in an educational context where National Curriculum pressures can beg the question by immediately supporting a skill-set that includes reasoning skills, enquiry skills, creative thinking skills, evaluation skills (Winstanley, 2008, p. 92), skills which present a series of attractive outcomes to funding agencies but which also eclipse the vulnerability of learning itself. When it gets to this stage, philosophers readily object to the trend, saying that rationality cannot be reduced to the paradigm of mathematics and geometry (Smith, 2011, p. 362) but the damage has been done when we overlook the value of wonder itself as a nebulous, vaporous experience to be discarded as soon as possible. So it seems that proper mediation needs to be designed to cater for vaporous exploration and a more gradual and strict application of a method whereby a channel has been opened backward to the half-thoughts that are at the origin of the process. Once that element is assured, effort can be directed at polishing those concepts which one hopes will be there at the end.

This question of method, however, is really one of axiomatic importance for those who ask whether it is appropriate for children to do philosophy.

The bane of dogmatism

Granted that the child is not engaged by anything quite so 'old' as the breakdown of old prejudices or habits of thought that found expression in debates of previous centuries, the issue of dogmatism is always a live issue. The child's business deep down is more likely to find a way to populate a 'void', to query 'toothless' energies, to challenge the word 'you' when applied to themselves. Who is the 'you' that is presented as a 'good' child, a 'kind' person, a 'clever' child, 'mummy's little darling' or perhaps the 'lazy' student or the 'disruptive' pupil? The teenager's task is to deconstruct the messages newly admitted into the psychic sphere from siblings and friends and to begin to establish the 'I' on autonomous grounds. The teenager allows the 'I' to be populated from the 'concepts' that appear within its unsatisfactory 'bubble' world. Ultimately these concepts derive their 'gravitas' or what Augustine once called 'weight' not from social forms but from some other reference point, such as parents or trusted friends. For Deleuze and Guattari, however, an underlying emptiness points to a basic vulnerability in every child.

This reference point is the plane of immanence, the original pre-philosophical and indeed pre-human plane from which arise the figures, forms, myths or what our writers call, *vapours* that are essential to philosophy. The journey from outside self to inside self will involve incorporating the environment in which the child regains contact with its own plane of immanence. A loving human community offers more to the child than the caring environment of animals because of the way humans speak to their children and introduce them to a life of cultural exchange. It is a mistake to think that 'I' am a ready-made identity, a fixed point of origin. The child has difficulty in understanding the properties with which it has been identified: 'kind', 'clever', 'beautiful' or 'stupid', 'disgusting', 'ugly' so that while an entire content has become woven around the self, some kind of conceptual clarification is necessary. And it is not the conceptual clarification of dispassionate inquirers that is required. Rather it is something that has the power either to compromise or promote in some serious way the child's own self-understanding. Philosophy may be 'the art of creating concepts' (Deleuze and Guattari, 1994) but this art requires both the deconstruction of dogmatism and the skilful congealment of vapours. And it is a matter of difficulty to find out how this might happen in the best interests of the child.

So vapours are required and need to be rediscovered somewhat against the grain. Since they are vital to the formation of the self, they must be allowed to form themselves into many playful shapes and sizes. This vaporous experience corresponds hugely to the experiences of children, particularly teenagers in classroom who constantly present themselves as people in search of themselves, people still vulnerable to malevolent influences and identity remarks. The question closest to the hearts of these children is to learn who they are or might become in the future. Accordingly, concepts still need to be defined, closed down, shaped, even if they retain a certain vitality due to their original formlessness and 'vaporous' state. Learners know the significance of true concepts by the manner in which the latter dominate their lives, give their lives meaning and energize all their projects, although they do not know whether they do them good. The paradox is that sometimes they are unable to put words on these concepts and this is where myth comes into play. Despite attitudinal rigidities which find their source in the emotional life and intellectual rigidities which prevent them from changing their minds, tweenagers or teenagers are attracted by myths and stories and above all, metaphors. These are the privileged means for the child to achieve its first steps in wisdom. They are naturally attracted by myths and marvels because these stories occur in a secure setting which enables the readers to play with them safely, to test out identities without too many consequences. Deleuze and Guattari speak of the first filaments of an identity, the first congealment of the vapours which rise up from what they call the 'plane of immanence'. A closer examination of this idea might be appropriate now.

Arising from the plane of immanence

According to Deleuze and Guattari three aspects are required for proper philosophical engagement: 'the pre-philosophical plane it must lay out (immanence), the persona or personae it must invent and bring to life (insistence), and the philosophical concepts it must create (consistency)' (Deleuze and Guattari, 1994, pp. 76–7). As thought extends, three domains intersect. There is the philosophical plane, which largely gives rise to reflection on the plane of immanence, the plane of science and the plane of art (p. 198). The main events in philosophical thought are called 'concepts'; the main events in scientific thought are called 'functions'; the main event in artistic thought are called 'sensations'.

The pre-philosophical/philosophical plane is a plane of immanence and means the very condition for philosophical reflection, its origin if you like, not a point of origin, such as a 'subject', for that would suggest that there is such a point. All philosophy must lay out a type of pre-philosophical ground (the plane of immanence) against which the self can form or more accurately, the plane against which the conceptual personae can be invented and brought to life (insistence). It is difficult to do this when one has been locked up in a dark room for years on end or if one has been raised by dogs. However, under normal circumstances, the concepts that follow normal inquiry can be philosophical. Indeed the experience of becoming philosophical is an experience of de-territorialization and re-territorialization. It is at once the experience of de-territorialization from the hominid (but not yet human) plane of immanence, which is as yet undefined, may detour through patterns of invisibility before re-territorialization once again in the logical sphere aided by the achievement of autonomy or selfhood. The claim to be human can now be made. The child becomes human by taking up its animal being, locating itself by means of a transindividualization process that includes machine elements before locating itself in a conceptual persona which it gradually learns to unify. It is then enabled to become that persona's perspective while constantly reviewing its own foundations. This is why philosophers lead such uneasy lives, for philosophical concepts constantly reveal an instability through reflection until finally (although perhaps never fully!) one single directional idea or concept emerges to guide the philosophers life and thought. Like Frodo's ring in *Lord of the Rings*, the one ring establishes itself to rule all the others, becoming the singular idea of a life, a lifetime's commitment going forward. This is how the great philosophers achieved their wisdom even if not all the famous philosophers led wise lives as becomes clear from reading their life stories. They were nonetheless dedicated to some kind of wisdom as an ideal.

The second aspect discussed is art and art deals with sensation. Sensations are also known as *affects*, a word which ties them in to a field of philosophical reflection that takes its modern inspiration from Spinoza. What deals with sensations is art in its many forms – performative and literary arts in addition to which are the fine arts of painting and sculpting. Every work of art is, our authors say, a monument which rather than referring to a commemoration of a past event, represents 'a bloc of present sensations that owe their preservation only to themselves' (p. 167). It is not memory that is invoked by means of art, but 'fabulation'. Art is capable of returning us to the first steps of human becoming from non-human to human because it enables the viewer, the reader, the listener to melt into the origins of 'man's nonhuman becoming' (p. 173). Art enables this vaporous pre-human existence to manifest itself. Ahab does not contemplate Moby Dick from a distance but relates to Moby Dick as a participant in the same world just as a reader of the text enters into Ahab's all-consuming passion to kill the whale. In art, the life of what is described becomes indistinguishable from the life of the reader. And so it is with lovers of art who in a sense are induced to melt into a landscape or a face or some horror-filled Baconian grimace in order to contemplate the universal.[1] One needs to be careful in speaking here about contemplation because one is invited not simply to appreciate the folds of the face but to become them in a great moment of undifferentiated significance. We are drawn in to a time before human time began to a world where distinctions no longer apply and we emerge from this experience with a greater appreciation of the human world.

For this reason I would like to think that the crossover between philosophy and art is quite significant because both must point towards the plane of immanence out of which the vapours arise. When Lipman constructed his works, he took pains to create a story. Gareth Matthews and Robert Fisher have likewise favoured stories while Karin Murris has found it beneficial to use picture books with young children. Established texts, children's books and even the Harry Potter series have been used to good effect. I have used Harry Potter with much success both at adult level and at junior high and senior high school levels. The story draws the child/teenager into a safe world where exploration is possible. This would be sufficiently removed from the anxiety-filled contexts of school texts to allow the mind to play about and consider possibilities. The child's mind wanders sufficiently widely to recognize itself, in the words of Mercon and Armstrong, as a 'rational transindividual system from which relatively stable singular and collective forms emerge' (Mercon and Armstrong, 2011, p. 253). Hence what I have called in a previous chapter, the invisibility of the child, operates in favour of the freedom to discover an identity which is both organic and particular. Philosophy becomes an important help in the struggle of the teenager to discover an identity as mediated through the labyrinthine connections with the environment that are now possible in a world of complex social connections.

The third aspect our authors mention is science and science deals with functions. Functions derive their power from the axioms that are assumed at the outset and so functions can be presented 'as propositions in discursive systems' (p. 117) or as 'states of affairs in a system of reference' (p. 127). The advantage of scientific thinking is its well-defined evidence base and its strict method of exploration. Its main enemy according to our writers is its own speed, a speed which tends to eliminate historical awareness from its procedures and leaves researchers with the sense of riding on the crest of a wave, an impression that often leads mathematicians to grow impatient with the systems they invent. Speed opens up its own zone of indeterminacy, as functions clearly understood at the outset blend into sketches, guesses and not so clearly defined hypotheses. Clarity is forced to battle with its own nemesis – conjecture, contrived solutions, unjustified speculation – due to pressure to offer value for committed research monies. There is no time for philosophical reflection in a wide sense only for the reflection that improves methods or discovers short-cuts. The atmosphere is breathless. Mathematicians are obliged to take risks, being compelled to take key calculations for granted as they build their systems quickly and attempt to capture a fleeting thought. Sometimes the inspired insight, which is already disappearing beyond the horizon, has been all too briefly glimpsed, for 'chaos is defined not so much by its disorder as by the infinite speed with which every form taking shape in it vanishes' (p. 118).

If we recall the issue of empowerment treated earlier, then it is interesting to ask whether philosophy shares with art the initial contact with the pre-human. Their planes intersect more closely than either of them intersect with logo-centred reason because in comparison to the bracketed character of scientific work, they range over the manifold in comparative freedom. Our writers explain this by saying that '[t]he plane of composition of art and the plane of immanence of philosophy can slip into each other to the degree that parts of one may be occupied by entities of the other' (Deleuze and Guattari, 1994, p. 66). One example of this is the way that complex and abstract concepts in philosophy can be represented in images and poetry often better than by dialectical argument. So, for example, Plato's myth of Er, which he borrows from his tradition, becomes the vehicle for a reflection on the nature of justice and the quality of political leadership he had come across. Similarly the myth of Gyges presents the basis for a reflection on morality and invisibility while the famous parable of the cave becomes the opportunity for reflection on the nature of truth and the benefits of goodness to the mind. These stories broaden the appeal of logic and 'work' for apparently 'no reason' but this may be because they manage to capture the intersection of art and philosophy. This is evidence for the claim that '[p]henomenology needs art as logic needs science . . .' (p. 149). Of course there is a crossing between the plane of sensation pertinent to art and the plane of reference pertinent to science but art induces the participant to melt into the non-human conditions of life while science induces the participant to leave the plane of immanence aside in the desire to capture and describe the contours of an objective landscape. This is further evidence of an intersection between the planes of art and science which may give rise to the controversy about 'learning to paint by numbers' etc. We now have to see in what sense this intersection can be relevant to the child's overall development.

Intersections

Ultimately children may then come to appreciate that questioning lies at the heart of human culture, arguably separating human culture from other hominids and facilitating the flexibility that has enabled the survival of *homo sapiens*. The lack of sacred cows is the price we pay for our flexibility and yet sacred cows are everywhere and dogmatism still prevails as the dominant attitude of this age group. For this reason I am reluctant to press philosophy into service as the instrument that will shape up or 'correct' any half-baked thoughts by comparing them to some tight logical presentations found in the tradition. I need to respect and nurture something like a *princeps incipiens*, an *arche – logos* (Foucault), an 'originator instinct' (Buber), a principle of newness (Nietzsche), natality (Arendt) and the half-glimpsed forms that arise from the plane of immanence (Deleuze and Guattari). Philosophy then needs to build on these architectonic beginnings while children have the prerogative in the protected space of classrooms to scuttle the tradition. If there is no set formula for human nature, it might be tempting, as Biesta has suggested, to 'think of education as being interested in how new beginnings and new beginners come into the world' (Biesta, 2011, p. 313). Learners always build on what is fragile when they move into thought and for this reason they return constantly to check that everything is okay. A toe dipped in the water is retrieved; a half-baked idea is aired and withdrawn. This return to an origin of thought is a constant requirement for philosophy. At such moments learners may need to return to an original philosophical vapour that has motivated them through the years, such as the fear of death or the sense of growing up, and to verbalize this vapour in a way that might permit its abandonment. From time to time a philosopher must break free from the words created in order to reconvene at that point of origin where animal and human meet and where in a contemporary context both meet machines.

In a previous chapter we have seen how an anti-Aristotelian philosopher like Gilbert Simondon rejects both the monadic understanding of the individual and the hylomorphic theory of substance in favour of 'transduction', 'transindividuality'. This, for all its apparent complexity, is a theory that tries to describe the human milieu. Simondon, like his teacher Canguilhem, proposes that the purpose of education is to put in place an individuating system that is responsive to the human milieu rather than an ecstatic monad (as in existentialism) defining its freedom by reference to its own idiosyncratic power. I would have to conclude therefore, basing the idea of doing philosophy with children on this elaboration of the human milieu, that we need to acknowledge that philosophy arises from animal sources in humans. The only question asked by philosophy is what it is to be human and not animal. This is an impossible question to answer and it may not be asked specifically but it is always raised. The human itself has no adequate definition. If it were a scientific question, it could be expected to arise from the human logo-sphere but it has its origin instead in what one might call a Darwinian space between *homo sapiens* and those traces in the plane of immanence to which we are very closely related. Philosophy which once played a key role in the survival of the species by means of its ability to notice, encounter and accommodate to difference, is continually at work in every new generation to set out the limits of human life and either to widen or narrow the chances of its eventual survival.

Conclusion

Young people live in this place already and yet they may not recognize how to be human in it. This is something they must learn for themselves. Meanwhile they need teachers to join them in their struggle and to enter with them into 'a uniquely relational space where personal and communal intellectual transformations are rapidly and intensely experienced' (Mercon and Armstrong, 2011, p. 256). To engage philosophically with these young people means invariably to engage in time travel, to move, as it were, backward into the past and to join them in their teenage years and interests. It is to look forward to another's future. It is not a time for clearing up the confusions of adult language or sorting out the antinomies of reason but for encouraging the child to come into the reality of a verbalized world, putting words on experiences that are always somewhat vague, separating out experiences, learning from the accounts of others, learning to 'insist' on a perspective. These form part of the art of creating concepts, concepts which rise like vapours from the rough ground (Dunne, 1993), ground that is not yet populated by contemporary human beings. Children need to make these concepts clearer and more sparkling by the frequent massage of words. They come through conceptual confusions as a matter of course, provided they are allowed by an education system to do so. More refinements can enable learners to polish claims and to structure arguments. But to introduce polished claims too soon would ignore the important lessons of the vapour trails and the noisy interludes through which the best of ideas must pass.

Note

1   Francis Bacon, artist (1909–92).

10

The Ambassador's Secret

Immediately after his return the traveller must present himself before this Council to communicate any fresh notions he may have gathered in his travels on laws, education, or nurture.

Plato, *Laws*, 952b, translated by B. Jowett

Introduction

This chapter is a reflection on the role of theory and practice in learning. To explore this connection I use two metaphors. The first is suggested not only by Nietzsche's fondness for the mountains over Basel but also by Heidegger's rustic hideaway nestled in the mountainous retreat at Todnauberg. The second is the metaphor of the ambassador suggested by a passage from Plato's *Laws*, which was later taken up in Jaeger's reflections on education as we shall soon see. Both metaphors say something essential about the learning process. The mountain metaphor says that we need to leave our areas of familiarity in order to learn while the ambassador's secret describes the need for contact with something that is truly strange and different.

The typical in-service teacher who lands at my door is looking for 'relevant' information. The key issue of 'relevance' is always a stumbling block against learning. Sometimes my visitors are fixed in the perspective of a particular interest, dragging it around with them like an old sledge and asking for something that will help them move it about. When I invite them to leave the interest aside and to move up the mountain, many refuse, saying that to do so would be unwise since they want their own specific interests to be addressed. They want to follow the lines of their own inquiry; they want to stay living in a valley marked out by familiar boundaries. But then I say to them that if they want to understand the valley better, they should attempt to achieve a different perspective on it and this means leaving their interest behind and moving out of the valley. Some accept this adventure after a little persuasion and soon find that they are glad to have done so. They now have opened up a wider vista and, even though they know that they must soon return to the valley, they know that it will never appear the same as before. They give themselves permission to consider as 'relevant' what on the face of it first appeared plainly as 'irrelevant', namely, a different view from a different place. Nevertheless it is with this move that they open themselves to the important work of theory.

I labour this metaphor because children are involved in the process of mountain-climbing constantly and quite naturally. For them the invitation to move up the mountain is greeted enthusiastically and it never occurs to most of them to stay behind. They are less likely to object to the 'irrelevance' of the view from elsewhere whereas, as adults, we suffer from a constant inability to see what is relevant to ourselves. Our familiarization and our knowledge act as an obstacle to learning and if we are caught up in a society where adults are meant to be experts, we are prepared to think of ourselves in this way. We seem to think that operating is enough and that theory follows in some kind of magically transparent manner. Hence theory can be left to brainy people. And yet it is clear to children, for it is embedded in their natural attitude rather than in their words or concepts, that they want to further every opportunity to move up the mountain and explore perspectives and information that they never imagined before. They know instinctively that to safeguard their own inquiry they need to separate their action zone from their zone of thought.

Theory may initially characterize itself as a perspective that permits the procedural commentary on some familiar zone of action, a closely tagged reflection on daily happenings, for instance. Or else it might permit further exploration of the higher reaches of the mountain, taking up the perspective of a series of detailed forensic descriptions favoured by modern scientific method, or adopting a moral view of things in a place set apart in the spirit of someone like Michael Oakeshott, for instance (Williams, 2007) or the current, rather deceptive media-like divine view of everything. These perspectives are manifestations of theory at higher altitudes, warranted or not, and they may be devalued compared with the base-camp reflection 'in action' (Schon, 2005). Indeed one can debate whether or which of these are higher than others. The direction, though, is clear as well as the need to move away from familiar territories and thought-frames.

Perhaps then the first base camp is marked by what Beverley Shaw described as 'procedural' theory, a temporal commentary, indicating 'the procedures by which certain aims are to be achieved: if you want to achieve "p", do "q"' (Shaw, 1981, p. 19). Pure proceduralism if it claims to encapsulate the total remit of educational theory would be rejected by many educational thinkers (Smith, 2006), Pring (Pring, 2005) and Paul Hirst (see Hirst and Carr, 2005), all of whom in different ways argue for a greater tolerance for more generalized forms of theory in order to prevent the focus from falling exclusively on proceduralism. To abandon the aspiration to a greater generalism (or not to justify it properly) seems to leave theory vulnerable to forms of procedural thinking as it gradually slips back down into the valley, unable to answer the big questions. So it is perhaps the rejection of such a procedural world that animates Richard Smith and others to argue robustly for a broader view of theory. Educators, they feel, must move further up the mountain if they are to recognize their own historical and cultural limitations. Moreover big questions continue to be asked.

Having moved further up the mountain in order to take the perspective of general theory, the issue of time becomes less important and we come closer to a discussion about ultimate values. Aristotle's causes, material, final, formal and efficient as fields of inquiry, comment on the reality of change and offer a higher order commentary disentangled from the procedural issues from which they came. Facts then become less important beside the contexts or discursive procedures that logically accompany them. And yet facts achieve their meaning only from the perspective of some more general framework, a more general theory. Facts, as Tröhler says, are given meaning by discourses (Tröhler, 2007). A purely procedural place for theory would fail to notice the many biases embedded in the context itself. For instance Jan Wright's interest in knowing what assumptions underpin a research decision (Wright, 2008, p. 2) looks for a theory that disturbs while Stephen Ball wonders why social theory is often disturbing, sometimes even violent, or why it generally 'plays a key role in forming and reforming key research questions, invigorating the interpretation of research, and ensuring reflexivity in relation to research practice and the social production of research' (Ball, 2006, p. 1). An awareness is emerging among the theorists of every discipline of an educational need built into its own operation and it is this same attitude that links the concerns of contemporary writers to the concerns of the ancient world.

This is why we need to turn to Plato for guidelines. Plato recognized the need for the switch in perspective that is needed both by our valley-dweller, our coal-face practitioner and our fixated researcher. He inspires us to switch the metaphor from mountain to travel. His idea is that we cannot do theory from the place where we stand: we need to move. Plato's account of his troubles in the court of Dion, in the *Seventh Letter* reveals his dislike for Dion a politician with a closed mind and an exclusive interest in power, someone dedicated not to learning but to ignorance. Had Dion been inspired by a more foundational form of theory like ethical theory, for example, – one further up the mountain to use our first metaphor – he might have had a broader mind. Instead he was given over to the simple replication of Plato's thoughts and the attempt to usurp privilege on the basis of them. He might even have become open to a new order of *explanation* than the one he lived by.

So this metaphor of the mountain is particularly rich as an introduction to the meaning of theory and it functions not only in research but in society generally. The value of philosophy is that it attempts to gain a more general perspective by moving up the mountain and looking back not only on the valley below but also on the disciplines camped on the foothills. However our metaphor does carry with it a notable distortion stemming from the ancient world, the issue of contemplation. To avoid this danger it might be useful to switch metaphor from moving up a mountain to moving out into a strange land.

Plato's ambassador

We know that the word *theoros* refers to an ambassador or group of ambassadors who travel to another jurisdiction, learn about its customs and structures and return to teach something about the good to the local community. The word *theoros* in Greek might also mean a delegate to a feast, an ambassador to a strange city where games or ceremonies take place. Lobkowitcz likens *theoros* to a spectator at games, an envoy sent to consult an oracle, a visitor who travels to another country in order to learn more about its customs. One aspect of this work is reflected in the term *theoria* or watching over, participating in the ceremonies available, honouring the local gods to be worshipped or the local laws enacted as servicing the good of the people. It is only to be expected, as Lobkowitcz says, that these customs and practices present themselves as strange, as foreign and as critically competitive with the world view of the ambassador (Lobkowitcz, 1967). The purpose of the ambassador, however, is not to agree with what is on view or to consume it, as one might consume quirkiness in a holiday resort, but rather to change, to shift one's feet from the familiar to the unfamiliar and back again, to run the risk of doing this. Ambassadors must be willing to undergo this risk for the sake of their own community. Movement outward is now specifically set in relation to Plato's educational vision to bring goodness into the lives of the citizen. In Plato's *Laws*, 952b, we read:

> To this Council, then, the observer of foreign customs must proceed as soon as he gets back. If he has come across people who were able to give him some information about any problems of legislation or teaching or education, or if he actually comes back with some discoveries of his own, he should make his report to a full meeting of the Council. If he seems to be not a whit better or worse for his journey, he should be congratulated at any rate for his energy; if he is thought to have become appreciably better, even higher recognition should be given him during his lifetime, and after his death he must be paid appropriate honors by authority of the assembled council. But if it seems that he has returned corrupted, this self-styled 'expert' must talk to no one, young or old, and provided he obeys the authorities he may live as a private person; but if not, and he is convicted in court of meddling in some educational or legal question, he must die. (*Laws*, 952b–d in Cooper, 1997)

This text in Plato invoked by Jaeger (Jaeger, 1986, pp. 259–60) impresses the reader by its curt severity and ominous atmosphere. The 'observer of foreign customs' is the description of what I want to call a 'theorist' but this observer does more than simply observe. This observer must also judge and communicate. A theorist in its modern manifestation is essentially someone who travels by means of books and ideas and perhaps even physically sets out to explore customs, ways of life and ideas that are not native or locally familiar. Armed with this knowledge, he returns to promote the good of his own people. Educated in this way and prepared to experiment with ideas within his own value system, the ambassador is prepared to turn his own personal experience into an experimental site and to return to his native city a wiser person. His travel is a test of his own wisdom.

Ambassadors must be prepared to exercise their judgement, for a city must be assured that their ambassadors have *not* been corrupted by their experience. Hence a community needs to select only those trustworthy characters respected in the community for this task. The ambassador is the representative of the tradition of his native city. In a similar manner, the educator is the one who must hold the past and the locality in trust for future generations. Plato's text refers to important risks that every educator runs, especially the ultimate risk of corruption. It also implies that such an ambassador would require refined political skills to assess competing theories and competing claims on the good ambassador's sense of appropriateness. In the midst of these claims and presentations of what is the best way to govern a state, the ambassador must negotiate between local preferences and other values. He must then mediate other visions of the good back to his own city. The educator follows this same ambassadorial praxis because all theory continues to bear the imprint of a political engagement that lies at the heart of the educational endeavour, whether this means the local classroom, district or local area.

Ambassadors must be willing to undergo this risk for the sake of their own community just as educators must be willing to enter different arenas, arenas of the autistic spectrum, for instance, arenas of abuse, arenas of depression, arenas of privilege, arenas of lifestyle and value clearly different from their own. These are not arenas for agreement or argument: the ambassador has no role in making them different from what they are. Where the ambassador can make a difference is back on familiar soil. Ambassadors have to carry these lessons back to their own cities with their thoughts duly transformed (or not) as the case may be. Even if they recommend no changes in the native city, they are to be commended for undertaking this task of placing themselves in a foreign land and undergoing the test of travel. And if they come with suggestions, they are to be listened to with respect. While it would be reasonable to listen to these words as a commentary on a distant land, it would not be reasonable to think of them as expressing indifferent knowledge or what moderns call spectator knowledge. The *theoros* explains what he has observed but this only becomes theory when it is delivered with the intention of making the home community better. The laws make knowledge subservient to the political objective to enhance the well-being of a local society.

Certainly *theoria* is linked to the thought generated by spectation but when spectation is de-politicized and separated from the ambassador's political function and only identified as a perspective from the top of the mountain, without any obligation to communicate goodness to the people below, then a serious mistake is made and scepticism displaces inquiry. For this reason some suspect that too much theory opens inquiry to undue speculation, since the theoretician's view is held *prima facie* to be out of touch with the experience of learners. There are problems if we think of theory as a spectatorial event in this sense, or if we think of theory as 'the view from nowhere' or as Hannah Arendt (Arendt, 1958, p. 11) calls it, the Archimedean point, for then it can be roundly rejected as irrelevant. Similarly when Dewey argues in *Democracy and Education*, that 'thinking is often regarded both in philosophic theory and in educational practice as something cut off from experience, and capable of being cultivated in isolation' (Dewey, 2011, p. 153) his target is really a form of contemplation removed from learning situations. By rejecting theory as contemplation, Dewey can stress the importance of learning situations themselves in generating their own kind of theory. He can then urge educators to create a more active environment to allow learners convert their actions into occupations of active inquiry, and subsequently into theory.

But there are problems with this also. Education needs the challenge of the unfamiliar in order to operate in its own locality. Conversely there are signs that the reflective practitioner movement has opted for a one-source understanding of theory located in the learner's environment. It aims at better quality practice over a whole range of domains by measuring theoretical points by reference to the operation of practice. This experience-based approach, as explained by Collins, results in more credible eye-witness stances. Hence 'individuals who have lived through the experiences about which they claim to be experts are more believable and credible than those who have merely read and thought about such experience' (as quoted by Ladson-Billings, p. 472) while at the back of every experience a contemplative kind of theory could still make a claim for peripheral attention. From the perspective of ordinary practice, the 'reflective teacher' and 'grounded theory' movements tend to find theoretical material in the particular, the ideosyncratic, the biographic and the unrepeatable. Another way of pointing to this difficulty is to say that it engenders a one-source form of defence and justification strategy for educational theory (validating action-research, for instance, over any other kind of research method) and that in order to avoid theory as contemplation there is an overemphasis on the practice site. Accordingly when a particular change in the educational practice is suggested, there is a recursive appeal to the character of practice itself as the sole adjudicator of relevance, change and even theory.

Echoes of these swings between theory as contemplation and practice as its antidote can be seen in the recent controversy between Wilfred Carr and Paul Hirst. Wilfred Carr shocked everyone, particularly Paul Hirst, by announcing that he wanted to abandon theory altogether and replace the philosophy of education with a kind of new 'practical philosophy' of education (Hirst and Carr, 2005, p. 619). Car saw no valid alternative apart from the practice site. He invoked Dewey's idea of the 'reflective self-understanding of educational practitioners' (Hirst and Carr, 2005, p. 621). Theoretical reason, as supported by Hirst, on the other hand, he now described as 'outmoded and confused' proposing that theoretical ideas are 'inextricable from the parochial social and historical contexts in which they are posed and addressed' (Hirst and Carr, 2005, p. 623). It is the fact that the question of theory needs to be addressed from this one single-source perspective (the historicity of the practice site) that underlies Carr's argument. One leg, one source, only one possible occasion for theory (See Long, 2008).

On the face of it, theory construed in this way would be irrelevant if the key to all learning turned out to be the learner's experience or the localized familiarities which tend to ground learning in the normal sense. The drift towards considering local practice as the only viable arena of inquiry under pressure from pragmatism suggests the need for a third approach, an approach that combines both the traditional view of theory and the new concerns for reflective practice. This is the ambassador metaphor.

The teacher-ambassador

If the ambassador metaphor holds true, then educational theory involves locality in two senses. First there is the native locality of the ambassador (teacher or learner) and second there is the locality visited. The intervention of distance signals the risky process of gaining perspective from somewhere other than familiar ground. The ambassador must defend this process of perspective taking, revealing the essentially political character of educational theory, the fact that it involves a comparison between localities on the basis of a pattern of justification that is not monophoristic or single-sourced. The ambassador will no doubt soon come up against the elaborate 'relevance'-based discourse of single-source ideologues who can run a very successful campaign in defence of their own locality, institution, union or special interest lobby. On the face of it, monophorisms can make their case in a stronger fashion and their arguments may seem compelling. Education, however, cannot do this because education is essentially a relationship between the ambassador teacher and the child or in another context between the learner and strange and unfamiliar settings. Education needs multiple feet if it is to be true to itself and to do this it requires multiple views where the vision of the good is contested and debated. Not to do this or to support a view of theory that takes its justification from a single course ultimately props itself up on the basis of ideology or proceduralism or some such device. Trying to operate from a single source makes education vulnerable to sectoral take-over and decline.

Teachers are like ambassadors. They have journeyed through a discipline to a faraway place and then, having familiarized themselves with strange thoughts and customs, they have now returned to encounter youthful spirits in the classroom. Initially it is local knowledge which determines the norms of relevance and teachers can have difficulty in motivating learners to change their ways of knowing and thinking to accommodate another reality, which seems outlandish to everyone at first. The teacher-ambassador presents the need for learning to the local knowers, as well as presenting the knowledge which, with skill and insight, can be tapered to their appetites and purposes. Teacher-ambassadors are not culturally embedded in any very strong sense since they must take into account the information, insights and indeed values that they bring from elsewhere and they may well be inclined to value this learning when set against the operative schemes rationally supporting local knowledge. I still remember having a French teacher in school who seemed to eat, drink and live French culture, even though he was not French and neither were we. This mix of knowledge bases can enrich local reflection, improve local practices and sharpen the applicability of theoretical knowledge once the bipolarity of the ambassador's knowledge is respected.

Martin Buber once spoke of the teacher having to be in two sides of the teacher–pupil relationship at once (Buber, 1961, p. 123), obviously the teacher's side but then also the pupil's side, to act as a communicator between the adult world and the child's world. Similarly here, the ambassador's knowledge attempts to stand at two sides of a political divide and that is the divide between the alien and the familiar. This form of engagement with knowledge is dangerous, as Plato notes, since it involves the ambassador in calling his own values into account but it has the benefit of promoting the rule of goodness rather than the rule of familiarity and the promotion of this rule in judging which practices or thoughts might improve the lives of people.

The political task of teaching

Already theory here shows two *spatial* aspects of its political nature. It involves first of all thought in a *distant* place with a loss of native privilege and status but it also involves a continuing active *close* connection with one's native city. The ambassador has no authority to suggest alternative practices within the city where he is the guest, and to do so would be unwise, for his mandate is to observe and learn. In the context of his visit he may be graciously received and shown the hospitality reserved for ambassadors. In this event he encounters a *theorodoxos* or ambassadorial host who instructs him and answers his questions. In one way the ambassador is like a student in class, listening to opinions, offering his own if asked, learning from other perspectives, a learner in an alien place. In another way he is like a teacher, asking questions obliquely, probing for key information, also a learner in an alien place. The ambassador is not simply interested in accurate description, in precise observations but he is also engaged in piecing together a more complex picture involving what the host city intends to proclaim as its identity, its value-set, its answer to the question about what form of good life should be followed and what laws are appropriate to do this. He must learn what formative or educational structures are in place to support the ceremonies on view. The ambassador's evaluation depends on his ability to describe this complex mix of ideal vision and real institutions by means of a language that is aware of an alternative to what is on view in the ambassador's native city. Like the ambassador, the student or the tutor on her part must engage in a foreign environment and in subversive reflection. Otherwise insufficient risk is taken for learning to occur.

So, on the one hand, there is distance involving risk and the challenge going with distance; on the other hand, there is closeness and the challenge going with familiarity. Theoretical thinking requires a 'there' and a 'here'. The teacher-ambassador must be able to view the games or public display from two perspectives at once, the perspective of the city hosting the event and the perspective of the absent city of which he is the representative. It should be obvious, therefore, that theory people are unable to speak univocally. They do not produce the power discourse of a dogmatic thought frame since they are obliged to abandon familiarization, moderate contentious opinion, in short, learn from every situation in order to teach later with humility. And yet the good is one, not many. It is not the teacher's to own nor even to grasp fully. He must learn to keep all values in trust on behalf of his own city, which is also in quest of the good life. As a visitor, his business is to inquire and to listen; as a reporter to the elders of his own city, he is expected to be accurate, to bring something new back with him, to come offering insights of benefit to the city. His observations must remain decentred throughout, politically sensitive, even multicultural.

Strategic or tactical?

It might also be worth asking whether educational theory is tactical or strategic, using the distinction set out by Michel de Certeau in *The Practice of Everyday Life* (De Certeau, 1984). De Certeau explores the difference between a strategic relation to the environment and a tactical relation to the environment. A strategic relation presumes home advantage and takes account of prior knowledge of the power structures at work in the environment. Status quo action is usually strategic, supporting action designed to reassert the benefits of familiarity. Elaborating on this thought, De Certeau describes strategy as 'the calculation (or manipulation) of power relationships that becomes possible as soon as a subject with will and power (a business, an army, a city, a scientific institution) can be isolated' (De Certeau, 1984, pp. 35–6). A strategy assumes a place that can be described as one's own (*propre*) and thus serve as the basis for generating relations with an exterior distinct from it . . . political, economic and scientific rationality has been constructed on this strategic model. It is clear that many of the power/knowledge areas – academic disciplines, specialisms, etc. are promoted in ways that are strategic in nature, but our ambassadors do not operate with this kind of advantage and so their theory cannot be taken to be strategic in De Certeau's sense.

Tactical action, on the other hand, is necessary when the agent is obliged to work under rules set by others and this is closer to the actual experience of ambassadors. But not exactly. The ambassador is unable to set the rules and must negotiate his thinking in a foreign environment. This seems similar to the idea of tactic, namely, 'a calculated action determined by the absence of a proper locus' (De Certeau, 1984, p. 37) which cannot count on a location for its power nor impose any control in this space that is properly owned by the other. A tactic is powerless to direct its agenda because the 'place of a tactic belongs to the other'. Instead a tactic resists in a covert manner, insinuating itself into the other's place, fragmentarily and still without being able to take it over and also without being able to keep it at a distance. A tactic depends on time – it is always on the watch for opportunities that must be seized 'on the wing'. It 'creates surprises', retreats when pushed, attacks when least expected. In short, De Certeau says, 'a tactic is an art of the weak'.

Now at first sight it might be reasonable to think that ambassadors operate tactically since they think outside their own environment. But that cannot be right since their thinking is primarily influenced by the strategic shelter of their own native city and they have no interest in subverting the foreign city. They do not relate to arenas of inquiry as tacticians, biding their time, pulling and resisting, if needs be, in order some day to secure some power advantage. They have no power relation to this environment; their power derives from the home city where they have a position of authority and where they can then operate strategically when the time comes. So it is more accurate to say that ambassadors are displaced strategists, people who cannot be arrogant with host environments or they will risk learning nothing, people who function as patent learners in an alien space in order to accomplish the mission in hand. The exercise of theory in these locations is not an exercise of expertise but rather a form of listening, which translates not into power in the place of listening, but into learning. To extend this metaphor, theory is a stance of learning implying the experience of not being at home, not being an expert or a ruler with power and this apparent feebleness is the paradoxical key to its strength. The ambassador operates strategically in channeling the good for the child but does so through a mandatory detour through foreign experiences and information.

The dawning of theory in the child

The word which enlightens, which causes a 'dawning' of some kind to occur in the life of an individual, holds a person's life in the balance. Normality is in a certain sense like oblivion when it is contrasted with a 'dawning' of this kind. A dawning can have the effect of corrupting as well as maturing the individual. The invitation to theory, which Plato's prisoner easily grasped on his release from the cave, is always vulnerable inside the cave. The child too is lost in oblivion on certain matters without theory or the perspective that theory brings. Until she is released from ignorance, it is as if reality itself has been concealed from her and there might be good psychological reasons why this protection is naturally necessary. But out of this narrow world the child can step, given the proper kind of human nurture that all human children need. It is not what the child does that causes this, it is not what the child constructs that generates her own new insights. It is rather what happens to a child, a set of circumstances moving from the outside in, an invitation to theory. These are the factors that generate a new dawning in the child.

A new dawning has the same effect as the release of prisoners from their chains and their view of the entire cave in a newer light. While there may be uncertainty about this new world, it is certainly a move forward out of the staleness of the old world circling around local concerns. All parties recognize that something good has happened, that the quality of life has in some sense improved and that the life of the child has benefited from added colour. Perhaps the children do not have the excellent teacher who is prepared to inspire them and give them a direction in life. Ambassador educators are no gnostic seers, claiming expert knowledge of the good to return as Zarathustra to the benighted multitude on market day nor do they necessarily have Socrates' skill to ventriloquize Diotima when called upon to give a speech.[1] Instead, ambassadors too are searchers after truth much in line with the everyday educators of youth. They are the ones who seek out that word which, in the words of Peperzak, dominates all beings by 'casting truth and being upon them' (Peperzak, 1997).

Like the ambassador, the *theoros* awoken in the child is a new spirit of research which helps the child move out of a familiar landscape, perhaps exposing thought to the dawning processes of truth. For some moments, she lingers there learning from what appears, reassured by its warmth, attempting to hold on to this transfigured experience if possible but the time soon passes and she is returned to banality and to normal routines. Metaphysical theory has taught her to see her experience differently but *not to grasp* its truth. She still sees shadows instead of clear ideas, vapours instead of concepts. She still returns to limitations bounded by her own experiences. She still moulders in her own ethnocentric assumptions. But if she has learned something of the truth, she will be happy to shoulder the political pressure and to leave her securities in order to learn, simply because it is goodness itself that beckons. The truth has done her enough good to enable her to make light of the doxastic conventions or ideological posturing presented in its place. The light will not light her way sufficiently but it will offer her the dialectical spring from which to evaluate her situation. She will always encounter in herself many voices which advise her to take other paths and many which advise her to avoid engaging in dialogue but the ambassador's secret will continue to invite and to reassure.

Conclusion

Will this ambassador fear the death penalty when he returns to his city and advises the senior Council who are meeting secretly at night, as Plato recounts in the *Laws*? The punishment is death (*Laws*, 952c–d). But perhaps Jaeger is wrong to focus too much on the negative side, on penalties faced by the ambassador for getting his report wrong. The important point is that the ambassador has exercised a theoretical mission and has been courageous enough to return as a bearer of new ideas. As an observer, a spectator, he is now a returned ambassador and law maker, a bearer of secrets which only he can tell for they require an intimate knowledge of two sources at least. As a political actor, if he has learned to be open to the intricate implications of the good life, he can bring possibilities to the children he teaches that they could not have imagined. Children are bound to benefit.

Contemporary writers, unlike perhaps their counterparts from the ancient and medieval worlds, have a different view of what lies at the top of the mountain. And that is understandable. Neither modern nor postmodern writers are particularly interested in contemplation, the organizing concept of theory in the ancient world. For the ancients, the issue was how to wrest theory from the gods and to grasp it for humankind. Their concern was how to negotiate some kind of Promethean gesture or else how to persuade the Muses to offer their inspiration through poetry and art without antagonizing them or causing them to disappear. Indeed they wanted the mind of their poets to soar to the heavens and commune directly with the gods. In the medieval world the ultimate endgame of knowledge was to contemplate God as the source of all knowledge, suggesting that theory already had its ultimate destiny, that all discoveries had already been inscribed in a general teleology of the intellect, which manifested itself in a process that took its earliest motions from the life of plants, the movement of animals, to culminate ultimately in the beatific vision. Modern culture by contrast is fixated on the journey inward into inner transcendental regions where the human can declare itself the centre of the world. This Copernican irony, which is often presented as liberation from the gods, has become a backroom prison in our own times, and for this reason, because the modern spirit has tried to use up the world, a postmodern spirit has arisen to wait for the gods that are yet to come, as Heidegger once remarked. General theory is being affected by these trends and theory beckons to us in the postmodern world to set out from our familiar spaces to act as ambassadors for the next generation. The postmodern mind has to try to disentangle itself from the foothills preoccupation with procedure and try once more to grapple with the human quest for learning:

The ore is homsesick. And it yearns

To leave the coin and leave the wheel

That teach it to lead a life inane. (Rilke, as quoted in Heidegger, 1971)

Note

1 In the *Symposium*, Socrates uses the speech of Diotima to issue a proclamation on love.

11

Mind Games and Philosophy

One and the same are thought and that whereby there is thinking.
Parmenides, Fragment, translated by T. Davidson

Introduction

I have often been puzzled about the idea of thinking itself. Thinking seems to float over knowledge picking at what is known, undermining its pretentiousness or checking its validity. It does the same for behaviours and beliefs and anything that can result in cognitive content. Heidegger's point that thinking is a response to what is thoughtful may not be as trivial as it seems, even though, on the face of it, such a definition seems circular and unrewarding. I like, however, the idea of thinking as a response. Thinking might well be a response to some universal quality in a work of art or a response to something that might 'get you thinking' by which one means an event that has life-altering significance.

On a visit to a single sex boys school in the centre of Cork city, I found myself in a class of 13-year-olds, asking them in general about wisdom. As a member of the Board of Management of the school, I had asked the Principal for permission to do a 'philosophy' session with these children who were neither used to me nor to the method I intended to use. I found myself having to establish my own authority with them, as I was alone with the class group, rather than focus entirely on the issue at hand. Indeed the boys automatically assumed I was an inspector who had come in to examine them and they were initially wary and a little hostile, despite the Principal's reassurances to them. They were nearing the end of their first year in the school and did not see how philosophy fitted in with their plans. The school was a DEIS school (Delivering

Equal Opportunity in Schools) and the class group was of mixed ability. As far as I could see, their day tended to be dominated by the examination culture of the school and firm discipline. Initially they sat silently waiting for me to make some announcement to them and when I announced that I wanted to do some philosophy, they looked perplexed. I asked them to think about a few questions I was about to ask.

I wanted, of course, to get them to think or to see if they were thinking already. But rather than beginning with a story, I began rather unwisely with an abstract question: 'what is wisdom?' I was met with silence. So after a few moments and in order to soften the atmosphere, which had grown tense, I switched tack to the question: 'can you give me an example of a wise person?' The class exploded with suggestions. Answers (excuse colloquialisms) included 'a very old person', 'my mam', 'my nan' [gran]. I asked why they were wise, what made them wise and was told that 'my nan gives my mother everything', and then someone piped up 'street-wise', 'the three wise men' (it was a Christian school) and then a flow of associative ideas like 'knowledge and stuff', 'knowledge and books and what you find in libraries'. Dewey would easily have dismissed these ideas as simple associations (Dewey, 2010). Then someone blurted out 'a wise football player . . . has to know when to pass the ball' (this led to a laugh and the pupil visibly shrank in the desk, muttering 'but it could be . . .'). This 'slowish' pupil was nevertheless very 'street wise' in judging what was acceptable to say and what was not, but it was obvious that his influence did not extend to school matters. The other pupils seemed surprised that he had volunteered anything. Pupils soon ran out of examples suggested by whatever thoughts they associated with whatever had just been said a second before. They began to rustle in their seats, as if to tell me that now that all the answers had been given, what else was there to say? I should give them the answer and be done with it. Their main concern was to say something roughly cognate with previous suggestions and also acceptable in the group. They began to get a bit bored. I will speak more about boredom shortly but most pupils were so sensitive to this sense of boredom, whatever it was, that in the absence of hints from myself as to what to say, I noticed them getting more and more anxious and my own control began to slip. The momentum had slowed dangerously. So it was time to move on.

Then I asked the question: do people have to be old to be wise? But there was a unanimous agreement that no, young people could be wise too. A few moments earlier, given the opportunity without my prompting to say anything they liked, not one boy (except the boy who suggested the footballer) had associated wisdom with youth. They had all assumed and tacitly agreed that to be wise, one had to be old. Now when I mentioned this, they began to get anxious again. Maybe this was the wrong answer they had given. Had I been tricking them? They were already losing interest because the activity was losing momentum for them and they had begun to run out of ideas. Besides they had answered the question to their own satisfaction, even if now they began to scramble with the young versus old idea. A few began to say that everyone can be wise and then that there was no difference between the old and the young and indeed that everyone was wise. The concept seemed to slip out of anyone's grasp and the teacher was not helping! As the concept flattened out and became shapeless, the whole class now erupted in general agreement that everyone was wise. But when I asked them why if everyone was wise, they should have singled out grandparents and the like, the anxiety returned. They needed an answer and I was not giving it. Perhaps I was only playing a game with them? Perhaps I had found a way to laugh at them? Or else they found that they had no alternative but to think the matter through.

I reassured them and said that it was a very difficult question that many people had asked before without coming to any definite conclusion but they did not feel reassured. Teachers, after all, are the ones with answers. So why ask questions if you don't have answers? Sensing that I might lose control, I asked them another question 'Where do you find ideas?' Again there was a flurry of hands and they felt relieved that I had changed the subject. Again the answers came out thick and fast: 'ideas come from when you are thinking', 'ideas are thoughts', 'ideas are notions', 'ideas come in dreams'. Once again they preferred to give answers suggested by previous answers as if their suggestions tagged on to acceptable answers given by the group like a continuous collective stream of chained ideas. One pupil whom I had to address directly, for he had said nothing up to this, said that wisdom could be found in 'listening'. I was taken aback. This silent child had been listening all along and had obviously thought about the question while the general chatter continued. It was a very 'thoughtful' comment to which I needed to return but before this idea could be considered, another pupil blurted out 'reading' and then, returning to an acceptable idea, added 'ideas are found in books and libraries' and then another chirped up with 'listening' again. They found it difficult for a moment to reconcile the associations of wisdom with knowledge and the 'content' found in books and libraries while at the same time dealing with something quite as personal and self-referencing as 'listening'. Ideas in books had come suddenly into conflict with ideas in people but this conflict could not be resolved without further thought and a new kind of stress began to build in the group. This was a connection that many of them had not made before and they needed more time to think. Someone said everywhere, that is, wisdom is everywhere, and all agreed, everywhere. The concept once again flattened out and had become shapeless. So we were back to a consensus answer which, like the wisdom question, led to an 'everywhere' kind of answer and the abolition of all distinctions. I wanted to return to the quiet pupil who mentioned listening first because it had stirred up thought, but I sensed that, after a minute or so, the noise level would have risen again and while this pupil might have had very good thoughts on why he thought ideas came from listening, very few would actually be listening to him as he spoke about them.

Now the point is that a stranger to the class asking these strange personal questions could not expect anything more. Over time I am sure the issue would change as the pupils became more familiar with me and with the strangeness of the questions. But at this initial encounter within this culture, these pupils were not happy to construct thoughts without the reassurance that answers lay around the corner. Was this because their intellectual lives had made them used to forming and shaping answers to suit curricular needs in which case to take away this framework would make them feel lost. They knew what could be said in the group and what could not. Most pupils (even the most apparently backward) filtered what they wanted to say through this 'street sense'. Indeed were they not wise to do so?

The group tended to follow the status of the person who gave the answer rather than weighing up the pertinence of the response. They were involved in comparing worlds and the status of worlds, but did not feel that they had any particular authority to adjudicate on the matter. In this initial session my authority still dominated the exchanges, predetermining what others said and what could be expressed. At the same time the most original contributions came from the boy who spoke about the footballer and the one who would only speak when addressed. The pupil, however, who suggested that footballers were wise and drew a chuckle from the class, never tried his luck again in that lesson, although in a follow-up lesson he participated in a dominant role when I took up the idea again, unfortunately without much insight. Indeed what I judged the more thoughtful contribution in this group, the comment about 'listening' was subsequently ignored by the group as it seemed to cause turbulence or had come from an unpopular source. Instead the pattern was to support the conventional answer by association and to follow the member with the most status or the answer that relieved the stress of perplexity. Later on when a questionnaire was handed out, it seemed to me that they had settled down and their minds had shut down completely or at least that certain mind games had been selected and others excluded. When confronted with a task based on a Matthew Lipman exercise, some of them proceeded to fill in the boxes at speed. The better ones (in my meagre judgement) were only one-third of the way in when the others had finished. The better ones had been wondering about some of the answers; the speedier responders had just given them a brief glance.

Mind games and thinking positions

In the chapter on Vapour Trails, I already referred to the benefit, using Deleuze and Guattari, of the vapours rising up from the plane of immanence, and I pointed to the vocation of philosophy to apply pressure to stabilities wherever they arise and to return all concepts to their vaporous origins in human experience. This particular approach to thinking needs careful consideration and may be considered unfit for learners in certain circumstances. As Socrates found to his cost, parents are not too enamoured if their own trusted values and concepts are 'questioned' in this way. Parents might characterize serious questioning as corrupting and disruptive and they might advise against introducing children to philosophy too young, if such 'questioning' is promoted. However, this latter course of action would prevent the development of appropriate critical capacities in the young where it is most needed, for it is not only the world 'out-there' but it is also the world 'in-here' that must be considered. I wish to turn my attention now to some of the ways that this inner world is characterized. Three separate mind games might be in play, although in our example it was the first one which predominated with some aspects of the third. Each in turn calls for a different way of positioning the self, the first as a god who surveys the world and for whom therefore the problems of the world do not exist, the second as an actor who engages in the world and presents a heightened political sense and last as someone who positions himself as homeless in the world.

The first thinking position: The self as a god

As I have already spoken of this position earlier in Chapter 9, I will only make a few brief comments here and move on. Western philosophy has perhaps suffered unduly from its attempts to mimic the way in which Homer presented the Greek gods on Mount Olympus as 'contemplators' of the world. Similarly, in the tradition, 'concepts' have been presented to children from the top down, as it were, as if the concepts had a clarity and an endurance which could be used as a measure of thought by those 'only' learning. A number of metaphors could be used to express this idea: the apparent haste to dispel the fog of ignorance as soon as possible; the urge for everyone to move quickly out of the shadows into the clear light of day; the urge to find one's way in some hardened landscape. Where is the perplexity when children are encouraged to move from one hardened landscape to another, from one adult thought to another, from one adult scientific shaping to another? It may be preferable to handle concepts as finished products but they actually begin their lives as vapours rising from underneath. As vapours, however, they do not serve the same function of shaping and refining and defining boundaries as the mature concepts. Instead they perpetuate confusion, cause unease and open up rather rough ground to the sense of mystery and wonder. This is the process which many people identify as philosophy. Avoiding the property of rigid concepts which have the power to clarify and to petrify, vapours refuse to act as petrifications in a child's life.

Although human knowing is not identical to the divine knowing of the Greek gods, philosophers have tried to replicate the stability of the contemplative state by means of a 'transcendental' turn in human knowing. In other words, the stability sought is claimed to exist in the mind already in the form of its categories of understanding. Aristotle mentioned ten of these but Kant enhanced their status and increased their number to twelve so that they could withstand any sceptical claims. Categories of the understanding like necessity and possibility, unity and plurality – serve as observer posts from which the world can be contemplated and understood and without which the world cannot be known at all. Transcendental structures like these categories effectively offer humans a way of thinking like the gods and ensure them security and godlike knowledge, should they finally wish to replicate the imagined magnificence of the Greek gods. Because the scientific revolution has also invented a method to enable humans to imitate this kind of contemplation by bracketing off a whole range of questions that could never come into focus, perplexity can be factored out and one disciplinary account of the world can be used to view everything that is. Then the task is simply to contemplate from a calm perspective all the many items of evidence which have been arranged without mystery in some systematic fashion. When Socrates explored concepts, on the other hand, he did not promise this level of control. Even though his disputations, as remembered by Plato, constantly tried to arrive at a definition of the concept concerned, the experience proved sometimes harrowing for his interlocutors. It might have seemed unusual or even demeaning for humans to be happy with imprecision and vagueness when in fact they seemed to have the aspiration to survey the whole world.

The second thinking position: The self as actor

Hannah Arendt's great example of a thoughtless person was Adolf Eichmann (*The Life of the Mind*, p. 4) who showed his thoughtlessness, not by being a cruel and vindictive man, but simply by living carelessly, by surrendering his own will totally to a dominant authority figure. Arendt judged Eichmann to be thoughtless because he refused to appear as an actor in his own life – someone capable of action and speech – and became instead a talisman, a representative of power, a neutered advocate of impersonal forces. A thoughtless person on her terms was someone incapable of any singular action. When people later confronted Eichmann with his crimes, he could only sit bemused and puzzled. He did not see himself as a killer; he did not think of himself as bearing any personal animosity towards Jews. And yet, as SS-*Obersturmbannführer*, he had organized the deportation to the death-camps of countless Jews. He did not claim any special powers for himself. He had simply done what he had been told to do in the service of the Fatherland and because he was a good soldier. So what was the problem? The problem in Arendt's view was that he had reneged on the human requirement to think. His use of stock phrases, clichés, standard codes of expression, demonstrated repeatedly his absence of thinking, an inability to decide on right and wrong. But, in Arendt's view, human society has a right to demand more from people than Eichmann's particular kind of thoughtlessness, especially since thoughtlessness is quite capable, given the appropriate context, to lead to the massacre of millions and the destruction of the world itself.

To Hannah Arendt, human society has a right to demand of every human being that they learn to think in relation to the world and not only in relation to their own ego-space, for setting aside for the moment discussion of people with brain abnormalities, thinking is the very condition of the moral fabric of society.

In *Between Past and Future*, Arendt makes it clear that children are essentially people who are becoming, growing, changing and moving into the public world (Arendt, 1968, p. 185). They need to learn to think. They still require concealment and darkness in order to grow. A choice must be made between exposing them to the light of the public world or leaving them voiceless as individuals. But a proper education must prepare them to become voices in the public world. They cannot be exposed directly in the political interchange of the public realm for they must be allowed to change and to become different. And yet some features of this political engagement must find a home in their way of thinking. Under ideal circumstances, schooling forges this political structure. Children are not introduced into the political world per se when they are introduced to school but some version of this world must form part of their experience (pp. 188–9). The school is not there to further the life of the child as a child hidden away in the private space of the home but rather to develop the talents and powers that are ready to appear as relevant to the public sphere. Indeed responsible parents must take it upon themselves to safeguard their children against the world and to act also in defence of that world against their children. Parents are door-keepers, in a sense, assuming responsibility not only for the children but also for the world – the public world – the world in which a proper polity functions. She argues that to create a 'world' in which children can operate according to their own chaotic instincts does a disservice to this door-keeping function.

Left to their own devices, children are even more tyrannical than adults and they need proper training in public thinking to be otherwise. Arendt rather famously recognizes that the abandonment of children into the authority of the peer group places the child as a minor figure within a tyranny. She complains that children, not yet complete, still in the process of becoming, are 'forced to expose themselves to the light of a public existence'. Where ideally the school provides a middle ground between home and world, Arendt complains about teachers who only take responsibility for the talents of the child, not for the polity of their appearance. The task of educators is to bring the child's newness into relation with the world and this is a political task. The new must be introduced into a pre-established polity, while adults must conservatively preserve the old world in order to allow the new to appear (p. 193).

Arendt's account presumes that children with proper guidance and with the powers conferred upon them by the guided polity of the situation in which they find themselves, will learn to make use of their own voice. Understanding this voice metonymically as the child's ego, Arendt expects this voice to display some of the qualities of an adult ego. The child is supposed to speak in a contest where everyone listens. It is supposed to listen in a context where everyone can learn. Lipman and Sharp envisaged that this kind of context would describe their community of learners and I have to confess to be being drawn to this idea where there is respectful exchange between individual group members (Lipman and Sharp, 1978). But the adult model does not exactly work for children, even teenagers who are very sensitive about who it is that says what is said. This might indicate that some force more primitive than the basic elements of a polity are at work here, which might refer back to original empowerment, but which can be distorted by means of tyranny. Not everyone can speak in a tyranny. Nor are the best ideas necessarily recognized. The esteem in which the voice is held by the group counts for more than its logic, content or argumentative polish. Even Seneca was careful not to appear too perfect to the youthful Nero.

The pupil who is silent by convention will be silent now or else ventriloquize the opinion of the dominant speaker. Skilled facilitators are required to handle these pressures on the polity by encouraging the silent participant to speak and by linking comments and reasons given by the most timid to comments and reasons given by greater status members. However, the group is never a polity in an adult sense (speaking ideally) simply because the ego is particularly pliable and changing at this time. The child has to learn what opinion rings true to itself and to do that it must, as it were, express the view in public, face the challenge to clarify the opinion and ultimately, as in all games, abandon it if necessary without losing face.

As I see it, Arendt's polity has one advantage and one disadvantage over the mind game of thinking of the self as god. The advantage of Arendt's position is that she situated the self and indeed thought itself in a value-laden environment. Thoughtful persons are now expected to be thoughtful of others and thoughtful for others in ways that exposed Eichmann not only as an amoral person but also as a thoughtless person. Being thoughtful in Arendt's sense means contributing to the value-laden conversations of people who have no clear overall view of the truth but who must work together in order to achieve some kind of consensus about what the truth might be. This may also apply to the truth about themselves, to the issue of identity and the various postures which teenagers play around with and to which they do not relate as a simple series of choices.

The disadvantage of Arendt's polity is that it presumes that some field of inter-subjective experience can be automatic, given the right political conditions and the same criticism might be levelled at some versions of sociocultural theory. If the polity is robust enough to allow for what Arendt calls action and speech, then the individual forms its own voice by association in such a context. This, however, may be problematic for children who have not found their own voice but rather need to experiment and play with proposed identities before being held to account for them. It might be an over-statement to consider such a context as exhibiting an economy of choice, suggesting, for instance, that such a child chooses this type of identity or that (see Hall, Murphy and Soler, 2008). An over-early politicization of the young has the same dogmatic effect as an over-early banishment of the vaporous origins of concepts. It is surely not enough to provide the right external conditions for the child to appear as a happy individual. The context is therefore only a negative condition for the appearance of a happy individual child, a necessary but not a sufficient condition for the successful appearance of the humanity in the child to which Arendt refers. Some further condition is required to build up the individual child. One needs to ask then some kind of questions about the genesis of the child's position in society, perhaps pointing to signs of some kind of prior 'empowerment' that enables it to take place. The element that gives a child the confidence to have an authentic opinion in the first place (as distinct from a bogus or ventriloquized opinion, which is also commonly found) also serves as a condition for the recognition that the child is able to give to other authentic viewpoints and opinions and to listen respectful to those of others. The ethical stance of any thought is arguably based on an appreciation of the fragility of one's own opinion and the recognition of the fragility of the opinion of others whereas dogmatic opinions are flung across the room with no sense of fragility on either part. Facilitators of philosophy in classrooms recognize this difference because often the most vocal opinions are the most conventional and the least thoughtful. Perhaps Judith Butler expresses my misgiving better when she writes in reference to Axel Honneth's work on recognition, 'Do we need to know both how the *I* is formed and how it achieves separation from others before we can ask how it comes to adopt the point of view of the other?' (Honneth, 2008, p. 112). The answer to this question is surely yes, because the invariant 'I' can rather worryingly appear too early in the life of the child and become determinative of the future positions of the child. The problem is that if the child belongs to a Hitler youth group or a Pol Pot camp or becomes ensnared by something like Joseph Kony's Lord's Resistance Army, the identity is forged too fast to avoid the dogmatisms of thought that go with the dogmatisms of behaviour. Of course an objector might argue that these examples are extreme and do not reflect the type of polarity that Arendt is talking about. True, but it is the 'timing' of the identity that is the moot question.

The third thinking position: The self attuned or bored?

The third mind game acknowledges the self as an actor but sets out to soften its contours as it appears, to allow it to appear in a way that matches awareness of self and awareness of world. Hegel's philosophy might be interpreted as an attempt to explain how we might ever reach an objective picture of the world from a human perspective. Leaving aside the perspective of the gods, his question is how humans can allow the world to appear in itself without prejudice. Given that we start off in something of a fog, what generally happens in consciousness is that both the world and the observer appear together, each marked by its own frontier and yet each dependent on the atmospheric conditions to maintain both object and subject in place. There is a vulnerability about this. It seems to be a philosophical requirement due perhaps to the training philosophers receive that they are amenable to allowing the world to appear without presuming its appearance from the start. Following this kind of philosophical asceticism every objective appearance becomes dependent on subjective perspective and vice versa.

Moreover there is no Greek god perspective on the world. Hegel's reaction against the supposed transparency of the empirical method simply tells us something which we know already from a further 200 years of empirical research. For a scientist to achieve 'objective' knowledge of the world other scientists must agree. Other scientists are only too quick to suggest that a researcher is imagining things if the researcher's results vary greatly from theirs. All knowledge must filter through historical conventions. Ultimately the most valued scientist is the one who manages to describe some aspect of the world itself without prejudice, someone whose results are unproblematic because they can be replicated by others without difficulty not someone who has been given access to secret knowledge known only to the gods. But the point is that this ability to view the real world is a function of some kind of process that enables the separation of self from world. Taking another option, Hegel prefers to begin as Spinoza suggested with a monism of sorts:

> Hegel, in order to do away with the Kantian separation of form and content, interprets any and every existing thing as something that is at the same time spiritual. (Adorno, 1993, p. 57)

The word 'spiritual' in this quote is misleading to English language readers for it is a translation of the German word '*geistlich*', meaning mental in the sense of human, not natural and not conventionally religious. Hegel's interest, as Adorno explains, is to oppose static models of knowledge, to oppose the idea that knowledge is in some way dead or 'reified' and as a result to oppose the model of the self or consciousness as 'reified'. For Kant, the role of consciousness is to link one distinct field to another, to link concepts by means of proper judgement to percepts, but for Hegel such a static schema is impossible. Hegel's argument is that self and world are always bound up together: each is a function of the other until the endgame when all alike are taken up into a total picture, which he calls the absolute. In the meantime, consciousness is a process both of separation and of unification in which there is no remainder. What is excluded by means of separation is included in another way – niggling questions which may once have been excluded remain to nudge a theory out of its complacency and return to be included, partial formulations and half-ideas eventually participate in the clarity achieved. These phases of consciousness derive their energy from the development of consciousness itself while clarities can never declare themselves as absolute, finished, fixed. Similarly identities are generally only partially formulated, half-developed, full of contradictions while the remainders are taken up with the self as part of its own life history and they play their part. There is a beautiful scene in *Babette's Feast* when the Lieutenant stands to speak and, although he never married the lady of the house he loved, he incorporated this unrequited history into the story of his own life and the life of the sisters who hosted the meal. This scene and the Lieutenant's speech capture the essence of what Hegel is saying. We take up the remainders of our life as part of ourselves much as we take up the half-thoughts and conceptual misunderstandings of our inquiries as part of our eventual understanding. Identity and conceptual understanding work together as long as we are prepared to allow their mutual becoming.

Reflection does not work like a physical mirror enabling the exact replication of something that stands apart from it. The business of reflection is to allow consciousness to come alive. And so our young philosophers are in the business of defining how they stand in relation to the world, now that the adults are silent on the matter to be discussed. Like the feral children, they have grown accustomed to experiencing themselves as subordinates to the alpha itself. Hegel's thoughts can inspire us to say that the field out of which consciousness arises is already dialectically structured. Like the vapours that arise to disturb and melt childish thoughts, so the art of dialectic when managed in a playful way, can arise to melt and disturb personal assumptions about identity.

In the same spirit, the spirit of Hegel, that is, 'words in empirical languages are not pure names but always *thēsei*, positings' (Adorno, 1993, p. 107) and there has been much discussion of terms like 'positings' in post-structuralist philosophy. Positings are not thoughts taken out of the air on the basis of some supposed authority. Nor are they the fruits of some kind of subjective *Weltanschauung*, Adorno suggests (p. 138). Rather they are the hard-won expressions of experience that are always marked by the vestiges of a hidden undergrowth and are never as flippant as they might seem. The 'immanent approach' of Hegel (Adorno, 1993, p. 146) announces a different kind of critique by allowing for the softening of positions and the removal of references to authorities that are outside the context of inquiry:

> Anyone who judges something that has been articulated and elaborated – art or philosophy – by presuppositions that do not hold within it is behaving in a reactionary manner, even when he swears by progressive slogans. (Adorno, 1993, p. 146)

The engagement of the self in thinking is complicated by the fact that the self is never fully solidified. The self is a transcendental reality that is, not transcendent, and so the problem is how to develop a 'method of immanence' that will respect the establishment of this transcendental reality rather than assuming some a priori principle called the 'I' already established. To imagine some clarity on this matter before its time is really the problem. We are back to child soldiers willing to offer their lives for the sake of some charlatan or local war-lord. And yet it is easier to identify with some outside authority than to take this challenge on board as the child's identity is still quite fragile. And yet it seems far healthier to begin by thinking in a more playful way. Team work has often proven to be successful as a way of establishing identities in the young. Being a member of a group and having some definite function within it can paradoxically help to establish individual identities, provided these identities can be set aside. Added to this are the many experimental identities which the young can play with and which are facilitated by human culture. Children of all ages sometimes 'put on' identities that they can subsequently 'take off' when the game moves on. There are no signs here of mastery over self or world and that is as it should be. But ultimately it is the engagement with thinking itself that is the telling factor. We are, after all, thinking beings, as Descartes rightly remarked.

The paradox of attunement

To advance this argument further, I have to borrow from Heidegger's theory of attunement which, quite contrary to the impression it might make, does not connote some harmonic concordance with the world as a state of affairs already existing. Attunement indicates the 'openness' to the world particular to humans. 'Openness' can be understood in two senses, either in the sense that there are no barriers preventing the individual from identifying with the world in its totality so that the individual completely 'fits in' with the world and may well become its clear representative. Alternately it might mean standing at the border of the world as one knows it and looking outwards into different worlds. If 'openness' means the former, the individual is fully at home in the world and does not experience the world as anything other than some superstructure entirely consistent with its own identity – the Hitler youth sees himself as the representative of the Fatherland. While mallards and chimpanzees may be entirely happy to live their lives within the programmed indices of the world into which they have been thrown in this sense, many humans, especially teenagers have a more 'out of place' feeling, envying those who seem to fit in while feeling themselves alienated. Heidegger's theory may explain why this is the case.

The human heart is restless because humans stand at the borders of the familiar and they want to be other than they are. We have seen how Nietzsche expressed his envy for the unhistorical way cows lived in the field and were able to conceal themselves totally within a world. Humans however are historical in the sense that they stretch between the past and the future. Teenagers in particular are living a period of transition between the past of a known family world and a future they cannot foresee. Their openness means that they are on the move in this metaphorical sense between worlds and they are not at home in the world as an animal might be at home in the world. Being attuned as a human being does not mean being static or anonymous within the world but rather being uneasy within it. Heidegger rather abstractly speaks of 'the fundamental ways in which we find ourselves disposed' (Heidegger, 1995, p. 67). By contrast animals are in an important sense 'captivated' in their world. For Heidegger it is the fundamental mood of boredom that brings humans face to face with their own lack of fit with the world that surrounds them. Boredom calls for ego change and ego adjustment so that paradoxically, the world can be experienced as a challenge, as an alien place. Removed from this excitement, however, time drags, routines suffocate and the being of humans simply hollows out into some kind of painful emptiness which intensifies slowly either until depression takes hold or else the option is taken to accept the need for ego change. A boring activity invites the person to accept the openness of the human world by challenging the person to change in some fundamental way.

There is no need to elaborate hugely on the three types of boredom Heidegger says impinge on human existence because they each goad the self into some kind of further development. Whether you are caught in a small rural train station waiting for several hours for a train with nothing to do or whether you find yourself at a party where the jokes do not amuse or the conversations do not engage, the experience is like the withdrawal of the world and a real sense of emptiness that follows (Heidegger, 1995). We may be suddenly struck by the emptiness of experience (p. 119) and it is this self-forming emptiness that is boring (p. 120). He elaborates further by linking the experience of emptiness to the general withdrawal of *things*, as characterized by the disappearance of an entire horizon or world (p. 147). Boredom arises in a first phase when things lose their ability to excite us and captivate us and instead draw us into a 'bubble' world which does not suit us because that is the animal world from which the human has come.

Constant bombardment by information particularly if this is responded to by a strategy of contact or tactility might simply 'captivate' a surfer in a world. This captivation can mimic the 'openness' of the human world but without the challenge, giving the impression that Dasein itself is prepared to live openly on the border of many worlds but in actual fact is not doing so. The problem here is similar to intoxification by drugs or alcohol which effectively shuts out the demands brought to light at the borders of the world. Animals do not have such problems because the 'specific character of animal capacity' (Heidegger, 1995, p. 231) keeps the animal captivated (hence interested) in its own setting. For humans, things call us into thought, things that challenge us to play the mind games that help illuminate the way we think and act. Intoxication in one way or another fixes us into such an unquestioning state and results in a deepening of the emptiness we feel. It makes us 'poor in world' like animals. To be free of this boredom, Dasein must express its own relative nothingness and indeterminacy in its struggle to resist 'captivation' by a prescribed world. It needs to do this by means of a resolution (*Entschlossenheit*) or in Heidegger's words, to create 'a moment of vision' in which 'the full situation of an action opens itself and keeps itself open' (Heidegger, 1995, p. 149). Reflecting on Heidegger's point here, Agamben summarizes the issue:

> Dasein is simply an animal that has learned to become bored; it has awakened *from* its own captivation *to* its own captivation. This awakening of the living being to its own being-captivated, this anxious and resolute opening to a not-open, is the human. (Agamben, 2004, p. 70)

Those children whom I tried to engage with philosophically stood at the threshold of an important discovery about themselves and the world. But they were not yet at the stage of saying to the world, 'let me in, let me in'. Some of them preferred to remain unconscious for the most part. They retained belief in a black and white world, even after the first hint of colour had begun to strike their retinas. Those willing to turn away from the dogmatisms of an earlier age were, however, trying to readjust to a new world. As they sought to engage in a rather personal form of dialectic, they needed the support of teachers who accepted something of the reality of living on the rich borders of worlds.

Conclusion

In this chapter we have seen that the developing mind can play tricks on itself. It sometimes imagines that it is a god who either has the answers or can achieve them easily and without distortion. It just needs to remember them. Rote learning simply panders to this illusion but so also do patterns of learning that are not challenging, like surfing the net and selecting only what appeals to you. There is a problem with any assumed stability of knowledge due to the vapour trails of thought which refuse to harden in time and into some coherent shape. This model spends its energies trying to defend the stability claimed for the ego at the outset and prevents the impression being given that there might be some vulnerability about the 'opinion' being defended. The ultimate defence is to say that everyone is entitled to their opinion but this is equivalent to abandoning the quest for precision of concept – wisdom means anything, anyone can be wise etc. The context hardens straight away. Because the children in the session described above had had no experience of listening to each other, they experienced stress at being asked to think for themselves without the safety cover of the teacher's prompts. Where there are answers to every question on demand, the vulnerability of thinking seems pointless. What is the point of thinking if the information is stable and readily available? It is in this context that the unexpected experience of boredom hopefully continues to threaten this 'captivation' and 'fascination' and may throw the learner back in search of something human.

12

Conclusion

He made several trials of the ring, and always with the same result – when he turned the collet inwards he became invisible, when outwards he reappeared.
Plato, *Republic*, 360a, The Ring of Gyges, translated by B. Jowett

Brief remarks

Any estimation of whether children live visibly or invisibly outside themselves or inside themselves is bound to be frustrated because of the complexity of it all. The Ring of Gyges now enables children to appear in several places and under several aspects at once but it also enables them to disappear and to postpone their appearance if needed. On the face of it, what could be more private than the sounds going on inside one's own head and yet everyone knows how suddenly the skull can fill with sounds that are both intimately experienced and yet open to public tracking as one streams songs from the internet. Such a simple action of listening to music has been rendered complex by the realization that 'childhood' itself, as currently understood, is now a 'public' event anyway and perhaps even a discretely public event. From a time when education normally built itself up on the private spaces of childhood, a time when children had been kept in the privacy of the home until judged ready to move on, a time when various systems of schooling gradually traced this historical and linear movement of the child's gradual independence, we now have emerged into a circular time where the father is the child of the child. The linear logic of preparation for adult life has been overtaken by the speed of cultural change and the fact that children due to their control of communications technology are now more likely to be the adept cultural players than their parents and perhaps their would-be educators.

Despite this the emotional support of this 'developmental' structure, which has been apparent over the years, is still as necessary as ever and the reason for this is that the child only has the confidence to grow and learn if empowered to do so. Some kind of biological empowerment, which has little to do with culture but which is so universal that it might point to a principle underlying all animal nature seems to hold sway. The term 'nature' may seem a strange word to use in a book about postmodern issues since a 'postmodern' metaphysics is generally thought to exclude such a category. Yet the evidence reflected upon in this book suggests that the human child shares some significant psychological structures with some other animals. Company is so important that the child will seek it whether with human beings or not. The *being* of the child is not separate from this association process, indicating that underlying emotional support, as we have seen in some dramatic cases, is a significant feature of the human collective, although not exclusive to it. We come back to Spinoza's key discovery that something essential to humans (namely Nature) is not unique to humans and that the 'cultural aspect' is rather less central to human life than might have been thought. This implies that individual identity is only one feature of a general collective.

In normal circumstances, children play happily by imitating segments of what they see, and they do this best in an environment of togetherness with other juveniles and usually under the watchful protection of adults. These webs of relation are inter-specific (and thus blunt) and yet crucial for social success and probably ultimately for survival. The social imperative seems to transcend human contexts and relies continually on some kind of pre-mentalist biological set of circumstances. Harlow's experiments have shown the importance of play in chimpanzee socialization and there is no reason to think that this condition is any less applicable to the socialization of humans. Language and culture add a further layer to this, as we have seen, but the reality is the same. For biological and cultural reasons, the private/public dichotomy is important because it marks off the juvenile from the adult and gives the juvenile the chance to grow. Under ideal circumstances all these supports line up to deliver one consolidated result – the self-confident individual child.

Switches between the private and the public also affect the general architecture of play. Traditionally human play has been associated with the child's own private space and its early attempts to negotiate its entry into the outside world. By engaging in meaning-making activities that promise mastery over a small, knowingly limited segment of experience, the child learns to negotiate a measure of emotional self-confidence necessary to emerge into the real world. The traditional character of play is that it sets up a world over which the child has full control but which is paradoxically recognized by the child as limited and which can be abandoned at will. The game is a limited space operation, controlled by the children themselves, where illusions of mastery are toyed with – literally, where unhelpful details about the real world can be 'simplified', or even cut out and removed. These moves enable the child to invent the illusion of mastery as an antidote to their fear of the outside world. They facilitate the child's journey from the child's private world to the outside world. The child is not fooling itself cognitively for it knows that there is a Reality, to capitalize the word Lacan uses, outside its current scope but it needs to 'fool' itself emotionally that the world will always appear on its own terms.

One of the conclusions of this book is that the postmodern child is beginning to lose touch with this linear logic and with a sense of the private. Mastery now seems too easy to achieve – instant celebrity, instant pop stardom, instant millionaires. One needs to heed Hannah Arendt's warning that there are dangers in exposing the child to public life too early. In postmodern culture, thanks to extensive communications technology, an entire range of influences swarm into the consciousness of the computer literate child at an ever earlier age. By contrast with a child's game, the global world is instantly available. The web of potentiality is extended infinitely through the world-wide web, for instance, or various social network technologies. The exposure of children to the world of fashion is direct and without the mediation of any local influences. In extreme cases, children may well be *constituted* by this public world of brand names and commercial norms. The game is experienced as a surfing experience that is already infinite and does not admit a world 'outside'. It is the world, after all. The experience of immediate power is satisfying but soon curiously disabling, if we think back to the normal ways in which children use play. And the linearity of exposure has been lost. It is in this context that other webs of relation come into the picture, playfully exchanged for the empowering world known to humans and animals. These new webs are presented as a series of counterfeit securities that consolidate the child's new positioning as a member of the public world, a being who has already positioned itself as adult in this sense.

The problem for educators is how to plot a graph from this global space back to the bypassed local space in such a way that it re-engages with those centres of empowerment, which have traditionally served as the context for learning about self and world. The educator is busy trying to reconnect the child to its roots and to the tried and tested historical patterns of its development. In Chapter 1, I spoke of a time when this empowerment mapped easily into the local collective as children supported family welfare and saw themselves as part of the family with a duty to help in the upbringing of younger siblings. But a new mindset is also in evidence among teenagers. Now the talk among street rioters is about themselves, their lack of jobs, their careers, their lack of educational opportunities, their own disgruntlement or general detachment from society. There is no talk about the past or the present. Only the future counts.

I had hoped that this was all a kind of exaggeration and so I was happy to read Honneth's reflection on recognition theory and the fact that empowerment is a deep-rooted function of the social collective and not a function of the individual child. I noted links between empowerment and emotion using modern reflections from Honneth, Fonagy and Target and older reflections from Bettelheim and Lorenz. Empowerment comes not as an emotion from the child to the carer but rather as a participation by the child in something pre-existing which can be linked to some kind of group identity. Buber had a real sense of this too. In its initial instance, the affection (if this is what it is) comes from outside towards the infant that is measured and reckoned as life-giving, even if that affection comes from a dog or a monkey rather than a human. Honneth's argument is that juveniles who are empowered are paradoxically happy to be vulnerable. A certain detachment from mother is accompanied by feelings of vulnerability but these are okay once the confidence of the juvenile is robust enough to experience the withdrawal positively.

Even if educators reinvent the educational spiral, allowing for possible future child-identities that are less biological and more cybernetic, the graph must *begin* in those centres of biological empowerment that humans share with animals. There is every sign that this event is an educational imperative and also that it is not happening. Evidence is showing that the precociously 'public' child is uneasy and declares its unease in bodily sicknesses, intoxications, binge drinking sessions, health anxieties, eating disorders, all of which are fuelled by a denial of the biological origin from which humans benefit (and suffer). These manifestations reflect the attitudes and sufferings of biological refugees, those whose very lives are now called to account by public 'concern' or 'surveillance'. In a new transductive reality where animal, human and machine all intermingle and declare a new identity for the human species, the educator needs to be able to map this imaginary state of affairs back to the linear logic he always presupposes unless that is, he has found a way to cope with the logic of early 'public' identity.

In Part II, I set out to show how children happen to appear in postmodern culture. As talented people they are asked to show and to believe themselves talented in the public arena almost straight away. Talent shows and X-factor hysteria or even 'private' presentations on highly rated YouTube videos are all attractive rituals in the cult of appearance. To be is to be perceived, as the philosopher Berkeley rather alarmingly suggested – *esse est percipi*. As people with contacts and value sets that have already crossed borders, children are invited to be global and dismiss local roots. They wear brand-name jeans; they respect labels; they even use public categories as ways of withdrawing from public scrutiny, visibility against visibility as we have seen in the discussion on Foucault. The invisible still finds ways to break through but, in general, a shifting public space, continually invigorated by an infinite series of stimulating impressions, deflects its insistent pressures. As public beings, children's patterns of visibility have been unknowingly set by commercial interests and by peer pressure while their invisibility still manifests itself in bodily ways. As public beings, they are invited to be in touch always but without local substance this has little depth while the focus is on currency and the immediacy of the moment rather than on history and memory, the underlying ingredients of the ego. Rhizomatic knowledge is knowledge without any predictable pattern.

History was important to Nietzsche because it provided the key to the manifestation of genius. Genius is not only the power to stand out from history between the past and the future, but it is also the power to participate fully in the historical moment. It is interesting that T. S. Eliot argued along similar lines, complaining that some young artists in the twentieth century operated without a strong sense of history, resulting in their creativity being compromised and their talent for expressing the time-now being curiously muted. Like Nietzsche's description of a historical culture or education – *historische Bildung* as a plastic power (Nietzsche, 1983, p. 62), Eliot's vision of creative word-craft involved the comparable struggle to find 'an arrangement of the right words in the right order. When you have the words for it, the "thing" for which the words had to be found has disappeared, replaced by a poem' (cited in Zilcosky, 2005, p. 28).

But rhizomatics tends to make nonsense of the right words in the right order just as it tends to make nonsense of any form of memorization as a linear ordering of events. The point for rhizomatics is not to straddle an epoch in history, even a short moment, but rather to dip in an out, to become entirely subjective in one's relation to information and events. Unlike genius in Nietzsche's account, which needed to be thickened by history in much the same way as the ego is thickened by history, the tactile perspective of rhizomatics is contact without personal thickening. Traditionally however, education has relied on historical thickening to chart the linear logic of learning and this is why learning has been stratified in curricula. A recent Vygotskian scholar has presented this historical view in a nutshell, describing the learning patterns of children in terms of specific learning and teaching steps, saying that if we are justified in talking about steps of learning, we must also be justified in talking about time (Zaretskii, 2009, p. 71). An engagement in time at the precise historical moment of development is recognized. The child's talents need to unfold in historical ways in order for the child to achieve independence. In this example, Vygotsky imagines four levels of support for the child's learning:

> We show the child how the problem should be solved and look to see whether or not, imitating what he's been shown, he completes the problem. Or we begin to solve the problem and allow the child to complete it. Or we give him problems that are beyond the bounds of his mental age to solve in collaboration with another, more developed child, or, finally, we explain to the child the principles for solving the problem, pose a leading question, break the problem down into pieces for him, and so forth. In short, we ask the child to solve problems that are beyond the bounds of his mental age using one form of collaboration or another (Vygotsky as cited in Zaretskii, 2009, p. 76)

Contrasted with this linear learning pattern is the extreme subjectivism of rhizomatic learning which can make its own brilliant appearance but soon proves to be flimsy and transitory. It is perhaps useful then to consult Baudrillard for a theory of this kind of appearance. Baudrillard warns us that there seems to be no way to distinguish between real historical appearance and the false kind of mimicry into which the young as imitators have been led. To Baudrillard, it is a general feature of society that patterns of visibility, indeed all rules of appearance, have become so vacuous that they do not have any normalizing grip on practice or people or bodies. Although the young may play games with these appearance rules, they basically only experience a chaotic range of symbols, lose themselves in a vast inter-textual play with concepts and ideas that can be dropped, exchanged, switched, substituted like a rhizome that turns and twists. They find it more and more difficult to declare themselves in the here and now. The next thought is just a click away. The last thought is easily forgotten. Life begins again with every passing second. This is what Nietzsche would call unhistorical appearance, being of the same status as cows in the field. This reality is not committed to history and, for this reason, the child experiences a form of extreme subjectivity and 'power' which does not allow itself to be consciously 'subjected' to anything. The irony is that the postmodern child is becoming used to the circular logic of starting anywhere and going anywhere and this may be affecting the way the child's ego is currently being constructed – public, powerful and unhistorical.

In Part III I ask what role philosophy might play as part of a possible reconstruction of the historical mindset. The questioning of philosophy constantly breaks down the hard concepts and the readily acceptable meanings that need to be critiqued and returned to their natural vaporous state and in this regard there seems to be a certain synergy with the postmodern appetite for the unhistorical. Experience of vapours brings children to an understanding of the 'plane of immanence' described so well by Deleuze and Guattari and it is from this that they might begin to trace a line of development, moving from impressions and half-thoughts to more solid concepts. Implied in this process is the fundamental question of 'world' or in other terms the distinction between the animal in man and the human, a question all too readily avoided by information culture.

Another function of philosophy is the way it promotes dialogue, perhaps between a teacher and a student or between one student and another. This is not simply an issue of argument shape. Dialogue does not replicate the contours of a mock television debate, dividing those who propose from those who oppose. Philosophical talk is something more radical and important, indicating a process whereby the 'thought would flow, rather than there being a lot of different people, each trying to persuade or convince the others' (Bohm, 1996, p. 30). Learning a lesson from the physicist-philosopher David Bohm, educators who have glimpsed these things in classrooms are proud to value the contribution of philosophy to the vaporous destiny of authentic thought. Thinking in such contexts announces the need for inquirers to move upward on the mountain to view the local situation better or it needs to be open to views from elsewhere. To do this, education needs more than a single-source foundation, that is, more than practitioner experience, lest the dogma of relevance comes back into play, crippling new ideas and inhibiting change.

The education of the postmodern child is caught at the moment between the circular attractions of the rhizome and the more traditional linear attractions of the arboreal or historical. Evidence is showing in some cases that the precociously 'public' child is uneasy and declares its uneasiness in bodily sicknesses, intoxications, binge drinking sessions, orgies, health anxieties, eating disorders, all of which are fuelled by an eclipse of the animal origin from which humans have come and which they have chosen to part. These manifestations reflect the concerns of the biological refugees we may have become in our postmodern age.

Human culture has traditionally built up the historical texture of the ego, presuming little in the child but an empty space which has to be loved into shape. If we were able to use a 'modern' philosophy of consciousness to explain these things, we could incorporate an older language of subject and object. Then we might be able to express the issue as Von Balthasar did, saying that the subject 'is unformed [*ungebildet*] until it finds itself performing the work of knowledge' (p. 68). This idea of the work of knowledge performed by subjection to a 'motley jumble of objects that get thrown into the subjective unoccupied space' (p. 68) suggests that the 'subject' must do something with this jumble by means of some kind of cognitive process that sifts, prioritizes and analyses in order to regain some actively ordering shape on the potential chaos of experience. The key word is order but not the circular order of the rhizome. For Von Balthasar, it is the work of agency to hold the world in this inward space (subjectivity) in order to put a shape on this chaotic invasion, to lessen the enchantment of its novelty, even if novelty is enjoyable, to move away from the pool of Narcissus where novelty has the power to hold the human spirit spellbound. On this account, language helps children to shape the elements of their inner world in a way that is 'more and more informed by the truth of the world' (Von Balthasar, 2000, p. 70) but this private world is carefully protected by carers to guarantee the safe presentation of the world and a return to a basic order of historical stabilities. Words so presented describe a gentle dialectic between inner and outer. They show the mediation of carers according to a formula expressed by Von Balthasar as the unity of the concept [*die Einheit des Begriffs*] (p. 73) for it is only some loving texture that holds these separations in place and prevents the world from becoming immediately overwhelming for the child. It is from this unity, Von Balthasar explains, that the essential separation between child subject and the objective world can occur. In other words, as Hegel suggested, the subject comes to be, and with it comes the independence of the objective world. The child has to have the confidence to allow the world to appear as it is in itself. Otherwise the world will only appear as a construction of its own needs and the truth of the world will be constantly submerged behind the ego's petty constructions. In this case, subject to the constructive whims and meaning-making exploits of the individual, who wrongly identifies learning with meaning-making, the individual child tends to lose itself in a world it does not know and cannot understand, for the world will always remain a function of its own egocentrism.

Under the sway of the rhizome, however, 'subject' and 'object' cannot be used as categories without qualification because they do not boast the same stable borders or architecture as proposed by Von Balthasar. Different factors now seem to be implicated as emptiness beckons on both sides, the side of the subject and the side of the object. And yet there may be some resonance with Von Balthasar's remarks about acknowledging the emptiness signalled by the clicking of computer keyboards. Similarly, basing his thoughts on Heidegger's analysis, Agamben has pointed to the need for a spiritual awareness that controls genius in its most anarchic manifestations. It is a spirituality that points backwards towards 'a certain non-individuated share of reality, which must not only be preserved but also respected and, in a way, even honoured, as one honors one's debts' (Agamben, 2007, p. 12).

Even consciousness in its brighter moments does not seem capable of capturing this paradox completely. Individuals experience a set of given facts that at one and the same time say why they are unique and also why they are the same as others. And yet they are aware that they are not entirely self-created, that, using Agamben's words, ego and genius are separate (p. 13), for genius, despite its timeliness, knows time and relies on history to set itself apart while ego, for all its proposed uniqueness, reflects the constant resonance of the whole ensemble.

Bibliography

Adler, M. (1957), The questions science cannot answer. *Bulletin of the Atomic Scientists,* 13(4), 120–5.

Adorno, T. W. (1993), *Hegel: Three Studies.* Cambridge/London: MIT Press.

Agamben, G. (1995), We refugees and European Jewry. *Symposium-a Quarterly Journal in Modern Foreign Literatures,* 49, 114–19.

—(1998), Homo-sacer: Sovereign power and bare life. *Revista De Occidente* (208), 63–76.

—(2000), *Means without End: Notes on Politics.* Minneapolis/London: University of Minnesota Press.

—(2004), *The Open* (K. Attell, Trans.) Stanford: Stanford University Press.

—(2005), *State of Exception.* Chicago/London: University of Chicago Press.

—(2007), *Profanations.* New York: Zone.

Arendt, H. (1958), *The Human Condition.* Chicago: University of Chicago Press.

—(1968), *Between Past and Future.* Harmondsworth/New York: Penguin.

Ariès, P. (1962), *Centuries of Childhood* (R. Baldick, Trans.). London: Jonathan Cape.

Aristotle (1902), *History of Animals* (R. Cresswell, Trans.). London: George Bell and Sons.

—(1907), *De anima* (R. D. Hicks, Trans.). Cambridge: University Press.

Aronowitz, Sand Giroux, H. (1985), *Education under Siege.* New York: Bergin and Garvey.

Ball, S. J. (2006), Introduction – symposium, educational research and the necessity of theory. *Studies in the Cultural Politics of Education,* 27(1), 1–2.

Barone, T. E. (1992), Beyond theory and method: A case of critical storytelling. *Theory into Practice,* 31(2), 142–6.

— (2007), A return to the gold standard? Questioning the future of narrative construction as educational research. *Qualitative Inquiry,* 13(4), 454–70.

Baudrillard, J. (1983), *Simulations.* New York: Semiotext(e).

—(1987), *Forget Foucault.* New York: Semiotext(e).

—(1996), *The Perfect Crime.* London/New York: Verso.

—(2005), *The Intelligence of Evil or the Lucidity Pact* (C. Turner, Trans.). Oxford/New York: Berg.

Bendle, M. F. (2002), Teleportation, cyborgs and the posthuman ideology. *Social Semiotics,* 12(1), 45–62.

Berkowitz, P. (1996). *Nietzsche: The Ethics of an Immoralist.* Cambridge, MA: Harvard University Press.

Best, S.and Kellner, D. (1991), *Postmodern Theory.* London: Macmillan.

Bettelheim, B. (1950), *Love is not Enough.* New York: Free Press.

—(1959), Feral children and autistic children. *The American Journal of Sociology,* 64(5), 455–67.

Biesta, G. (2011), Philosophy, exposure, and children: How to resist the instrumentalisation of philosophy in education. *Journal of Philosophy of Education,* 45(2), 305–19.

Blondel, M. (1984), *Action (1893)* (O. Blanchette, Trans.). Notre Dame: Notre Dame University Press.

Bohm, D. (1996), *On Dialogue.* Oxford/New York: Routledge.

Bronson, P.and Merriman, A. (2010), The creativity crisis. *Newsweek,* 156, 44–9.

Brown, T. (2008), Desire and drive in researcher subjectivity: The broken mirror of Lacan. *Qualitative Inquiry,* 14, 402–23.

Bruner, J. (1983), Play, thought, and language. *Peabody Journal of Education,* 60(3), 60–9.

Bruner, J. S., Jolly, A. and Sylva, K. (eds) (1976), *Play: Its Role in Development and Evolution.* Harmondsworth, UK/New York: Penguin.

Buber, M. (1961), *Between Man and Man* (R. Gregor Smith, Trans.). London/Glasgow: Fontana.

Buckingham, D. (2007), *Beyond Technology: Children's Learning in the Age of Digital Culture.* Cambridge,UK/Malden, MA: Polity.

Burbules, N. C. and Torres, C. A. (eds) (2000), *Globalization and Education: Critical Perspectives.* New York: Routledge.

Callister, T. A. and Burbules, N. C. (2004), Just give it to me straight: A case against filtering the internet. *Phi Delta Kappan,* 649–55.

Child, B. J. (1998), *Boarding School Seasons.* Lincoln/London: University of Nebraska Press.

Conroy, J. C. (2008), Philosophy, wisdom and reading the great books. In M. Hand and C. Winstanley (eds), *Philosophy in Schools* (pp. 145–57). London/New York: Continuum.

Conroy, M. A., Sutherland, K. S., Snyder, A., Al-Hendawi, M. and Vo, A. (2009), Creating a positive classroom atmosphere: Teachers' use of effective praise and feedback. *Beyond Behavior,* 18, 18–26.

Cooper, J. M. (ed.) (1997), *Plato: Complete Works.* Indianapolis/Cambridge: Hackett.

Cooper, J. M. and Procope, J. F. (eds) (1995), *Seneca: Moral and Political Essays.* Cambridge: Cambridge University Press.

Cramond, B., Matthews-Morgan, J., Bandalos, D. and Zuo, L. (2005), A report on the 40-year follow-up of the Torrance tests of creative thinking: Alive and well in the new millenium. *Gifted Child Quarterly,* 49(4), 283–91.

Cunningham, H. (1995), *Children and Childhood in Western Society since 1500.* London/ New York: Longman.

— (2002), Beloved children. *American Historical Review,* 107(2), 655–6.

— (2009), Designing modern childhoods: History, space, and the material culture of children. *Journal of Social History,* 43(1), 210–12.

Cussen (1936), *Commission of Inquiry into the Industrial and Reformatory School System.* Dublin: Government of Ireland.

Davidson, T. (1870?), *The Fragments of Parmenides.* New York: John Wiley

De Certeau, M. (1984), *The Practice of Everyday Life* (S. Rendall, Trans.). Berkeley/Los Angeles/London: University of California Press.

Debord, G. (1983), *Society of the Spectacle*. Detroit: Black and Red.

Del Lucchese, F. (2009), Monstrous individuations: Deleuze, Simondon, and relational ontology. *Differences-a Journal of Feminist Cultural Studies*, 20(2–3), 179–93.

Deleuze, G. and Guattari, F. (1987), *A Thousand Plateaus: Capitalism and Schizophrenia* (B. Massumi, Trans.). Minneapolis: University of Minnesota Press.

—(1994), *What is Philosophy?* (H. Tomlinson and G. Burchell, Trans.). New York/ Chichester: Columbia University Press.

Demos, J. (1971), Developmental perspectives on the history of childhood. *Journal of Interdisciplinary History*, 2(2), 315–27.

Department of Education and Science (2012) www.education.ie/home/home.jsp?pcateg ory=17216&ecategory=33128&language=EN. Retrieved 3 January 2012.

Dewey, J. (1988), *Experience and Education*. New York/London: Collins Macmillan.

—(2010), *How We Think*. US: Dewey Press.

—(2011), *Democracy and Education*. US: Simon and Brown.

Dreyfus, H. and Rabinow, P. (1982), *Beyond Structuralism and Hermeneutics*. Chicago: University of Chicago Press.

Dumouchel, P. (1992), Simondon, Gilbert Pleas for a philosophy of technology. *Inquiry – an Interdisciplinary Journal of Philosophy*, 35(3–4), 407–21.

Dunne, J. (1993), *Back to the Rough Ground: 'Phronesis' and 'Techne' in Modern Philosophy and in Aristotle*. Notre Dame, IN: Notre Dame University Press.

Dweck, C. S. (2007), The perils and promises of praise. *Educational Leadership*, 65, 34–9.

Ebenkamp, B. (1998), Fashion en mass. *Brandweek*, 39, 32.

Edwards, R. and Usher, R. (2008), *Globalisation and Pedagogy: Space, Place and Identity*. London: Routledge.

Elwes, R. H. M. (1901), *Improvement of the Understanding, Ethics and Correspondence of Benedict de Spinoza*. New York: M. Walter Dunne.

England, E. B. (1921), *The Laws of Plato* (Trans.). Manchester: University of Manchester Press.

Evans, J., Rich, E. and Holroyd, R. (2004), Disordered eating and disordered schooling: What schools do to middle class girls. *British Journal of Sociology of Education*, 25(2), 123–42.

Fisher, R. (2008), Philosophical intelligence: Why philosophical intelligence is important in educating the mind. In M. Hand and C. Winstanley (eds), *Philosophy in Schools* (pp. 96–104). London/New York: Continuum.

Fonagy, P.and Target, M. (1997), Attachment and reflective function: Their role in self-organization. *Development and Psychopathology*, 9, 679–700.

Foucault, M. (1979), *Discipline and Punish* (A. Sheridan, Trans.). New York: Vintage.

Fowler, J. W. (1995), *Stages of Faith: The Psychology of Human Development and the Quest for Meaning*. New York: Harper.

Frost, J. L. (2010), *A History of Children's Play and Play Environments*. New York/ Oxford: Routledge.

Gadamer, H.-G. (2004), *Truth and Method* (J. a. M. Weinsheimer, G. Donald, Trans.) London/New York: Continuum.

Gay, V. P. (1983), Winnicott's contribution to religious studies: The resurrection of the culture hero. *Journal of the American Academy of Religion,* 51(3), 371–95.

Giroux, H. (1992), *Border Crossings: Cultural Workers and the Politics of Education.* London and New York: Routledge.

Givens, P. R. (1962), Identifying and encouraging creative processes: The characteristics of the creative individual and the environment that fosters them. *The Journal of Higher Education,* 33(6), 295–301.

Goleman, D., Kaufman, P. and Ray, M. (1992), *The Creative Spirit.* New York: Penguin.

Grimstad Klepp, I. and Storm-Mathison, A. (2005), Reading fashion as age: Teenage girls' and grown-up women's accounts of clothing as body and social status. *Fashion Theory,* 9(3), 323–42.

Hakanen, E. A. (2002), Lists as social grid: Ratings and rankings in everyday life. *Social Semiotics,* 12, 245.

Hall, K., Murphy, P. and Soler, J. (eds) (2008), *Pedagogy and Practice: Culture and Identities.* London: Open University.

Hand, M. (2008), Can children be taught philosophy? In M. Hand and C. Winstanely (eds), *Philosophy in Schools.* London/New York: Continuum.

Harlow, H. F. and Zimmermann, R. R. (1958), The development of affectional responses in infant monkeys. *Proceedings of the American Philosophical Society,* 102(5), 501–9.

— (1959), Affectional responses in the infant monkey. *Science,* 130(3373), 421–32.

Hayles, N. K. (1996), Simulated nature and natural simulations: Rethinking the relation between the beholder and the world. In W. Cronon (ed.), *Uncommon Ground.* New York/London: Norton.

Haynes, J. and Murris, K. (2011), The provocation of an epistemological shift in teacher education through philosophy with children. *Journal of Philosophy of Education,* 45(2), 285–303.

Heidegger, M. (1971), *Poetry, Language, Thought* (A. Hofstadter, Trans.). New York/ London: Harper Colophon.

—(1976), *What is Called Thinking?* (J. Glenn Gray, Trans.). New York: HarperPerennial.

—(1995), *The Fundamental Concepts of Metaphysics.* Bloomington/Indianapolis: Indiana University Press.

Heidemann, I. (1968), *Der Begriff des Spieles und das ästhetische Weltbild in der Philosophie der Gegenwart.* Berlin: De Gruyter.

Hester, P. P., Hendrickson, J. M. and Gable, R. A. (2009), Forty years later – The value of praise, ignoring, and rules for preschoolers at risk for behavior disorders. *Education & Treatment of Children,* 32, 513–35.

Hirst, P. and Carr, W. (2005), Philosophy of education – A symposium. *Journal of Philosophy of Education,* 39(4), 615–32.

Honneth, A. (1996), *The Struggle for Recognition* (J. Anderson, Trans.). Cambridge: Polity.

—(2005), A physiognomy of the capitalist form of life: A sketch of Adorno's social theory. *Constellations: An International Journal of Critical & Democratic Theory,* 12(1), 50–64.

—(2008), *Reification.* Oxford: Oxford University Press.

Humphries, S. (1981), *Hooligans or Rebels: An Oral History of Working-Class Childhood and Youth 1889–1939.* Oxford: Blackwell.

Itard, I. M. (1932), *The Wild Boy of Aveyron.* New York: Century.

James, A. and James, A. L. (2004), *Constructing Childhood.* Basingstoke/New York: Palgrave Macmillan.

James, A., Jenks, C. and Prout, A. (eds) (1998), *Theorizing Childhood.* Cambridge/ Oxford: Polity Press.

Jowett, B. (1888) (third edition), *The Republic of Plato.* Oxford: Clarendon

Kennedy, N. and Kennedy, D. (2011), Community of philosophical inquiry as a discursive structure, and its role in school curriculum design. *Journal of Philosophy of Education,* 45(2), 265–93.

Kenway, J. and Bullen, E. (2001), *Consuming Children.* Buckingham/Philadelphia: Open University Press.

Kett, J. F. (1971), Adolescence and youth in nineteenth-century America. *Journal of Interdisciplinary History,* 2(2), 283–98.

Kobak, R. R. and Sceery, A. (1988), Attachment in late adolescence: Working models, affect regulation, and representations of self and others. *Child Development,* 59(1), 135–46.

Kohlberg, L. (1981), *The Philosophy of Moral Development: Moral Stages and the Idea of Justice.* New York: HarperCollins.

Lacan, J. (1966), *Écrits 1* (Vol. 1). Paris: Editions du Seuil.

Lankshear, C., Peters, M. and Knobel, M. (2000), Information, knowledge and learning: Some issues facing epistemology and education in a digital age. *Journal of Philosophy of Education,* 34(1), 17–39, 203–8.

Lipman, M. (1984), The cultivation of reasoning through philosophy. *Educational Leadership,* 42(1), 51.

Lipman, M. and Sharp, A. M. (1978), Some educational presuppositions of philosophy for children. *Oxford Review of Education,* 4(1), 85–90.

Lobkowitcz (1967), *Theory and Practice: History of a Concept from Aristotle to Marx.* Notre Dame, IN: University of Notre Dame Press.

Long, F. (2005), Thomas Reid and philosophy with children. *Journal of Philosophy of Education,* 39(4), 599–614.

—(2008), Troubled theory in the Hirst-Carr debate. *Journal of Philosophy of Education,* 42(1), 133–47.

Lorenz, K. (2002), *King Solomon's Ring* (M. Kerr Wilson, Trans.). Abington, Oxon/New York: Routledge.

MacKinnon, D. W. (1964), The creativity of architects. In C. W. Taylor (ed.), *Widening Horizons in Creativity.* New York: John Wiley.

Masschelein, J. (2001), The discourse of the learning society and the loss of childhood. *Journal of Philosophy of Education,* 35(1), 1–20.

McKeon, R. (ed.) (2001), *The Basic Works of Aristotle*. New York: Modern Library.

McMahon, F. F., Lytle, D. E. and Sutton-Smith, B. (eds) (2005), *Play: An Interdisciplinary Sythesis*. Lanham/Oxford: Univeristy of America Press.

Mercon, J. and Armstrong, A. (2011), Transindividuality and philosophical enquiry in schools: A Spinozist perspective. *Journal of Philosophy of Education*, 45(2), 251–64.

Milgram, S. (1974a), The dilemma of obedience. *The Phi Delta Kappan*, 55(9), 603–6.

— (1974b), *Obedience to Authority: An Experimental View*. New York: Harper and Row.

Murris, K. (2000), Can children do philosophy? *Journal of Philosophy of Education*, 34(2), 261.

—(2008a), Autonomous and authentic thinking through philosophy with picturebooks. In M. Hand and C. Winstanley (eds), *Philosophy in Schools* (pp. 105–18). London/New York: Continuum.

—(2008b), Philosophy with children, the stingray and the educative value of disequilibrium. *Journal of Philosophy of Education*, 42(3–4), 667–85.

Nelson, J. A. P., Young, B. J., Young, E. L. and Cox, G. (2010), Using teacher-written praise notes to promote a positive environment in a middle school. *Preventing School Failure*, 54, 119–25.

Nietzsche, F. (1973), *Beyond Good and Evil*. Hammondsmith: Penguin.

—(1983), *Untimely Meditations* (R. J. Hollingdale, Trans.). New York: Cambridge.

Nussbaum, M. C. (1990), *Love's Knowledge*. New York/Oxford: Oxford University Press.

O'Sullivan, D. (1979), Social definition in child-care in the Irish Republic: Models of the child and child-care intervention. *Economic and Social Review*, 10(3), 209–29.

Partin, T. C. M., Robertson, R. E., Maggin, D. M., Oliver, R. M. and Wehby, J. H. (2010), Using teacher praise and opportunities to respond to promote appropriate student behavior. *Preventing School Failure*, 54, 172–8.

Pearce, R. H. (2001), *Savagism and Civilization: A Study of the Indian and the American Mind*. Baltimore, John Hopkins University Press.

Peperzak, A. (1997), *Platonic Transformations: With and After Hegel, Heidegger, and Levinas*. Lanham/New York/Boulder/Oxford: Rowman and Littlefield.

Piaget, J. (1951), *Play, Dreams and Imitation in Childhood*. London: Routledge and Kegan Paul.

(1951/76), Symbolic play. In Bruner et al. (eds), *Play: Its Role in Development and Evolution*. Harmondsworth, UK/New York: Penguin.

Pletsch, C. E. (1977), History and Friedrich Nietzsche's philosophy of time. *History & Theory*, 16(3), 30.

Poster, M. (2004), Consumption and digital commodities in the everyday. *Cultural Studies*, 18, 409–23.

— (ed.) (1988), *Jean Baudrillard: Selected Writings*. Stanford/Oxford: Polity.

Postman, N. (1994/82), *The Disappearance of Childhood*. New York: Vintage.

Pring, R. (2005), Education as a moral practice. In W. Carr (ed.), *The RoutledgeFalmer Reader in Philosophy of Education* (pp. 195–205). London: Routledge.

— (2008), Philosophy and moral education. In M. Hand and C. Winstanely (eds), *Philosophy in Schools* (pp. 18–26). London/New York: Continuum.

Rapson, R. L. (1965), The American child as seen by British travelers, 1845–1935. *American Quarterly,* 17(3), 520–34.

Ribak, R. (2009), Remote control, umbilical cord and beyond: The mobile phone as a transitional object. *British Journal of Developmental Psychology,* 27(1), 183–96.

Rich, E.and Evans, J. (2005), Making sense of eating disorders in schools. *Discourse: Studies in the Cultural Politics of Education,* 26(2), 247–62.

Rohrer, T. (2007), The cognitive science of metaphor from philosophy to neuropsychology. *Neuropsychological Trends,* 2/2007.

Rolón, C. A. (2003), Educating Latino students. *Educational Leadership,* January, 40–3.

Rose, L. (1991), *The Erosion of Childhood: Child Oppression in Britain 1860 to 1918.* New York: Routledge.

Ruitenberg, C. W. (2009), Distance and defamiliarisation: Translation as philosophical method. *Journal of Philosophy of Education,* 43(3), 421–35.

Schaefer, C. E. (ed.) (2011), *Foundations of Play Therapy* (second edition). Hoboken, NJ: John Wiley.

Schell, C. O., Reilly, M., Rosling, H., Peterson, S. and Ekström, A. M. (2007), Socioeconomic determinants of infant mortality: A worldwide study of 152 low-, middle-, and high-income countries. *Scandinavian Journal of Public Health,* 35(3), 288–7.

Schon, D. A. (2005), *The Reflective Practitioner: How Professionals Think in Action.* Aldershot, UK: Arena.

Schor, J. B. and Ford, M. (2007), From tastes great to cool: Children's food marketing and the rise of the symbolic. *Journal of Law, Medicine & Ethics,* 35(1), 10–21.

Shaw, B. (1981), Is there any relatiionship between educational theory and practice? *British Journal of Educational Studies,* 29(1), 19–28.

Sloterdijk, P. (2004), Anthropo-technology. *NPQ: New Perspectives Quarterly,* 21(4), 40–7.

—(2009). Rules for the human zoo: A response to the letter on humanism. *Environment & Planning D: Society & Space,* 27(1), 12–28.

Smith, R. (2006), As if by machinery: The levelling of educational research. *Journal of Philosophy of Education,* 40(2), 157–68.

—(2011), The play of Socratic dialogue. *Journal of Philosophy of Education,* 45(2), 221–33.

Somekh, B. and Mavers, D. (2003), Mapping learning potential: Students' conceptions of ICT in their world. *Assessment in Education,* 10(3), 409–20.

Sook-Yung, L. and Young-Gil, C. (2007), Children's internet ue in a family context: Influence on family relationships and parental mediation. *Cyberpsychology and Behaviour,* 10(5), 640–4.

Sprehe, J. T. (1961), Feral man and the social animal. *The American Catholic Sociological Review,* 22(2), 161–7.

Sternberg, R. J. (2002), The psychology of intelligence. *Intelligence,* 30(5), 481.

Sternberg, R. J. and Davidson, J. E. (eds) (2005), *Conceptions of Giftedness* (second edition). Cambridge/New York: Cambridge University Press.

Sugai, G. and Horner, R. R. (2006), A promising approach for expanding and sustaining school-wide positive behavior support. *Social Psychology Review,* 35, 245–59.

Suissa, J. (2008), Philosophy in the secondary school – A Deweyan perspective. In M. Hand and C. Winstanley (eds), *Philosophy in Schools* (pp. 132–44). London/ New York: Continuum.

Sutton-Smith, B. (1997), *The Ambiguity of Play.* Cambridge, MA/London: Harvard University Press.

Touher, P. (2007). *Fear of the Collar.* Reading: Ebury.

Triebenbacher, S. L. (1998), Pets as transitional objects: Their role in children's emotional development. *Psychological Reports,* 82(1), 191.

Tröhler, D. (2007), Philosophical arguments, historical contexts, and theory of education. *Educational Philosophy & Theory,* 39(1), 10–19.

Valcke, M., De Wever, B., Van Keer, H. and Schellens, T. (2011), Long-term study of safe internet use of young children. *Computers and Education,* 57, 1292–305.

Vansieleghem, N. (2005), Philosophy for children as the wind of thinking. *Journal of Philosophy of Education,* 39(1), 19–35.

Vanzago, L. (2005), Presenting the unpresentable: The metaphor in Merleau-Ponty's last writings. *Southern Journal of Philosophy,* 43(3), 463–74.

Von Balthasar, H. U. (2000), *Theo-Logic: Truth of the World* (Vol. 1). San Francisco: Ignatius Press.

Wheatley, R. K., West, R. P., Charlton, C. T., Sandeers, R. B., Smith, T. G. and Taylor, M. J. (2009), Improving behavior through differential reinforcement: A praise note system for elementary school students. *Education & Treatment of Children,* 32, 551–71.

White, J. (2011), YP4C? What is philosophy for? Paper presented at the Institute of Education Philosophy Research Seminar.

Wilson, B. (2003), Of diagrams and rhizomes: Usual culture, contemporary art, and the impossibility of mapping the content of art education. *Studies in Art Education,* 44(3), 214–29.

Wilson, K. and Ryan, V. (2006), *Play Therapy: A Non-directive Approach for Children and Adolescents.* London: Bailliere Tindall.

Williams, K. (2007), *Education and the Voice of Michael Oakeshott.* Exeter: Imprint Academic.

Winnicott, D. W. (2000), *The Child, the Family and the Outside World.* Hammondsmith: Penguin.

—(2005/1971), *Playing and Reality.* London/New York: Routledge Classics.

Winstanley, C. (2008), Philosophy and the development of critical thinking. In M. Hand and C. Winstanley (eds), *Philosophy in Schools* (pp. 85–95). London/New York: Continuum.

Wright, J. (2008), Reframing quality and impact: The place of theory in education research. *Australian Educational Researcher,* 35(1), 1–16.

Zaretskii, V. K. (2009), The zone of proximal development: What Vygotsky did not have time to write. *Journal of Russian & East European Psychology* 47(6), 70–93.

Zeidner, M. and Schleyer, E. J. (1999), The big-fish little-pond effect for academic self-concept, test anxiety, and school grades in gifted children. *Contemporary Educational Psychology,* 24(4), 305–29.

Zembylas, M. and Vrasidas, C. (2005), Globalization, information and communication technologies, and the prospect of a 'global village': Promises of inclusion or electronic colonization? *Journal of Curriculum Studies,* 37, 65–83.

Zilcosky, J. (2005), Modern monuments: T. S. Eliot, Nietzsche, and the problem of history, *Journal of Modern Literature,* 29(1), 21–33.

Zingg, R. M. (1940), Feral man and extreme cases of isolation. *The American Journal of Psychology,* 53(4), 487–517.

Ziser, M. (2007). Animal mirrors. *Angelaki: Journal of the Theoretical Humanities,* 12(3), 11–33.

Žižek , S. (2009), *The Parallax View*. Cambridge, MA/London: MIT Press.

Index

i 22 3 69 4 82